THE INTEGRATION OF POLITICAL COMMUNITIES

Karl W. Deutsch
YALE UNIVERSITY

Philip E. Jacob
UNIVERSITY OF PENNSYLVANIA

Henry Teune
UNIVERSITY OF PENNSYLVANIA

James V. Toscano
UNIVERSITY OF PENNSYLVANIA

William L. C. Wheaton
UNIVERSITY OF CALIFORNIA, BERKELEY

The Integration of Political Communities

EDITED BY

PHILIP E. JACOB AND JAMES V. TOSCANO

UNIVERSITY OF PENNSYLVANIA

J. B. LIPPINCOTT COMPANY

PHILADELPHIA AND NEW YORK

SECOND PRINTING

Library of Congress Catalog Card Number: 64–21042

Printed in the United States of America

Preface

THIS GROUP OF ESSAYS IS AN OUTGROWTH OF AN UNUSUAL interdisciplinary faculty-graduate seminar on research in political integration conducted at the University of Pennsylvania in the fall and winter of 1961–1962.

Using the analogous settings of the nation-state system and the fragmented local government system in the United States participants of the seminar developed hypotheses and theoretical perspectives concerning the achievement of integrated political behavior within and among communities at the international and metropolitan levels. Models were designed to analyze quantitative and qualitative data bearing on the development—and the frustration—of integration at these different political levels.

The implications of a wide range of relevant empirical studies were assessed in the fields of communications, international relations, planning and regional science, local government, social structure, social psychology, and cultural anthropology.

Preliminary experimental tests of certain hypotheses were undertaken applying similar methodology in a comparative analysis of national and local patterns of political relationships.

On the basis of their experience in the seminar, further study of the proceedings (which were recorded, mimeographed, and exchanged), and extensive mutual consultation, the five authors responsible for this volume prepared their individual papers. These reflect a substantial refinement, coordination and extension of the thinking that went on in the seminar. Although the authors have worked closely together and exchanged criticisms and editorial suggestions, each has expressed independent judgments in the chapters for which he was responsible. Hence, significant differences in perspective, conceptual framework, terminology, and sometimes in basic conclusions appear among the essays—even though the authors believe that they share in large measure the same commitment to rigorous empirical inquiry, a common concern for uniting the varied disciplines of social science in the exploration of political phenomena, and a profound interest in understanding more clearly the influences which can produce more viable and mutually beneficial human communities.

Professor Karl Deutsch of Yale University, Department of Political Science, served as Research Consultant for the seminar. Its co-directors were: Philip E. Jacob (Political Science and International Relations), William L. C. Wheaton (City Planning), and Henry Teune (Political Science) of the University of Pennsylvania. James V. Toscano, then Ford Research Fellow in Public Affairs and now Assistant Professor of Political Science, University of Pennsylvania, was rapporteur. His extraordinary effort in editing the transcript and drafting coherent reports of major segments of the material was the indispensable foundation for this publication.

Other participants in the seminar were, from the University of Pennsylvania faculty: Harold Herman (Fels Institute of Local and State Government) and Paul Davidoff (City Planning); predoctoral candidates and research fellows: Thomas Dye and David Livingston (Fels Institute), Donald Martin and Janet Reiner (City Planning), Thomas Reiner (Regional Science), Joan Gotwals (Polical Science), Hedvah Shuchman and Robert Pfaltzgraff (International Relations), and Norman Schwartz (Anthropology); and Cyril B. Roseman (Princeton University, Politics).

The seminar was made possible by a generous grant to the

University of Pennsylvania by the Ford Foundation to stimulate interest and training in public affairs research. This grant led to the launching of a broad program of studies concerned with the influence of social values on the determination of public policy. The seminar was designed as an integral part of this program, to advance interdisciplinary cooperation in such research as well as to contribute substantively and methodologically to greater understanding of the nature of the integrative process at different political levels.

The authors wish to express particular appreciation to Mrs. Lucy Daghlian for her tireless and devoted assistance in the preparation of the manuscript for this volume, as well as in serving as the all-important secretarial pivot of the Public Affairs Research Program.

PHILADELPHIA, PENNSYLVANIA
JULY 23, 1963

PHILIP E. JACOB

Contents

I

The Integrative Process: Guidelines for Analysis of the Bases of Political Community

Often cited in literature concerned with the development of political community and coordinated collective action, the concept of political integration is neither very well defined nor very clearly understood. Here, Philip Jacob and Henry Teune set forth the problems of defining the concept and systematically investigate the variables associated with political integration in the light of existing studies contained here and in other sources. Serving as both a summary of previous research and an introduction to the succeeding chapters, Chapter I "integrates" the existing knowledge about political integration into a conceptual framework. Ten factors that may exert some degree of integrative influence are examined in the chapter. The various research studies employing these factors are evaluated, and some potentially rewarding areas for future research are explored.

THREE LINES OF POLITICAL DEVELOPMENT HAVE CONVERGED TODAY to lend new urgency to the problem of political integration.

First, the unprecedented pace of urbanization has produced a logjam of complex human necessities that are overtaxing the established forms of local governments; yet new patterns of government suitable for the metropolitan era have not emerged, and political fragmentation of responsibility now threatens elemental living conditions as human congestion increases.

Second, the rapid rate of birth of new nations, often without a firm political tradition or unified communal base, has suddenly confronted many peoples and governments with responsibilities of extraordinary difficulty. The need for coordinated collective action to meet these demands often runs athwart hard-set lines of social organization to which people have been accustomed and which have conditioned them to pull separately rather than together.

Third, in the realm of international relations, the incredible technological transformation of the means of communication, production, and annihilation, which has created relationships of mutuality among people, has at the same time precipitated a crisis of survival for mankind. Most people continue to place their ultimate hopes and loyalties in separate nation-states and are not disposed to function as fellow-members of a world community. As a result, the instruments of international cooperation and political organization are so poorly supported that they cannot fulfill the political, economic, and strategic requirements of a world that has become, by force of circumstance, interdependent, but refuses to recognize its interdependence and act accordingly.

How can human beings develop effective political communities? What are the conditions of integration among communities —and within them—that will meet the essential problems of contemporary human relationships? Social research is now belatedly giving increased attention to these issues. The purpose here is to examine the significance of what has been done to date and draw together some of the principal implications for further research. At the same time we would expect that the urgency of new insight into the bases of political community will prompt large-scale, systematic empirical inquiry to this end.[1]

1. This appraisal is based in large measure on the interdisciplinary seminar on research in political integration conducted at the University of Pennsylvania, 1961–62 (see Preface). The authors of this chapter assume personal responsibility, however, for the conclusions which are expressed here.

Fundamental problems confront the social scientist who explores this area. Among these problems is the very definition of the subject matter. Just what is the phenomenon of political integration? Are we all talking about the same thing when we speak of political integration among nations, or within nations?

A second group of problems concerns the identification of variables that have an influence in producing integration or inhibiting it. What circumstances of social organization and behavior lead people to hold together as a community or form ties with other communities? How can we tell whether a given set of circumstances will encourage integration? How can one identify precisely the variables that do have influence?

A third set of problems lies in measuring the impact of each variable and of all the variables in combination upon the political process. We need to know not only that a particular condition or factor *has* some influence upon political behavior, but *how much* influence it has, in what *combination* it functions with other determinants of interaction, and in what *sequence* of circumstances it must occur to be influential.

The Phenomenon of "Political Integration"

The concept of integration, though widely used to describe closely knit political and economic relationships, has not been

---

References to major recent research on political integration at the international, national, and municipal levels will be found throughout this volume. The range and depth of such studies has been increasing rapidly during the last few years. Pioneer works include: Karl W. Deutsch, *Nationalism and Social Communication* (Cambridge: Technology Press, and New York: Wiley, 1953); Ernst B. Haas, *The Uniting of Europe,* (Stanford: Stanford University Press, 1958); Lucian Pye, *Politics, Personality and Nation-Building* (New Haven: Yale University Press, 1962); Rupert Emerson, *From Empire to Nation* Cambridge: Harvard University Press, 1960); Karl W. Deutsch *et al., Political Community and the North Atlantic Area* (Princeton: Princeton University Press, 1957); Lloyd Rodwin (Ed.), *The Future Metropolis* (New York: George Braziller, Inc., 1960); John C. Bollens (Ed.), *Exploring the Metropolitan Community* (Berkeley and Los Angeles: University of California Press, 1961); Raymond Vernon, *Metropolis 1985* (Cambridge: Harvard University Press, 1960).

precisely and consistently defined even in some of the important recent research and statements of public policy concerning it. It is one of those terms whose meaning we often take for granted. We think we know what it is when we see it. But faced with the task of rigorous empirical research, in which political integration is the critical dependent variable whose growth or decline, existence or non-existence is the central object of inquiry, we need to start with a clear understanding of what constitutes "political integration."

Political integration generally implies a relationship of *community* among people within the same political entity. That is, they are held together by mutual ties of one kind or another which give the group a feeling of identity and self-awareness. Integration, therefore, is based on strong cohesiveness within a social group; and *political* integration is present when a *political*-governmental unit of some sort is cohesive.

The Focus of Cohesion. This broad definition, however, leaves open several key questions. First, in respect to what *kinds* of group behavior does the existence of cohesion constitute political integration? In other words, what are the particular *objects* of cohesion which result in political integration? What ties are the critically important ones from the standpoint of constituting a political "community?"

One approach to this question is the concept of a "security-community" advanced by Deutsch and his fellow authors of *Political Community and the North Atlantic Area.*[2] Within a given territory people will have attained a "sense of community and institutions and practices strong enough and widespread enough to assure for a 'long' time, dependable expectations of 'peaceful change' among its population." A security-community, these authors explain, is "one in which there is real assurance that the members of that community will not fight each other physically but will settle their disputes in some other ways."[3]

2. Deutsch *et al., Political Community in the North Atlantic Area, op. cit.*

3. *Ibid.,* p. 5. Non-violence in the resolution of group conflict is also considered a critical component of political "community" by Ernst Haas in his studies of international regional organization. Haas adds to his definition the

Thus the object of cohesion in this view is limited to the resolution of conflict without violence.

Valuable as is this clean-cut definition, it is probably too narrow to cover many of the situations with which people studying political integration are concerned. An alternative, though looser, definition would include a much greater variety of objects of common action or corporate behavior as indicators of an integrated political community. The essence of the integrative relationship is seen as *collective action to promote mutual interests.* A broad range of social activities carried out or supported by members of a community would indicate a high degree of integration among them—the operation of schools, provision of social welfare benefits, maintenance of fire and police protection, recruitment of defense forces (particularly if accomplished by voluntary enlistment), building of highways, obeying of traffic signals, undertaking of collective commitments such as contracts and treaties. The basic test is whether the people do function together as a coherent social group on a significant number of tasks. It is both the *range* of functions in which they engage corporately, as well as the particular *kind* of function they undertake, which is important.

This approach leads easily to another which identifies political integration with certain kinds of outputs of policy in a society. From this point of view, cohesion is politically integrative if the political unit acting through its governing organs,

element of loyalty to common institutions. See *The Uniting of Europe, op. cit.*, p. xv. Objections have been voiced by Herbert J. Spiro on the grounds that these criteria are too narrow to encompass the range of relationships which ought to be analyzed in a comprehensive comparative approach to the study of political systems. Violence, he maintains, may be a characteristic "style" of conflict resolution in some social groups which should nevertheless be considered communities. He would extend the notion of community and require as a minimum condition only "awareness of the pursuit of common goals, and of members' inability to solve alone the problems arising out of these goals." See Herbert J. Spiro, "Comparative Politics: A Comprehensive Approach," *American Political Science Review*, Vol. 56, No. 3, September, 1962, p. 589. This seems to broaden the concept of community so much, however, as seriously to impair its usefulness in research.

adopts public policies that commit the resources of the community to common purposes. Thus, if a high portion of total community income is spent by the government, this could indicate a high level of cohesion within the political community—or at least evidence of the readiness of the community to acquiesce in the particular corporate commitments represented by those expenditures.

The use of governmental expenditures as a measure of integration hardly seems applicable at present, however, in the area of international relations. Even within a nation, the size of the government's outlay is not an unqualified indicator of the degree of cohesion. It must be determined whether public expenditures really do reflect widely felt agreements within the community.

Western industrialized nations with mature political systems do tend to devote a much larger proportion of their income to government programs than do less developed countries; and, judging by other indices, they appear to have correspondingly greater cohesion.

On the other hand, it is questionable whether state-managed societies, which absorb an even larger proportion of the national income in government expenditures, are more cohesive than the Western democracies. The problem is that authoritarian governments may employ high public expenditures in order to offset conditions of serious *dis*integration. Anxious to maintain themselves in power or to promote ideological objectives, authoritarian regimes may try to overcome great internal dissension in the society by force and repression.

Another illustration that suggests caution in this matter is the frequent absorption of a large portion of government revenue in empire building and various other forms of external exploitation. Sometimes such action may demonstrate a strong base of common interests and aspirations in the community. People may indeed be drawn closely together in a vicarious experience of rulership over others, pride of empire, and the like. On the other hand, empire building may actually be the preoccupation of a few, while to the many it represents a burden of life and treasure which they would prefer not to carry.

Degree of Cohesiveness. A second definitional problem concerns the *degree* of cohesiveness necessary to constitute integration. How many things must people do together for their society to be considered integrated? How persistently must they continue these common tasks? Does integration require that most of these things be done by most people voluntarily and habitually, rather than under compulsion? Or, on the other hand, may compulsion be needed to cope with those who deviate, and, if so, how much force can be applied to how large a minority before disintegration sets in? Or may compulsion, *applied to a majority,* actually induce voluntary and habitual compliance by most of the people in the course of time? To these questions no precise answers are evident at the moment.

Integration is a relative, rather than absolute, term. Instead of considering political integration as a specific condition that exists or does not exist, it might be more useful to envisage a set of relationships which are *more* or *less* integrated, or a progression of events leading to an *increase* or a *decrease* of integration. A rough test of the degree of cohesiveness necessary for integration might then be worked out on a comparative basis, using the broad notion of functional agreement or cooperation mentioned above. The test would be the proportion of "public-oriented," cooperative, corporate activities in which people in various political units engaged, as against actions that were non-corporate, or "privatistic" (concerned with personal or special group interests rather than the general well-being).

Such a test should surely be refined, with greater weight given to certain kinds of activities that are more crucial to the survival of the community than others. This would probably lead to some more precise measures, such as those proposed by Deutsch *et al* in the inquiry previously mentioned. Engaging in acts of violence as opposed to accepting peaceful change is certainly a far more telling indicator of the degree of cohesiveness than popular agreement on means of common sewage disposal or international postal communications, important as these activities may be.

Here the concept of a "threshold" of integration is relevant. The threshold—that is, the point where a group of people have become sufficiently integrated to be considered a community—may be fixed arbitrarily. One might simply designate the threshold as the point where the amount of corporate activity overbalances the noncorporate. On the other hand, a comparison of the situation of various political units might reveal a sharp breaking point in their scale of corporate activity. The threshold would then be distinguished by a marked increase in the amount of corporate activity as revealed by empirical data. Or again, we might think of the threshold of integration as a zone that might be entered, or even crossed or recrossed, more than once during the halting and uncertain progress of a community toward integration.

The degree of cohesiveness necessary for political integration is ultimately made evident in each case by whether a social group "jells" and holds together as an identifiable and functioning political unit. The Austro-Hungarian and Ottoman empires did not maintain sufficient cohesiveness to remain integrated political communities; most metropolitan areas have not yet achieved sufficient cohesiveness to become integrated.[4]

But this ultimate test has limited usefulness to students of the political process and especially to formulators of policy. We do not want to wait for a final verdict. We want to know in advance of the final curtain whether action is moving toward or away from integration. Hence, we try to predict the degree of cohesiveness necessary for integration, at least in terms of probabilities: What are the *chances* of a group's achieving and maintaining a communal relationship, or, conversely, of an existing community breaking up?

The Levels of Integration. A third definitional question: What is the *level* of cohesion among people at which political integration functions?

4. See Chapter 5, Wheaton, "Integration at the Urban Level."

Studies of political integration have been conducted at at least four political levels: the local community, the metropolitan or provincial level, the nation-state, and international organization, including both regional and global relations among states. Are we dealing with the same phenomenon at all of these levels? Is political integration at the local level clearly the same thing to which we refer when we talk about international organization, agreement and collective action? A distinction between the two is important.

At the lowest level of political organization, the local community, integration involves relationships directly among persons. At the higher levels there is an additional dimension: integration concerns the relationship of community to community. This distinction may not rule out the possibility that we are confronting essentially the same process. For what is going on at each level is the development of corporate functioning; and ultimately, whatever the political level, it is individuals who are involved in these activities.

To be sure, political integration among political communities, in contrast to integration within them, must harness the actions of people who already are incorporated and function collectively through established governmental institutions. The problem is to integrate the already integrated. The situations are not dissimilar, however. A major part of the integration process within a community involves intergroup relations establishing patterns of overriding corporate endeavor among the vast array of primary and secondary groups which are themselves integrated social units.

On balance, it appears that the differences between relationships within communities and those among communities are not so great as to indicate that political integration is a different phenomenon in the two types of situation.

Structural Characteristics of the Definition. There are certain structural characteristics basic to the definition of integration: The terms "political integration" and "cohesion" are (1) dispositional, (2) involve a concept of comparative rank, and (3) are relational.

People are *disposed* to respond in an integrative way toward certain objects or stimuli under certain conditions. Thus, integration cannot be "seen"; it must be inferred from certain observations. This is analogous to concepts of intelligence and I.Q. "Intelligence" can be defined as the disposition to learn easily and rapidly. It can be predicted that a person who has this disposition will probably do well in school, will solve problems easily, will remember abstract stimuli, and the like. Are these things indicators or definitions of intelligence? The paper and pencil tests of intelligence are treated as both indicators and definitions. In order to distinguish clearly between an indicator and a definition, however, a clear statement must be given of what it is that an indicator indicates. But definitions of dispositional terms, and this is the important point, will appear to be indicators.

Political integration is a concept of rank. It is defined by a ranking of entities, in this case communities. Communities are *more* or *less* integrated. We know, in short, the degree of integration by observing those things which manifest integrative behavior. We do not define at this stage any zero point or point of critical degree of disintegration.

Finally, "integration," like "cohesion," is a relational term. It refers to what happens between communities or persons. Just as the term "father" implies another person, so "political integration" implies something about two or more political actors or communities.

Political integration, defined roughly as a state of mind or disposition to be cohesive, to act together, to be committed to mutual programs, refers to more than one aspect or dimension of behavior. It has no one best indicator. Despite these various facts about definitions of political integration, indicators are often used as definitions.

In summary:

(1) More rigorous research on political integration should

sharpen the definition of what is being analyzed: identifying the properties of this pattern of social behavior, specifying the degree of cohesiveness necessary to achieve or promote integration, and finally, stating the level of such behavior in terms of the political system or structure within which political integration is being examined;

(2) Full agreement on a definition is neither likely nor necessary, but it is essential that there be understanding of the different usages of the term "integration";

(3) Useful research can develop around the concept of cohesion, indicated by overt or passive agreements for collective action of various kinds (as well as agreements not to act, such as pledges not to commit acts of violence);

(4) In respect to the question of degree, a useful working procedure is to adapt to this research the view of "system maintenance" in the field of systems theory research—in other words, enough cohesion to hold the group together as an identifiable entity for some forms of political action, at least to the extent of being self-identified;

(5) In regard to the level of analysis, research on integration can profitably be conducted at all levels of political organization, since we have no reliable knowledge that the phenomenon is substantively different at the various levels.

A Systematic Concept of the Integrative Process

To understand how and why political integration develops, or is inhibited, it is necessary first to identify other phenomena associated with it; second, to establish the interrelationship among factors that appear to exert an integrative influence.

Previous research indicates ten factors that may exert integrative influence upon people: (1) geographical proximity; (2) homogeneity; (3) transactions, or interactions, among persons or groups; (4) knowledge of each other; (5) shared functional interests; (6) the "character" or "motive" pattern of a group; (7) the structural frame or system of power and decision-making; (8) the sovereignty-dependency status of the community; (9) governmental effectiveness; (10) previous integrative experiences.

The enumeration of these variables does not mean that the list of influential factors has been exhausted, nor that their integrative influence has been conclusively established. Research procedures designed to test the significance of these variables have been explored along the following lines: (1) hypothesizing a relationship between integration as the dependent variable and other phenomena that appear to be influential; (2) determining appropriate indicators for each of the independent variables; (3) measuring the extent to which each variable is present in a given political community; (4) where possible, establishing an interrelationship among variables and the relative weight of each in the total situation; (5) establishing correlations with the degree of integration present in each community.

The extent to which research of this type has proceeded varies greatly among the ten variables, as the review later in this chapter will indicate. Truly comprehensive and definitive research on political integration will require both intensive work to identify and establish scales for particular variables and once this is done, the examination of enough cases in widely differing settings to make possible reliable generalizations.[5]

5. In order to avoid circularity in the pattern of research, particular attention needs to be paid in selecting indicators to make sure that the same index is not being used to identify different variables. For instance, in research on political integration there is often a tendency to use a phenomenon as an indicator both of *integration* and of some variable affecting integration. If an inter-community or inter-jurisdictional agreement is accepted as an indicator of integration, it ought not simultaneously to be used as an indicator of homogeneity which is being examined as a possible variable indicative of influence. An attitude of social acceptance toward other members of a political community, which is used to indicate a degree of homogeneity, should not simultaneously be used as an index of the degree of integration when one is trying to determine how much of an influence the factor of homogeneity has in encouraging integration. Confusion on this point seems to us to have muddied the water and limited the rigor of some of the work previously done in this field. The problem becomes peculiarly acute in comparative research on integration at different political levels and in different

Table 1 attempts to envisage in comprehensive fashion the relationship between these integrative factors and the degree of integration actually achieved at four different levels of political community. This conceptual framework provides for the discovery of important differences in the mix, or combination, of integrative variables that are influential at different political levels; it also suggests the possibility of weighing the respective influence of each variable against the others, though instruments of measurement are not yet refined enough to permit a reliable assignment of weights among the variables. Indeed, comprehensive research on political integration has hardly yet been undertaken. Data on the various indicators have not been gathered in sufficient volume to make possible factor analysis of the relative impact of each variable.

The Interaction of the Variables. Ultimately it will be necessary to answer at least four questions before arriving at a composite assessment of the integrative process.

First, how much of a given factor must be present in the total situation of a community for it to cross the "threshold" of integration? In other words, what is the "critical mass" of each factor necessary for integration to occur?

Having considered the question from the standpoint of each separate variable, it is necessary to face the problem of the necessary combination or "mix" of variables to produce integration. What is the integrative "syndrome?" What is the formula of combination? Or are there several such formulas that seem to work, and what are they?

The third question returns to the problem raised earlier of the level of political relevance. We cannot at this stage predict that every integrative factor will be equally potent at each political level. Can we discern at what political and social level each factor becomes significant? A preliminary exploration of this problem

---

cultures. Indicators used to identify one variable in a given study may in another study be used to identify a completely different variable. An early step in the advancement of research on integration could therefore be a systematic overview of the variables and their corresponding indicators.

TABLE 1

THE INTEGRATIVE PROCESS: A CONCEPTUAL FRAMEWORK

		Political Level			
		International (between nations)	National (within nations)	Metrop. Regional (bet. local communities)	Local (within local communities)
Integrative Factors	Proximity			Ch. 3, 4	
	Homogeneity	Ch. 2, 6, 8, 9	Ch. 2, 6, 8	Ch. 2, 6	Ch. 9
	Transactions	Ch. 2, 3, 4	Ch. 2, 3, 4	Ch. 2, 3, 4	
	Mutual Knowledge	Ch. 2	Ch. 2	Ch. 2	
	Functional Interest			Ch. 5	Ch. 5
	Communal Character				
	Political Structure	Ch. 7	Ch. 7	Ch. 5, 7	
	Sovereignty (autonomy)	Ch. 2, 6	Ch. 6	Ch. 2, 6	
	Governmental Effectiveness	Ch. 6	Ch. 6, 9	Ch. 6	
	Integrative Experience	Ch. 3, 4	Ch. 9	Ch. 3, 4	
Impact Formuli	Combination				
	Sequence				
Indicators of Degree of Integration					

NOTE: Analysis of the operation of these integrative factors is provided in this volume where indicated by the chapter references noted.

in reference to the influence of values in the political process is undertaken in Chapter 8.

The fourth question is whether there is a particular sequence of steps or ordering of variables upon which integration is conditioned. It may be essential that certain acts or conditions precede others before the succeeding variables can become effective as integrative forces. This requires not only a quantitative estimate, in other words, but also a time process analysis.

A Costing Model of Integration. In an attempt to arrive at an overview of the integrative process, the University of Pennsylvania Seminar on Political Integration tried to develop a kind of "costing model" which would relate variables to one another and assess their respective integrative impact.

In the model, the impact of each of the variables was evaluated in terms of costs, or conversely benefits, to the members of a community. "Cost," used here in a non-monetary sense, expresses the degree to which people are willing to expend effort and concern to accomplish or work against a given objective.

The first step in developing the model is to appraise the cost of each variable to those persons or communities involved in a particular issue of integrative relationships. A demonstration of how this might be done was carried furthest in reference to transactions (see Chapters 3 and 4).

Second, it is necessary to differentiate the price of a particular variable as it appears to different individuals and groups. People make sharply different appraisals of what they are willing to expend in order to achieve a given goal or to prevent its achievement. The differential impact of various types of government services upon different elements in metropolitan communities, for instance, is pointed out by Wheaton (see Chapter 5). From a political standpoint it is necessary to differentiate further the cost of the integrative variables according to the political influence of the various groups in a community. One must discount the cost estimated by those with a limited amount of political influence, whereas one must increase the weight attached to the cost estimated by those who are elite or in positions to influence strongly the course of public events.

Finally, an over-all costing or estimate would attempt to balance the costs of all elements in the integrative process against the rewards or benefits which the acts of integration might be expected to bring. At the point where the benefits exceeded the estimated costs (after allowing for the differential elements previously mentioned) a "price of merger" would appear. If cost exceeded anticipated benefits for the people affected, the price of merger would not be met and integration would not occur.

One must emphasize that in this type of model we are asking for data which at the moment it is impossible to supply with any degree of assurance that it represents the real situation in any political community. Nevertheless, the model does perhaps indicate what kinds of data must be sought and who it is that ultimately must supply the necessary information—the people in specific communities who have it in their power to make or influence decisions and who thus control their relations with each other and with people in outside communities.

Identifying Integrative Factors

Essential to the development of sound research on political integration are reliable methods of identifying and measuring integrative factors. In the following discussion some prevailing hypotheses concerning the ten integrative factors mentioned above are first set forth; indicators of each of these variables are proposed and appraised, and some lines of research to test the hypotheses are explored.

1. ***Proximity.*** The hypothesis is that the closer people live together geographically, the more likely are integrative relationships to develop among them; and the closer communities are to each other, the greater the likelihood of their political integration. This hypothesis is usually qualified by recognition of a close

relationship to other variables such as homogeneity, interaction or transactions, and mutual knowledge.

There is a noticeable difference between studies of international integration and integration at the local or metropolitan level in the attention given to proximity. Preoccupation with international regionalism, especially since the Second World War, has led to a kind of rough geopolitical calculation that international integration among nations is facilitated by their regional contiguity. Curiously, this assumption has not been subjected to rigorous testing, and the argument remains largely in the realm of pitting cases against each other to support or refute the proposition of a regional imperative to international association. Against the experience of contiguous "little Europe" is cited the experience of the British Commonwealth or the Organization of American States whose members are widely dispersed. When such reservations are met by refinements of the regionalists' hypothesis, the purely geographic element is in effect qualified by reference to other kinds of proximity.

Regional science intra-nationally, however, has prompted a serious and sophisticated analysis of the proximity factor, although its relationship to political integration has only begun to be explored intensively.[6]

Procedurally there is every reason to move ahead on both the international and intra-national levels to determine the influence of the factor of proximity on political cohesion. With enough cases, it ought to be possible to control other variables sufficiently so that definitive conclusions can be reached about the influence of physical distance, *per se*.

Among indicators used to measure proximity are contiguity (see the case study of Philadelphia suburban communities reported in Chapters 3 and 4), physical distance separating communities from one another, using either boundary to boundary, or center to center; time to travel from one community to another by available transportation (the value of this indicator is

6. See Walter Isard, *Methods of Regional Analysis* (New York: Technology Press and John Wiley, 1960).

that it reflects more realistically the possibility of physical contact between people or communities than does the raw index of distance); cost of transportation; and number of "intervening opportunities" or choice points—such as intersections, traffic lights, shopping centers, etc.—along the way. Distance, in other words, is a function of technology, density of population, or some combination of these indices.

For the moment, we conclude that geography becomes significant only as it engages the motivation of human behavior. Its integrative impact is indirect and must be mediated through other factors.

2. ***Homogeneity.*** The problem here is essentially to identify the social boundaries of a community and to see to what extent they correspond to the effective political boundaries. In other words, how much of a difference does it make in holding a group together as a functioning political unit if its members have similar social, economic, or other characteristics?

The hypothesis is that social homogeneity will contribute strongly to the feasibility of political integration and, conversely, that communities whose members are very different from one another will have a very hard time achieving or maintaining political integration. Viewing the problem in inter-community terms, the hypothesis holds that the more that communities are similar, the more successful are attempts to build integrative relationships among them.[7]

The choice of indicators for social homogeneity presents an immediate and large research problem. There are ten different elements that have been used as tests of homogeneity: wealth or income, education, status or class, religion, race, language, ethnic identification, attitudes (a catch-all of different types of dispositional factors such as perceptions, fears, aspirations, loyalties), values, and "character" (which in the sense of social or

7. The term "homogeneity" for purposes of empirical research involves the use of statistical measures both of central tendency and dispersion of specific characteristics. For an example of research procedures on homogeneity using socio-economic characteristics, see Eshref Shevky and Wendell Bell, *Social Area Analysis* (Stanford: Stanford University Press, 1955).

communal character is taken to be a composite of traits held to distinguish a particular group). Each of these has been applied as a test of homogeneity without much regard to whether similarity or likeness has in fact been associated with a *feeling* of homogeneity—that is, a sense of belonging to the group that shares the particular characteristics.[8]

This has been particularly true in the case of use of economic indicators of homogeneity. Some studies have seemed to take for granted that wealth, income, occupation, and so forth, automatically establish a common social outlook or class affiliation. There is enough empirical evidence, however, to contradict the extreme versions of economic determinism and to call for explicit testing of the degree of interrelationship between economic factors and other elements of social homogeneity.

One approach that can help indicate how people actually feel toward others is to use the well-established concept of "social distance" in measuring attitudes and values. One's readiness to associate with others in a variety of situations is scaled and compared. Similarity in people's expressions of social distance toward one another and toward persons and groups outside their community is taken as evidence of a *feeling* of social homogeneity. If people are wide apart on the social distance scale, one assumes that they are not very homogeneous socially and, hence, according to the integration hypothesis, that political integration among them would be difficult to achieve. The closer the readiness to associate, the stronger the presumption of political cohesion within the community.

If economic indicators are to be used as indicators of homogeneity, it is important to introduce several measures to supplement raw figures of wealth or income level in a social group. We need to know, for instance, not only how equal or unequal people

8. See, for instance, the conclusion of Cantril and Buchanan that people within nations feel they have more in common with their fellow nationals than with people of a similar social-economic class in other countries. William Buchanan and Hadley Cantril, *How Nations See Each Other* (Urbana: University of Illinois Press, 1953).

are in their material status but what opportunities they may have to change their situations and to better or worsen themselves. In other words, one wants to have both a measure of dispersion or concentration of wealth and income and a measure of *mobility* among income brackets.[9]

The raw socio-economic indicators of homogeneity need to be supplemented by information concerning the attitude of different groups toward each other, for instance, haves to have-nots and vice versa. The society's homogeneity will be substantially affected even in the case of a large disparity of incomes if the have partners are strongly disposed to assume public responsibilities and, in particular, to be carriers of some of the burdens of the have-nots. Thus, inequality in economic rewards might be offset by readiness to share wealth or at least not to have wealth constitute a social barrier.

This leads the inquiry concerning social homogeneity more strongly toward attitudinal elements. For instance, if we have discovered that a particular group of haves accepts a large measure of social responsibility while others do not, we need to know what motives have persuaded each group to take their differing positions. What "payoffs" do they anticipate, or what norms are influential in one case or the other? It is possible that the more public-spirited attitude, viewed in long-term objectives, might not be an indicator of greater disposition for homogeneity but rather might represent a calculated attempt to prevent greater homogenization resulting from pressures which the intelligent and foresighted haves were clever enough to anticipate and try to forestall.[10]

This vital kind of understanding of motivating hopes and fears in human behavior is fundamental to determining whether homogeneity is deeply grounded and real or merely a surface illusion be-

9. The factor of mobility is also relevant to other economic indicators, for instance, in regard to class status, religion, and attitudes. The *fluidity* of a society—the ability of people to cross social lines—may be an important element in increasing the sense of homogeneity.

10. The implications of this factor are further explored by Deutsch in Chapter 6.

neath which people are not really alike at all. From this standpoint attitudinal research seems quite basic in establishing the presence of homogeneity. What is not too clear is whether some kinds of attitudes are more fundamental than others when it comes to ascertaining the social boundaries of a community. One is inclined to say that attitudes that reflect fears, fundamental aspirations, loyalties, and values are the critical ones, whereas those that are merely representative of various kinds of information or knowledge are not so.

The use of values as an indicator of homogeneity presents particular difficulties. There has been widespread and fundamental disagreement over what is meant by the term "values." Some of these disagreements are explored in Chapter 8. Probably the most important distinction from the standpoint of research on homogeneity is the distinction between values as goals, or preferred events, and values as normative criteria of action representing feelings of obligation, legitimacy, and the like. The distinction is important because goals and norms are fundamentally different kinds of phenomena and hence represent different social characteristics. Each may properly be examined as a human attribute which might have an important effect in establishing the homogeneity or heterogeneity of a social group. The methods of identifying and measuring norms and goals differ because the objects of observation are intrinsically different. Hence research on homogeneity of values must start with a precise definition of the phenomenon under investigation.

A second research problem concerns the identification of *group* values when values are peculiarly the attributes of individuals. There is often a tendency to think of groups or collectivities having a personality or a character of their own which represents something over and beyond the values of the individual members of the community. We can find at this stage no sound empirical foundation for such conceptions and see no way to use them as indicators of homogeneity. The existence of such collective values for groups seems more a matter of subjective impression than of verifiable observation.

On the other hand, if by collective values or value patterns we mean a modal distribution within a community of either goals or normative values, these can be made the object of empirical research. If either goals or norms are widely shared by individual members of the community (as against deviation from these goals or norms by minorities in the community) this might well be the most basic element of likeness or homogeneity. Shared values are close to the springs of motivation; thus if the basic direction of action is similar among the members of a group, one might expect them to constitute a firm and solid unit. Consequently, considerable attention is devoted here to the means of identifying and measuring the distribution of values within and among communities and the determination of the extent to which communities are linked by similarity of the values that prevail among the inhabitants.

In practice, research has moved much further in applying the indicators of wealth, education, class status, and religion, than in examining the impact of attitudes and values. It is important to plan to correct the balance and to conduct at the local level, the national level, and the international level systematic studies which will attempt to plot the map of homogeneity of attitudes and values; that is to say, to provide at least rough profiles of the degree to which members of a given community share or differ in the attitudes and values they hold.

Homogeneity should probably not be identified by any single index. The social boundaries of a community should be drawn on the basis of a composite profile of the various indicators previously mentioned. This raises, of course, the difficult question of whether a truly sound composite scale of homogeneity can be derived. At present it seems impossible to determine in more than an arbitrary fashion the proper weights to assign to each element in the total scale, especially in view of the strong probability that their influence will vary with different cultural situations and at different levels of political structure and organization.

Our conclusion is that current research procedures should treat each possible contributing element to homogeneity as a separate variable whose weight as a factor contributing to political integration would be assessed separately. This is particularly necessary if research on political integration is to become comparative across cultural lines and between different systems and levels of political organization.

3. *Transactions.* The influence of *transactions* as a factor of political integration is now the subject of intensive research, partly as a result of developments in the analysis of communications as a field of social behavior. The subject is extensively treated by Deutsch in this volume and elsewhere. In the most general terms, the hypothesis holds that cohesiveness among individuals and among communities of individuals can be measured by—and is probably promoted by—the extent of mutual relationship or interaction among them.

The range of transactions is, of course, tremendous. As in the case of the factor of homogeneity, it is important to try to determine which of the many forms of transactions may be most critical to the promotion of cohesion. Research has concentrated on three major types of interaction: *communications*—the interchange of messages (mail, telephone, radio, etc.); *trade*—the exchange of goods and services; and *mobility*—the movement of persons (a type of transaction that may be assessed also by frequency of personal contacts).

How much interaction among people is significant? At what point in the spectrum of transactions, from practically no interaction to the most regular and continuous interrelationships, does one decide to identify this factor as worthy of notice? Two approaches have provided useful data for analysis. One is to compare the amount of transactions of a given type among members of a particular community with the amount that is carried on by the membership of the community with the outside world. This ratio of "domestic" to "foreign" transactions can be ascertained for a community at the lowest or at the highest political level, the term "foreign" referring to all persons outside the given community. The second approach, developed particularly by Deutsch and explained in Chapters 3 and 4, uses an indifference model to arrive at a figure of expected transactions against which the actual state of transactions can be compared. That is, were there to be no intruding effect of community cohesion, one could calculate how the total body of transactions or particular group of transactions might be expected to be distributed throughout the population. To the extent that transactions exceeded this figure, they would measure the influence of community integration upon the flow of transactions—or conversely, the extent to which transactions could be considered an integrative influence. In either case, the hypothesis would require a demonstration of a close correlation between relative frequency of transaction and the amount of political agreement and corporate activity among the members of a particular community. The question would be whether one could, in effect, superimpose on political boundaries a map of transaction boundaries (representing points at which transactions exceeded either the "expected" rate based on indifference, or the actual rate of transaction outside a given area) and find that these boundaries coincided.

Exchanges or transactions between people in various communities have costs attached to them. Costs of transactions differentially benefit one community over another. Attempts to facilitate transactions, and thus political integration, would probably be resisted by communities whose income depends heavily on intercommunity transactions. Switzerland has a large stake in maintaining the nation-state system because it lives largely off international transactions. In much the same way, a local community in New Jersey living off the flow of such transactions as traffic tickets, restaurants, and gasoline stations has a direct interest in opposing reductions in transaction costs resulting from limited access highways, subsidized public transportation, and increased air traffic.

Cost accounting of transactions, then, could explain existing patterns of political integration as well as help predict where greater political integration is likely to occur. A simple scheme for cost accounting transactions between any particular set or group of political communities is presented in Table 2.

TABLE 2
TRANSACTION COSTS
FOR A SET OF POLITICAL COMMUNITIES

Technique of Transaction	Changes in Costs as Functions of: 1 Distance ($ per mile)	2 Political Boundary ($ per boundary)	3 Distribution of Control of Cost Decisions	4 Distribution of Benefits of Transactions
Communications (movement of messages—mail, telephone, and telegraph, etc.)				
Trade (movement of goods and services)				
Mobility (movement of persons)				

If costs of transactions are related to political integration, then the greatest amount of political integration should occur between communities where (1) distance and (2) political boundary factors are negligible, where (3) those who are affected by the changes in costs can participate in decisions relating to costs, and where (4) the benefits of the costs of transactions are rather evenly shared. The use of a particular technique of transaction should be greatest when, after the initial cost of the technique, costs do *not* vary with distance (holding short distances constant) or political boundary and when costs are determined by all those affected thereby and are mutually beneficial.

Research on transactions as a factor in integration has been carried farthest in the international field with reference to the analysis of colonial-empire relationships. Its application to the analysis of metropolitan areas is just beginning (see the experimental design developed by Toscano in Chapter 4). What is needed is a large-scale extension of this kind of research, now that its design has been sharpened, to situations at all political levels and involving a variety of cultural contacts.

On the basis of the limited evidence so far produced, it is not at all clear that the hypothesis can be sustained without considerable modification. It is apparent at both the international and local levels that intimacy of transactions does not always lead to political integration. The transactional influences, if indeed they do represent an integrative factor, may be conditioned by other variables; or other variables may need to be present for the transactions to have their integrative impact. Thus, the evidence is conclusive from Deutsch's studies of communications and trade between colonies and mother countries that transactions far exceeded the expected rate based on indifference; nevertheless, in most of these instances the empires have broken up, indicating that political integration never took hold in the face of both insufficient rewards for at least one party to these transactions and serious lack of homogeneity of values, attitudes, status, wealth, and other factors.

This suggests the great importance in future research of attempts to appraise the interrelationships of transactions with rewards and other variables and to develop estimates of the relative weight of the transactional factors in the total group of pressures and influences.

4. ***Mutual Knowledge* ("*Cognitive Proximity*").** Both attitudinal research and the study of transactions, as well as of the influence of proximity in a geographical sense, have indicated that something more than propinquity is necessary to induce people to work together closely and form a viable political community. Indeed, it is apparent that unless people are aware of each other and know a good deal about one another, they are not likely to enter into social or political partnership. However much alike they may be, in terms of the elements of homogeneity discussed previously, if they don't *know* that they are alike, the effect is lost. People may be next-door neighbors in an apartment house but remain complete strangers. When this occurs they are not inclined to become closely knit members of the same social group or community. The

hypothesis here is that mutual knowledge or understanding among people and groups of people is essential to their functioning together effectively as a political community. As a matter of fact, the argument for the integrative influence of all three of the previously discussed factors—proximity, homogeneity, and transactions—rests upon an assumption that they will induce greater mutual acquaintance and understanding which in turn will encourage a community association.

This proposition calls immediately for considerable refinement. First, how much understanding and knowledge and, second, what kind of knowledge may contribute to integration? How much do you need to know about someone else in order to feel inclined to join with him in a community? At the level of political communities, in contrast to more intimate social groups, the evidence suggests that people do not demand close acquaintance as a condition of association. At the international level, loose and informal attachments, including alliances, are formed with virtually no basis of acquaintance across national lines, though it is apparent that more enduring and demanding forms of political integration do not arise among groups that are relative strangers. Thus parochialism, ignorance, and apathy among large populations have often facilitated the creation and maintenance of empires by governing minorities. At the local level, however, some familiarity with the overt behavior patterns of one's neighbors seems to be an element in establishing community. We seem to want to know how people take care of their property, what their church affiliation is, how interested they are in education, and so forth, before we decide to move into their community or encourage them to move into ours.

This familiarity with overt behavior is supplemented by knowledge of certain physical or social characteristics which will enable us to determine whether the persons fit our stereotypes of desirable or undesirable neighbors. In other words, it is not so much knowledge about the specific *individual* which influences integration as it is knowledge about the *type* of person as identified by racial, ethnic, class, and other such group characteristics. Put another way, it is not knowledge *per se* about other people that is significant for political integration but knowledge that links up with a preconceived gallery of stereotypes which each of us holds and uses as a touchstone in determining whether we want to live and work together.[11]

These stereotypes—while strongly persistent—are not immune to change. Actually they may be very volatile. There are repeated demonstrations of people reversing deeply set images of other nations under the impact of new political alignments. A classic illustration is the transformation of widely held American images of Japanese and Germans within a few years after the Second World War and, conversely, of American images of Russians.

This suggests a third qualification. Mutual knowledge will not contribute to integration unless it is accompanied by or linked to experience or memories of experiences which have had a favorable impact. In other words, it depends upon the *quality* of our previous associations whether a fuller understanding of what another person is like will cause us to seek closer association, or on the other hand, to fear him, be contemptuous of him, or simply ignore him. Familiarity in itself seems to have little behavioral influence; it is knowledge which excites an anticipation of reward that exerts an integrative impact.

Finally, it is apparent that *accuracy* of mutual knowledge may have relatively little to do with determining its integrative effect, except to the extent that it enables knowledge to bear up under test and trial. The fundamental requirement is that knowledge

11. There is now available an excellent comprehensive review and bibliography of research on national stereotypes. See H. C. J. Duijker and N. H. Frijda, *National Character and National Stereotypes*, Vol. 1, "Confluence," (Amsterdam: North-Holland Publishing Co., 1960). See also the important work by Harold Isaacs and other associates of the Massachusetts Institute of Technology Center for International Studies who have developed techniques of interview and survey which effectively establish prevailing patterns of ethnic images. Note also the impressive "Proposal for Cooperative Cross-Cultural Research on Ethnocentrism" by Donald T. Campbell and Robert A. Levine, *Journal of Conflict Resolution*, Vol. 5, No. 1, March, 1961, p. 82. This is an effort supported by Northwestern University's Programs of African Studies, International Relations, and Comparative Politics.

will have conveyed *awareness* of others and, second, that it will have aroused favorable or unfavorable *dispositions.*

The object of inquiry, therefore, is not so much the range of mutual knowledge, nor its validity, but the evaluation of this knowledge by the members of the community. The indicators we use should relate, therefore, to ascertaining what people *think* they know about one another rather than what they actually do know and whether they obtain from this knowledge a sense of mutual appreciation or the opposite. Attitudes and images, therefore, are the most productive indicators, and the growing volume of research on stereotypes held by persons of what other people or groups are like is highly relevant.

5. ***Functional Interest.*** An important influence in the development of political communities may be the convergence of functional interests, that is, the interests to which people are prepared to devote major effort for fulfillment. Such interests might also be defined as actions for which they expect a substantial reward as a result of their efforts (if one assumes a view of human motivation consonant with the stimulus-response theory of learning). The proposition to test is whether the functional interests of the bulk of a community are sufficiently similar so that they will be advanced by the development of common political ties. Conversely, sharp diversity of functional interests within the society might be expected to limit the possibility that any corporate action by the government would be able to convey benefits widely and evenly throughout the society.

If the hypothesis is expressed in inter-community terms, integration would be viewed as dependent on the extent to which the dominant functional interests are shared in each community and thus could be advanced by inter-community agreement or association. By way of illustration, economic interest groups whose prosperity is contingent upon a high external tariff may not be amenable to international economic cooperation which involves a reciprocal lowering of tariffs. Effective economic integration would depend upon whether groups that would benefit in each country from an expansion of trade, or the development of joint investment policies, are more dominant than groups which feel they would not benefit—for instance, farmers who are at a disadvantage in competition with producers in other countries.

In international relations, an illustration of the influence of functional interest as an integrative factor is the alignment of nations in a war for national survival and now, in view of the development of the technology of mass annihilation, the strong pressures for international disarmament agreements for survival.

These converging functional interests, however, may not provide a firm and lasting basis for integration. They often tend to be transitory—people's devotion to particular interests switching as conditions change—and hence functional associations may be simply marriages of convenience.

Analysis of functional interests recalls the issue of homogeneity, raising the question of the extent to which people in the same or different communities share interests. However, considered in political terms, the issue is not so much the identification of *common* interests, as it is the assessment of the influence of *particular* interests in the decision-making process. We want to know not only whether a large number of people have the same stake in a given type of endeavor but what interest groups are politically dominant.[12]

Functional interest analysis should relate to the fancied as well as the real interests of people. Sometimes what people think will contribute to their benefit will not turn out to be beneficial and may even preclude any possibility of their obtaining the benefit they seek. They may see their interest only in the short run and be confounded by long-term developments; or they may accept a statement of some respected leader rather than try satisfying themselves directly that their interest is involved; or they may simply be badly misinformed and think that they are pursuing an interest when they are not. From a short-range action standpoint, and that is of course what concerns us in the analysis of integrative forces, it is the belief that counts most. The reality is significant only indirectly and in the longer run as it serves to reinforce

12. See Wheaton, Chapter 5.

or correct beliefs by facilitating or frustrating action based on those beliefs.

One further point needs to be made concerning functional interest analysis. In the political arena these interests are almost always funneled through *groups*. They represent in a sense embyronic communities or, indeed, may be highly organized and stratified communities operating as social and political forces within the broader political community. Hence, this kind of analysis is primarily concerned with interests as articulated by groups rather than by individuals.

Given these circumstances, appropriate indicators of functional interests are the policies expressed by organized interest groups and actions undertaken by them to advance these policies. One should recognize that these functional interests are by no means limited to economic stakes; they can be developed around a whole range of non-economic goals such as civil rights, education, peace, and civic improvement.

Although there is relatively little difficulty in determining indicators of functional interests, there is no clear solution for the problem of measurement. Mere numbers of people associated with a given functional interest group convey no understanding of their political weight. Political "power" is a highly volatile element, with no reliable indices, despite efforts to measure influence in terms of the subjective judgments of people who are considered by an observer to be influential (the approach taken in studies of community power structure).

Nor is there a good way to measure the *intensity* of the functional interest, that is, the depth of attachment to it of those who share the interest and their readiness to devote themselves to the advancement of their interest. For these reasons research on the influence of functional interest in political integration is handicapped.

An important task that can be undertaken is the identification of interests and interest groups that move the community toward or away from integration. One can also identify those interests that reach beyond a particular community and link up with corresponding interest groups in other communities to form a possible basis for inter-community integration. The studies by Ernst Haas of the functional bases of integration in Western Europe are an excellent pioneer effort in this direction at the international level.[13] Haas closely identifies the degree to which trade unions, business organizations, and other functional groups in the six countries of the European Community share the same objectives and the extent to which they conceive of their interests as being compatible with European integration or to depend on the maintenance of national autonomy.

To some extent the studies of voting behavior both in elections and in legislative activity can provide some measure of the relative political influence of interest groups. This is especially true in countries whose political systems enable major interest groups to dominate particular political parties or blocs—either at national or local levels. One trouble with using voting as a measure of interest group influence, however, is that the vote of an elector or legislator usually reflects a combination of influences and pressures; he is not the minion of a single interest group. In the absence of more adequate instruments, however, the measurement of functional interest by its capacity to command political support is justified, especially in determining its influence as a factor in political integration.

6. ***Communal "Character" or Social "Motive."*** Some major contributions to the study of social behavior in recent years have reconstructed the concept of social or group character to make it amenable to empirical research. These studies have empirically described modal distributions of attitudes, values, and patterns of overt behavior.

From a motivational standpoint these studies raise the provocative question of whether societies may acquire by cultural inheritance and learning a set of behavioral dispositions so pervasive and compelling that the whole group will tend to act in a distinctive manner. Community behavior will run, so to speak, in grooves which have been carved by the "communal" character.

13. Ernst Haas, *The Uniting of Europe, op. cit.*

McClelland, for instance, by content analysis of the statistical distribution of relevant symbols in appropriate samples of the community's communication stream, has successfully demonstrated differences among societies in the mix of three major motivational sets: an affiliation motive, an achievement motive, and a power motive. In turn, particular combinations of these motives seem to be demonstrably related to certain complexes of social and political action, such as economic development.[14]

Studies of communal character open a new dimension of analysis for students of political integration. If it is established that a community can acquire a collective motivational pattern that strongly influences its behavior on economic enterprise, it may be possible that it will have acquired traits which dispose it toward cohesiveness and integration or, on the other hand, toward anarchy within or belligerence without. Using techniques similar to those developed by McClelland, research should be able to establish profiles of communal character related not only to national entities but to sub-national communities and trans-national groupings. These characterological assessments could be compared with indices of community integration in the same manner that McClelland has linked motivational patterns to economic development.

To our knowledge, sound empirical research on national character has not yet developed evidence of a direct link between communal dispositions or traits and integrative behavior to the point where an integrative syndrome can be identified. Observations of the peculiar patterns of belligerence or cooperativeness, anarchism or responsiveness, of particular societies and national groups have, on the whole, been too impressionistic and scanty to sustain this kind of conclusion at present. This should not preclude an attempt, however, to salvage the concept of national character or communal character and to see whether, with available research techniques, a rough estimate can be made of the integrative force of acquired cultural characteristics or psychologi-

14. David C. McClelland, *The Achieving Society* (Princeton: Van Nostrand, 1961).

cal motives of various communities.[15] A point of departure for such research might be to build on McClelland's work and attempt to determine whether there are correlations between the mix of achievement, affiliation, and power motives on the one hand and internal and external community cohesiveness on the other. To put the research problem in hypothesis form, we might take McClelland's "affiliation motive" as the aspect of communal character most likely to be associated with integrative or cooperative behavior. We might then suggest that those societies characterized by a high proportion of affiliation motive, in contrast to achievement and power motives, would be both internally cohesive and strongly disposed to cooperate with other communities. The indices of communal character so construed have been specified and scaled with some precision by McClelland. A major set of indicators is to be found in the verbalization of aspirations and beliefs in stories used with children at an early stage of socialization.[16]

Another significant approach to the identification of communal character, this time at the national level, are the studies of aspirations and fears by Hadley Cantril and Lloyd Free using a self-anchoring scale.[17] Employing Cantril's and Free's findings on national differences in hopes and fears, one could establish

15. The communal character approach tends to discount the significance of leadership as a determinant of social action, for it generally implies an initiative stemming from the mass of society. To safeguard against the possibility of imputing to communal character an influence which in reality may come from leaders who are in a position to command the following of their society, the analysis of character, or motive, should be conducted in such a way as to permit separate identification of elite patterns, and comparison with the distribution of the motivational patterns through the society as a whole.

16. See McClelland, *op. cit.*, Chapter 5, in which he spells out his typology for content analysis.

17. This comprehensive program of research, conducted in seventeen countries, is summarized in Hadley Cantril and Lloyd A. Free, "Hopes and Fears for Self and Country: The Self-Anchoring Striving Scale in Cross-Cultural Research," *The American Behavioral Scientist*, Vol. 6, No. 2, Supplement, October, 1962.

whether they were significantly correlated with integrative behavior. In other words, do nations that have a generally pessimistic view of the future tend to be less or more cohesive, than those that are more optimistic? Are nations whose aspirations center largely on increases in economic welfare likely to be more cooperative in their international relations than those that are predominantly preoccupied with prestige, physical security, or political independence?

Each of the above sets of studies of what we have called broadly communal character already encompasses enough data so that it should be possible to take their findings as is and, by matching them with measures of both internal and external integrative behavior, conclude whether such characterological features do have significant influence upon the building of cohesive national communities and, further, upon the encouragement of association between nations.

7. *Structural Frame.* Analysis of the system of decision-making or the power structure within the community introduces a different kind of variable from those previously discussed. The question here is the organization or arrangement of political action, rather than behavioral characteristics of persons or groups.[18] We want to know whether the *system* makes a difference in the amenability of a community to cooperative relationships. If the community is pluralistic, rather than monolithic, if it is organized hierarchically or provides equality in decision-making, if it is socially stratified or mobile, if its political authority is centralized or dispersed—is the society more or less likely to be internally integrated and more or less disposed to be closely linked to other communities?

While research on social and political structure is voluminous, there has been little attempt to determine whether structural differences carry over into the influencing of community and inter-community cohesion. Prevailing democratic theory holds that consensus or, more explicitly, consent is vital to the growth

18. See the view expressed by Teune in Chapter 9 that structural arrangements can be treated as persistent behavioral dispositions.

of a healthy and united political community. Consequently, a political structure that permits wide participation in decision-making should be conducive to cohesion, whereas one that is authoritarian should invite dissidence and in time disintegrate as a result of pent-up frustrations exploding in violence. But this democratic hypothesis has not been systematically tested by applying a reliable measure of the degree of cohesion to communities that have differing forms of government.

In view of the recent evidence from the experience of new and developing countries, the hypothesis might be turned about. A proposition now frequently advanced holds that a structure of highly concentrated political authority, with strict limitations on general participation, particularly on the voicing of dissent, is almost a requisite of national community organization under conditions of threat and social change.

It should be possible to determine whether consistently clear differences in cohesiveness appear in communities at the same political levels which have marked differences in political structure. Thus one might compare a set of local communities in the United States in which political power was tightly held in a few hands with another set where it was widely dispersed with a large amount of public participation in decision-making. A similar comparison might also be undertaken among nations. Both the extent of *internal* cohesion and the disposition toward external cooperation should be examined.

Indicators of political structure would include: the amount of day-to-day decision-making power exercised by top leadership, the degree to which leadership is organized in a strict hierarchy of power, the amount of accountability of policy makers to others, the amount of organized political opposition tolerated, the degree of mobility within the structure of political power, and the amount of political influence exercised upon the leadership group by other segments of the society. A considerable volume of data is available, particularly at the national level, on these points, so that scales of political structure are feasible, enabling countries to be ranked according to some of the dimensions suggested. Correlation with integrative behavior could then be undertaken. It is probable that the analysis of political structure at the local or metropolitan level has also proceeded far enough in the United States and in a few other countries to make possible the same kind of analysis.

In the area of international relations it is hardly possible to test the hypotheses concerning the effect of different structural patterns on integration. International relations, as they are currently conducted, are set within the *single* political frame of reference of the nation-state system: diffused, pluralistic, non-authoritarian, and consensual, with the possible exception of the European Community. International institutions do not have a highly structured pattern of political organization, and they all function within the same over-all system. There are really no situations to contrast. Historically, it is true, there are instances of international association with varying degrees of integration and differing types of political structures—federal, confederal, and unitary. But it is hazardous to reason from such situations to the present state of international affairs because there are so many elements that differ. About all that one might profitably do is to note the extent to which integrative behavior has been able to develop under such pluralistic conditions. To the extent that it has, the democratic hypothesis would be sustained. But in fact, progress toward international integration is so tortured that the hypothesis may well be questioned.

There is another aspect of structural analysis worth exploring: The hypothesis has been advanced that structure results in certain ideological dispositions and that communities with a common or similar political structure have ideological affinities that make it possible for them to integrate more easily. The argument is that countries with democratic political institutions are likely to develop an attachment to these institutions and that this then tends to produce a favorable attitude toward other democracies. Thus, one assumes that the Free World will be able to hold together, and that the North Atlantic Community will become increasingly integrated because a common heritage of political institutions will have engendered devotion to the same set of political ideas. The same argument would hold for communist nations.

A test of this hypothesis would require carefully controlled comparisons of the degree of integration achieved among communities with like political structures in contrast to their relationships with countries whose political institutions differ. It would be vital, of course, to recognize the great differences among institutional arrangements which may be hidden by a common facade of ideological labels. The facts of political organization must be distinguished from the form. How truly similar are the political systems of the United States, France, and West Germany; or, on the other hand, the political systems of the Soviet Union, Yugoslavia, and Poland? Fundamentally, it is a matter of adopting reliable indicators of structural political factors. Sound research would require that we go back to the indicators previously mentioned and look at the informal structure of power to obtain our data, rather than at the formal constitutional arrangements.

8. *Sovereignty-Dependency Status.* A major assumption of political theory as applied to the modern state has held that the ultimate mark of a community's political integration is its attainment of a status of "sovereignty." The classic concept of sovereignty holds, first, that within a fully organized society all members of the community are subject to a supreme political authority; and, second, that the community as a political entity is independent of control by any one else. Classic sovereignty implies total *internal* political cohesion and complete *external* autonomy. Sovereignty is synonymous with absolute integration within a community and absolute disintegration among communities.

The classical conception, however, seems to bear little relationship to the realities of modern political communities. Political power within a community is usually dispersed to some degree, even in a nominally sovereign nation-state with an authoritarian system of government. Variations in the amount of concentration or dispersion of power are considerable, but rarely does the structure of power establish the point of extreme concentration called for by the traditional concept of sovereignty.

Sovereignty is also limited externally. A few states exercise a large degree of—but not complete—freedom from outside control. Most are heavily restricted in what they can do by the influence of others, which is often so great that countries are in fact, if not in name, dependent rather than independent.

Conversely, sub-units of sovereign states, such as local governments, may in fact exercise a substantial degree of autonomy in the making of political decisions, or at least certain types of political decisions, even though theoretically they should be totally subservient to the central political powers. Such a situation prevails not only in federally organized countries but also in those where expediency directs that the central government shall leave many decisions to the discretion of lower units.

It is therefore crucial to determine empirically the relationship between political autonomy and political integration, treating each as separate variables and assuming that political communities will vary greatly in the amount of autonomy that they in fact exercise. Sovereignty and dependency represent relatively large or small amounts of autonomy on a continuum of varying political conditions at all levels of government.

The question of sovereignty has an economic dimension as well as a political dimension. A community's autonomy is expressed not only in its control over political decision-making but in the extent to which the allocation of its economic resources may be subject to outside decisions. This aspect, particularly, needs to be observed in societies that are not totalitarian, where the direction of the economic life of the community is not completely under political authority.

In Chapter 6 specific attention is given to the problem of scaling the sovereignty-dependency status of communities with reference both to political and economic autonomy. Indicators of political autonomy include: (1) the extent to which decisions are subject to review by another political authority; (2) the extent to which discretion is limited by constitutional or contractual commitments which may not be set aside without serious consequences; (3) the scope of the decisions or range of the decisions which are subject to control by the community itself; (4) the percentage of community defense and law enforcement facilities that are shared with other communities; and (5) the percentage and kind of decisions made in one community that are enforceable in another and vice versa (status-of-forces agreements, narcotics control, etc.).

On the economic side, some of the following factors may be used as indicators of sovereignty-dependency: (1) ratios of mutual trade (exports plus imports) to total external trade and to total gross product of each partner; (2) percentage of tax base shared; (3) percentage of gross national product received in forms of loans, grants, or direct aid; (4) percentage of population directly dependent on (employed by or in) other political communities; (5) percentage of vital resources imported (vital in terms of the community's major economic activities).

The significance of political autonomy as an integrative factor may be tested effectively by comparing the degree of sovereignty with the degree of integration prevailing in communities at different political levels. If sovereignty is presumed to solidify a community, then one would expect to discover greater integration on a national basis than within a local community with a much more limited autonomy. If it should appear that there is not a significant difference in the degree of cohesion between a local community and the national community of which it is a dependent part, the sovereignty hypothesis would be seriously discounted.

This is not to suggest that comparisons among communities of the same political level would not be useful. To test the sovereignty hypothesis, great powers possessing a relatively high degree of autonomy could be compared with well-established but less independent smaller countries, such as New Zealand or Denmark, and also with new, small, and recently formed states still heavily dependent for their survival economically, and perhaps politically, on outside assistance or toleration. The question to be answered would be whether those states which were at the dependency end of the scale proved to be any less integrated or cohesive than those that were closer to the sovereignty end.

Another type of study might pinpoint the sovereignty variable while holding many of the other variables relatively constant. Integration within a community could be assessed before—and after—it had achieved political independence. To what extent, for instance, has the achievement of political independence in the new countries of Africa and Asia been accompanied by an increase in community cohesion? If it has not, this would tend to refute the sovereignty hypothesis.

A corresponding study at the local level could be conducted which would examine the degree of integration which prevailed in communities before and after they were granted "home rule" or, conversely, what happened to the cohesiveness of communities which became absorbed in metropolitan or other regional jurisdictions.

As for the influence of sovereignty upon inter-community relations, it is commonly held to be a major hurdle to integration. In the study of international relations, it is widely asserted that the more sovereign the state, the less disposed it will be to cooperate with others and in particular the more intensely will it oppose political arrangements that encroach upon its autonomy. This proposition, which has never been put to a systematic and comprehensive test, will be examined here by Deutsch and others; their preliminary observations throw doubt upon its validity.[19] The question is entirely amenable to research. For instance, using the dependency sovereignty scales suggested by Deutsch in Chapter 6, one could then see whether those states that were most

19. Deutsch *et al., Political Community and the North Atlantic Area, op. cit.*

sovereign were consistently most reluctant to enter into international agreements, to join international institutions, to accept as binding the resolutions of international organizations, to honor international commitments, and otherwise to demonstrate a disposition toward international integration.[20]

One problem with the analysis of sovereignty in the ways that have been suggested is that sovereignty may have more influence subjectively as a state of mind than objectively as a condition of autonomy. Some people are extremely sensitive about independence, yet have very little. From the standpoint of political impact, it seems probable that it is the *consciousness* of sovereignty that impels action rather than its actual possession by a political community. If such is the case, one needs a different set of indicators from those that have been suggested. One indicator might be the attention devoted by the members of the community to the issue of sovereignty. Another might be their sensitivity to assumed violations of sovereignty or, indeed, their actual claims that it had been violated or was threatened. The verbalization of community loyalties would be an appropriate index—expressions of "Americanism" for instance—or non-verbal expressions of devotion to the symbols of sovereignty, such as patriotic celebrations. It is possible that one is considering here a variable that is substantively different from actual autonomy; perhaps this is one aspect of social homogeneity. But because it is tied so closely in people's minds to the image or goal of autonomy, it should probably be kept very much in mind whenever the issue is raised concerning the possible influence upon community behavior of the degree of sovereign status which it enjoys.

9. *Governmental Effectiveness.* There may be a very close connection between the cohesion of a political community and the effectiveness of its government in meeting demands and expecta-

20. An exploration along these lines is reported by C. E. Carrington, "Decolonization: The Last Stages," *International Affairs*, January, 1962. Relevant statistical data on international agreements among European states is available in Arthur Henry Robertson, *European Institutions: Cooperation, Integration, Unification* (New York: Praeger, 1959).

tions of its citizens. This issue is explored in considerable detail in the chapter by Deutsch on the price of integration. Essentially, the hypothesis is that governmental effectiveness is necessary to retain the loyalty of the members of the community, and such loyalty is necessary to maintain internal integration in the community. Governmental ineffectiveness, on the other hand, will engender pressures for new, different, or external forms of integration. Citizens will look outward and pitch their loyalties to new forms of political organization or to other larger units of community.

Such hypotheses require both agreement on what constitutes governmental effectiveness and availability of indicators which can identify governmental effectiveness regardless of cultural or political differences between communities. We believe that governmental effectiveness can be measured uniformly both by objective indices (such as physical survival or increases in gross national product) and by subjective indices (such as feelings of well-being and belief in an ameliorative future). The problem with objective indicators is that they must be shown to correspond to evaluations of the people. This can be done by comparing what people expect of their government with what they think they are getting. Such a measure has the advantage of being "self-anchored" within each community.

While it is clear that this variable may be of vital importance in analyzing the degree of integration in communities that are already politically organized, there is a question as to whether corresponding research can be undertaken on situations, such as international relations, where central governmental institutions do not exist or are rudimentary. Two possible approaches may be considered. First, one could treat international institutions as a form of government, (inter-government) whose effectiveness would be measured in the same way as national or sub-national institutions and compared with them. Objectively, the contributions of the United Nations, NATO, or the European Community) to the physical survival and well-being of people could be measured against their failures and frustrations. Subjectively, popular expectations of the United Nations could be compared by means of survey data with their estimates of fulfillment. The second approach would compare the amount of governmental responsibility invested in international institutions with the amount kept strictly within the hands of national or sub-national units of government. Just as within the United States expansion of national government responsibilities has reflected confidence in the government's effectiveness, so an increase in the scope of political actions and economic activities undertaken by international bodies could be a measure of their effectiveness.[21]

10. *Previous Integrative Experience.* Some research on international relations, such as the studies of European integration by Haas, suggest that integration may occur more easily if there have been previous integrative experiences. This "spill-over" effect in Philadelphia suburban communities was examined by Toscano with results suggesting that its occurrence may depend critically upon the presence of other factors. (See Chapter 4.) Further research is needed at the international, national, and local levels to determine whether there is a geometrical progression in the building up of political integration, where, after a number of integrative experiences, further integrative acts follow more and more rapidly. A refined spill-over hypothesis would have some basis in learning theory as noted in Chapter 9. It would involve the principle of reinforcement. But the reinforcement principle is symmetrical. Integrative experiences, in order to contribute to a generalized habit of integration, must be rewarded. If they are not rewarded or are punished they may encourage habits which lead to disintegration. In this perspective, once having broken the ground of cooperation with someone else or with another community, a person or a community confronted with a situation in any way similar might be expected to follow in the path that has already been tried out.

Lines of research to test this variable of integration at both the

21. Care must be taken here to avoid using increases in governmental activities as indicators both of integration and governmental effectiveness.

international level and the metropolitan are now clear. (See Chapters 3 and 4.) This is one of the areas in which direct comparison between international and metropolitan experiences should be possible by use of parallel indicators and a common methodological design.

Communication Theory and Political Integration

At both the international and metropolitan levels, students of political integration have been experimenting with various bodies of theoretical knowledge to improve the depth and scope of the investigation of integration. Karl Deutsch, developing his own previous work employing the theory of communication and control in the study of nationalism and social mobilization, focuses upon transactions and other forms of social communication in his analysis of the integration of political communities. Recasting traditional concepts and propositions, he points out the relevance of communications theory to the explanation of integrative behavior in parallel relationships of nation-states and local communities. Salience, covariance, message, memory, response, and transaction emerge in the following chapter as useful conceptual tools in such analysis.

STUDENTS OF INTERNATIONAL AFFAIRS HAVE SPENT YEARS TRYING to find out why people insist at certain times upon having a sovereign state of their own which occupies a sharply bounded area of the world. They also have been occupied with the motivations of the rank and file of the population, who often show extreme resistance to their country's being amalgamated or merged with other governments. What motivates popular acceptance of a government, compliance with its prescriptions, and voluntary giving of support when that government needs support? Why do all these things seem to be limited to clearly defined political constituencies? This problem comes up in international politics in the study of nationalism, supernational federation, world government, and incipient international functional institutions.[1]

Students of local government, however, find something similar. They find that the metropolitan complexes of our modern industrial civilization have sprawled out to such an extent that large built-up regional areas are visible on aerial photographs.[2] There is, nevertheless, widespread resistance by particular constituencies to the acceptance of common political institutions, whether they be common over-all municipal governments or common functional agencies to operate facilities ranging from sewage disposal plants to integrated regional high schools. This resistance is quite relevant and determines what can and what cannot be done in metropolitan areas. In this double context this preliminary report attempts to bring these two areas of concern together to discover whether the study of the sources of the demand for sovereignty on the international level can in some way shed some light on the demand for quasi-sovereignty or pseudo-sovereignty on the municipal level.

The task of this inquiry will be to outline steps that have been taken by investigators on the international level in order to understand the problem and then to discover whether these concepts can be of use in the study of metropolitan integration.

1. This chapter is based on extensions of basic concepts in international political integration developed in an advanced interdisciplinary faculty seminar on Political Integration conducted by the author at the University of Pennsylvania under the auspices of the Social Values and Public Policy Study sponsored by the Ford Foundation. Most of the basic theoretical concepts were developed in a research program on large-scale political communities supported at Yale University by the Carnegie Foundation.

2. For an elaboration of this point see Jean Gottmann, *Megalopolis* (New York: Twentieth Century Fund, 1961).

The study on the international level began with description, as it so often does in social and natural science. A number of historians and others began systematically to gather descriptions of nationalistic behavior through the case study approach. Carleton Hayes and Hans Kohn were outstanding early representatives of this type of work.[3] Rupert Emerson and others have continued it.[4] One of the first results of this work was to show the great uniformity that characterizes the passionate assertions by nationalists of the uniqueness of their particular nationalism.

The insistence with which nationalists claim to represent a unique national spirit, a unique people, a unique nationalist movement, is in itself one of the most uniform characteristics of political behavior. Just as a classical case of illness could be described long before the virus theory of disease was formulated, so it is possible to describe step by step the symptoms of nationalism and nationalist awakening. Nationalist movements have sequences of development that are not invariable but which occur so frequently that they cannot be accidental. Political scientists, such as Rupert Emerson, have studied the spread and disintegration of empires. In his work and in similar studies symptoms are described, sequences of symptoms identified, and clusters of symptoms and signs associated with each other, resulting in the discovery of syndromes of nationalism.

The perceptive recognition of such syndromes then permits the cautious and judicious appraisal of probable future development and of the wisest—or in any event, the least unsafe—course of policy under the circumstances of each particular case.

3. Cf. Carlton H. J. Hayes, *Essays on Nationalism* (New York: Macmillan, 1926) and *The Historical Evolution of Modern Nationalism* (New York: Macmillan, 1948); Hans Kohn, *Prophets and Peoples: Studies in Nineteenth Century Nationalism* (New York: Macmillan, 1946) and *Nationalism, Its Meaning in History* (Princeton: Van Nostrand, 1955).

4. Cf. Rupert Emerson, *Government and Nationalism in Southeast Asia* (New York: International Secretariat, Institute of Pacific Relations, 1942) and *From Empire to Nation* (Cambridge: Harvard University Press, 1960).

Communication and Control

A promising body of theoretical knowledge that may eventually prove helpful in getting a more differentiated analytical understanding of national communities and governments has been developed in the theory of communication and control.[5] Modern communication engineers have developed a wide variety of machinery that controls itself to some degree. The more self-controlling machinery was constructed, the more it became possible to understand the essential elements of the processes of control and self-control. The technology of self-controlling systems has in some sense been the mother of general systems theory and, more specifically, of the study of communication and control called cybernetics.[6] Essentially, control involves the transmission of messages, and the understanding of control processes is a branch of communications engineering, not of power engineering.

This development has some relevance for the understanding of political problems. A great deal of political science has concentrated its attention on the problems of power and has slighted the questions of communication. More recently, however, political scientists are paying increasing attention to the question of perception, as well as to questions of communication, transmission of messages, distortion of messages, speed of response to messages, and memories that are being brought to bear upon messages for interpretation. If we look upon nations and governments as communication systems, impersonal, verifiable evidence can be obtained to check general descriptive or qualitative assertions about nationalism, about sovereignty, and about the merger of states.

For example, some nationalists may assert that countries A and B "naturally" belong together, whereas other nationalists assert

5. Cf. the first section of Karl W. Deutsch, *The Nerves of Government* (New York: The Free Press of Glencoe, 1963).

6. Cf. Norbert Wiener, *Cybernetics: Communication and Control in the Animal, the Machine and Society* (Cambridge: M.I.T. Technology Press; and New York: Wiley, 1948), and *The Human Use of Human Beings* (Boston: Houghton Mifflin, 1950).

that B "naturally" ought to be independent from A. How does one get any kind of verifiable evidence? The classic nineteenth century solution was to say: "Ask the population." Plebiscites, however, frequently became pretexts for civil wars. Furthermore, voters had an exasperating way of changing their minds. When the food situation in Germany was bad after the First and Second World Wars, certain Germans in North Schleswig decided that they were Danes. (Their exasperated countrymen called them Bacon Danes.) When Germany became prosperous, these people rediscovered their German nationality. Indeed quite frequently people vote for living standards; moreover, they may cast their ballot one way and act in a contradictory way, often reversing their allegiances.

The simple idea of Ernest Renan to consider nationality a plebiscite expressed in everyday life leads to a complication. If we apply Renan's concept and say national allegiance is not something expressed only with a ballot in peacetime—and perhaps once every ten or twenty years on a battlefield—then it should be possible to count, measure, and verify the daily acts of commitment that Renan might have had in mind. One could analyze the daily behavior of people to find out to what extent they belonged to a particular community. From this it followed that one could think of communities partly in terms of the probability of mutual transactions between residents because their transactions would be more frequent or important within these communities than within any others.

If one asks how salient a relationship is in an individual's life, one first asks how much of that person's time and resources will be taken up by the relationship. This opens the way to a study of the whole range of transactions in a society. For example, the question of unification between Thailand and Bolivia does not arise since the populations of those two countries have almost no transactions with each other. The question whether Thais like or dislike Bolivians, whether they find each other congenial, whether they would work well together in a joint service agency is academic, since there are so few transactions between the populations that could give rise to rewards or frustrations.

Salience

Transactions are therefore the first step to salience. The study of quantitative densities of transactions is the first step toward estimating the degree to which people are connected with each other. If there are three units, A, B, C, and at the beginning of the period, A and B are united and C is alien, while at the end of the period the link between A and C has become much stronger and the link between A and B has greatly weakened, the result may be a secession movement between A and B and an integration movement between A and C. In politics these events depend on leadership, parties, historical events, and so on, but they also must have a favorite societal climate, a condition that can be studied and forecast from transaction flows.

In 1754 there were closer links between individual American colonies and Britain than there were among the colonies themselves. Proposals for federation or union did not stir up any great enthusiasm. By the 1760's and 1770's, however, the ties among the colonies were strong enough for some linkages. There were sufficient societal shifts and increases in transactions among the colonies to support the American split with Britain.[7]

It is these mute forces of history, the societal shifts, which precede many of the more spectacular political actions. Hans Kohn's book, *The Idea of Nationalism,* shows that almost every nationalist group has some heroic forefather who was calling for national unity or national reassertion and whose voice died in the wilderness. At a later stage other leaders appear who say much the same thing, but then things begin to happen. The difference is that the societal climate has changed. Thus, the first conscious at-

7. Cf. Richard L. Merritt, *Symbols of American Community, 1735–1775* (Yale University, Ph.D. thesis, 1962), publication forthcoming.

tempts to unify Germany by political means came in the early decades of the nineteenth century, between 1807 and 1815. Before then, it was not even tried, and even as late as the middle of the eighteenth century there was still a war among the German states fought with great energy and bloodshed. In the second half of the eighteenth century, there was a sudden flood of German journals and periodicals that catered to an all-German reading public and crossed state boundaries. Publications increased from about ten such journals to several hundred in some fifty years. At the same time all-German publishing was introduced. The all-German book trade became financially successful and the rate of communications increased enormously. All this happened long before the political fireworks of the nineteenth century, but it changed the whole political situation. Similarly, the economic changes between Bavaria and Austria, which are Catholic, and Saxony and Prussia, which are Protestant, affected the country. Bavarian industry had become dependent on Prussian coal, not Austrian or Bohemian coal. By 1830 when the question of the customs union arose, Bavarians turned to Vienna and said they did not want a customs union with Prussia; what could the Austrians offer the Bavarians? Austria, however, had no substantial economic favors to offer, for its economy was not meshed with Bavaria. The Bavarians became involved with Prussia, joined the customs union, and ended up in the German empire. The underlying fact of economic and educational interaction, however, preceded most of the more spectacular political and military changes.

Governments with great power and discretion could deliberately try to do things which would purposely change the direction of communications and thus affect the direction of integration. The Bavarian education officials in the 1780's who decided to standardize Bavarian grammar according to the North German model could have tried to do the opposite. Such moments of decision can greatly alter the course of events. In contrast, the Austrians got the Slovaks in the 1840's to standardize their spelling on a dialect which was remote from that of the Czechs and therefore made for two separate languages. At certain turning points, a single decision can affect the climate for many years to come.

The Study of Covariance

The second step in measuring the degree to which people are linked is the study of covariance, that is, the study of joint rewards and penalties. Covariance is an old statistical term; the romantic German phrase "community of fate" sounds much more impressive, but the basic argument is the same for both: If your neighbor prospers, you will prosper; if he loses, you will lose. This is by no means always true. Marxists have long tried to argue that the wages of workers in all countries will fluctuate together, with their income varying inversely with that of the bourgeois exploiters. Nationalists from Napoleon III to Adolf Hitler have pressed the opposite argument: that the main patterns of covariance, the main joint rewards, cut across class lines by countries, regions, or nations. The assertions of these theorists can be verified or disproved by observable facts, by the observation of covariance of income among people in different regions or different social groups.

We can discover whether such covariance is perceived, and this will remind us of the dual character of every political or economic interest. First, the actual probability of a joint reward may be called "interest" in the objective sense. Second, the concentration of attention upon an expected joint reward or deprivation would be the subjective aspect of the problem. Thus to assert that people will unite or accept common governments if they have "common interests" is to say two different things. On the one hand, it is asserted that they have a joint chance of payoff; this is an objective empirical assertion that can be verified, usually by means of economic, political, or strategic research and analysis. On the other hand, it is said that they are interested in, and attentive to, such a supposed or imagined joint reward, although this perception of reward may turn out to be unrealistic. (They may get more of a reward than expected, or they may get much less.) Data on these matters of attention, perception, and expectations can be obtained from the content analysis of mass media or other messages, and through interviews and survey research.

The classic reinforcement or learning theory describes what happens when there are many rewarding transactions in a community. When there is a significantly high level of important transactions, many of which bring joint rewards, the people who have experienced these mutual transactions will like them. When these transactions are highly visible, easy to identify and differentiate, people may form images of the community or of the group involved in the transactions. If these transactions were rewarded, the image of a community may be strongly positive. Liking this kind of community, people may say: We belong together. In their favorable reaction to the community, they might then also say, I can see myself as a member of this community; I will call it "we" if I speak of a group. I will call it "home" if I speak of a territory. I will express and experience love of country (patriotism) or love of a group of people (nationalism), but in any case I identify with this symbol or this group. What is done to this country or to this group or to its symbol, such as the flag, is done to me. I feel diminished or enlarged, depending on the diminution or enlargement of this country or this group.

If psychological identification or psychological role taking has gone this far, people will be willing to remain with the group, even if they now experience deprivation. The learning psychologists have experimented with rats and have made them pull levers in order to satisfy their hunger for cheese. If a rat is invariably rewarded with a cheese pellet for pulling a lever, the habit of pulling the right lever will persist. But the psychologists also varied the experiment by rewarding the rat only on a probability basis. The rat would again confidently approach the lever and pull, but no cheese would be forthcoming. Undaunted, the rat would pull again and in accordance with the built-in probability device, cheese would be forthcoming. Rats taught to work on a probable-payoff machine develop more tenacious habits of pulling than rats spoiled by a soft machine that rewards them every time. The important point, however, is that even on the probability machine the payoffs have to come relatively early. If the probability machine does not reward the rat at all the rat will not go on pulling.[8]

This sounds simple for rats, but the generalization that follows is less simple. The first hypothesis that follows would hold that if people have experienced a high level of transactions, with substantial joint rewards at one time, they may be quite willing to accept joint deprivations at a later time, provided joint rewards come again still later. The second hypothesis, still generalized from the rats and the cheese, is that a group of people taught to identify with each other by means of initial joint rewards but then reinforced by a probabilistic mixture of joint rewards and joint deprivations will show greater cohesion and greater strength of habit than a group of people who have experienced nothing but joint rewards. This is now a restatement of the classical nineteenth century doctrine of nationalism as presented in the writings of Ernest Renan: a sense of national solidarity is produced or strengthened by the memory of joint victories and joint defeats, common triumphs and common sorrows. It sounds more elevated to talk in the nineteenth century rhetoric of nationalism than to speak of rats and cheese, but it may refer to the same probabilistic reinforcement mechanism.[9]

There is another immediate policy implication: rewards must come before the penalties, and rewards must be strong and frequent enough to initiate the habit. If one goes to the French and tells them to first set up a joint army with the Germans, which is not a reward, to give up their national military institutions, dissolve their officer corps, expose themselves to the possibility of warfare, and only at some later date obtain cultural, economic, and other kinds of integration, then this is just as unlikely to

8. Cf. C. B. Ferster and B. F. Skinner, *Schedules of Reinforcement* (New York, Appleton-Century, 1957).

9. On this point see Karl W. Deutsch, *Nationalism and Social Communication* (Cambridge: M.I.T. Technology Press; and New York: Wiley, 1953).

work today as in 1954. In 1954 the European Defense Community was not only turned down by the National Assembly but was conspicuously opposed by most of the French people.[10]

In a similar sense, if local governments were invited to share burdens, losses, or sacrifices at an early stage, according to the general theory, this ought to be much less successful than if one could devise a way in which local groups could first share joint rewards and only later be invited to make joint sacrifices. This is a set of propositions which begins with transition measurements, goes on with measurements of rewards and probability distributions, then proceeds to inferences about psychological responses to these measurements and probability distributions, and then makes further inferences about probable attitudes. Every link in this chain is measurable. The responses, rewards, perceptions, and identifications can be measured through sampling attitudes, and they can then be confirmed through the study of gross group behavior, political behavior, and voting behavior. If reality turns out to be more complicated than this tentative outline, a great deal may still be learned from analyzing the variant cases.

The Search For Simple Models

The next line of development is the crude modeling of this process of the learning of habits of community perceptions, community identification, community compliance, and community support. What is proposed is a primitive theory of the methods of learning to form a market for common political institutions. This, then, is in a sense market research for regional or international government.

On the metropolitan level research could be conducted into the acceptability of common institutions, based on the assumption that acceptability of a particular institution will not depend primarily upon the intrinsic merits of this institution itself but

10. Cf. Raymond Aron and Daniel Lerner, *France Defeats the E.D.C.* (New York: Praeger, 1956).

rather upon the context of community perception based on previous transaction flows and the previous experience of reward.

There is nothing in the model that would claim that if deprivation goes on indefinitely, self-interest will not reassert itself. In politics deprivation never goes on indefinitely. If the individual is deprived of food for too long, he might die long before he changes his mind.

It is perfectly possible, however, to learn a set of habits at an advanced stage which may then make it impossible for the person who has learned them to change his behavior in a way that would be in accordance with his changed interest later. This might be called "heroic learning" or "pathological learning," depending on one's point of view, but it is quite possible to teach people to have an image of themselves that they would rather die for than give up.

For instance, at an early stage a Bavarian might be convinced that he would be more secure from the encroachments of the French if he would join in the greater Germany. He might then actually join Germany, and Bavaria might then share in the unprecedented prosperity from 1871 to 1913. The result is that the Bavarians become only nominal particularists. They made a special point of telling everyone that if war should come Bavarian regiments would fight with the utmost heroism and self-sacrifice for the common German cause. Later when the Germans got into the war, the Bavarians did suffer very heavy losses of life. If the Bavarians had seceded from Germany, they might have been better off; but at that point the habit of thinking of themselves as Germans had gone far beyond the original dispute over customs unions, prosperity, and security from Napoleon III. All these issues, which had played a role in the learning of the habit of being Germans at one stage, were now irrelevant. The Bavarians now would rather die than give up their learned self-perception and identity as Germans. It is conceivable that under certain conditions the Bavarians might unlearn being Germans again; they could become alienated again, but it is quite unlikely that any intense short-range deprivation would do this.

On the metropolitan level, individuals might have such strong identifications with communities that they would prefer to endure certain irritants rather than accept membership in a new or larger community. Here might be the case of the suburban voter rejecting integration into a metropolitan area, even though in his present situation he is harassed by mounting taxes, crowded schools, and traffic-choked highways.

Institutional Attempts at Coordination

A different line of research converging with this would center upon some of the institutions and attempts to coordinate behavior in order to get certain things done. The classical political science textbook way of coordinating behavior consists in having a third party set up with supervisory power. The individual is envisaged as functioning spontaneously and more or less haphazardly; so an office, an institution, a function, a government must be set up, distinct from the individual or distinct from the smaller group, which coordinates their actions. Motorists are perceived as driving thoughtlessly, and traffic police then must enforce a traffic code that keeps them from crashing. This is by no means the basic doctrine of traffic engineering, but it is the basic theory of politics of Thomas Hobbes. Individuals behave spontaneously in random aggressiveness against each other, making each other's lives "solitary, nasty, brutish and short," therefore a sovereign must restrain these individuals and coordinate their behavior, at least to the negative extent of keeping them away from each other's throats.

The basic notion is that the function of coordination is taken away from the components and is located in a separate cell or unit of the system—the sovereign, the king, the monarch, the Secretary General of the United Nations, the United Nations Assembly, the Federal World Government, or the federated city government. Someone has to coordinate, and coordination is done by an agency external to the other components of the system.

But in what manner, by what means, toward what goals and

along what lines of policy does the coordinator coordinate? Hobbesian political science does not know. In a Hobbesian world, everybody is at war with his neighbor, except for the sovereign, who restrains everybody. These theories of amalgamated government—through the single sovereign, the single committee, the politburo, or the United Nations Secretary General—all these are theories which avoid the problem of coordination by consigning it to a small group or to one person who is then trusted to accomplish it by means of his peculiar nervous system and point of view.

Classical theories of coordination are thus not theories of political coordination at all. They are theories about delegating the problems of coordination to biology or to small-group dynamics, to the small committee, or to the single individual. One may ask: How does behavior get coordinated in the mind of the sovereign, among the members of a politburo, the U.S. Joint Chiefs of Staff, the National Security Council, or the Committee on Foreign Affairs of Congress? Or: How does behavior get coordinated among the electorate or among the population of the United States or among the hundred-odd governments of the world? One then begins to ask: How do messages flow? Where is past experience stored? How are decisions made? Actually one is looking for decision-making systems which can make possible requisite coordination, or the minimum of requisite coordination. The central questions involve how coordination is accomplished and how people, individuals, or smaller groups build larger systems or form larger systems in which a degree of coordinating performance is accomplished, requisite to their needs or better than what they had before.

Delegation of a particular function to an individual, to a group, to an office, to a bureaucratic organization, leaves coordination to the internal processes of this *amalgamated* agency.[11] In-

11. Cf. Karl W. Deutsch *et al.*, *Political Community and the North Atlantic Area* (Princeton: Princeton University Press, 1957) and *Backgrounds to Community* (forthcoming), for a further development of the concepts of amalgamated and pluralistic communities.

side the amalgamated agency it is assumed that there will be a tight control of power structure. The chief of the agency controls the agency; he in turn has great self-control, and one hopes that the Freudian super-ego controls the chief. The result is a pyramidal structure of authority. The amalgamated institutions do, however, require a degree of compliance and popular support for functioning, a fact which is usually taken for granted by theorists, but which is precisely the kind of thing which cannot be taken for granted and which needs study.

There is a second pattern of accomplishing coordination. Neither specialized functions nor the over-all function of making a general class of decisions is amalgamated; instead sovereignty or decision-making competence is left with the components of the system. In this process the communications equipment and capability of the components of the system are increased to exchange messages sufficiently to ensure coordination. For example, to get a dozen cars over 300 miles of road from Philadelphia to Boston, one can string them together, have one tractor or engine pull them, and have all the decisions as to whether they should go or stop, turn left, right, or go straight ahead made by the one man in the cab of the lead car. This is the typical image of the train with the amalgamated function of steering all the cars of the train. The alternative would be to have the cars driven in convoy. In this case, each car or truck has its own steering device, and decisions must be made in the cab of each truck as to which way to turn. If the drivers have been trained to stay in convoy, they will manage not to lose liaison. They will exchange signals; they will watch each other; the lead car will watch to see that he does not lose the cars behind him; the cars in back will watch the lead car; and, with luck, the whole convoy will get through traffic. This convoy is a *pluralistic* decision system. The decisions are made in the cab of each truck in the road convoy, or on the bridge of each ship in its maritime counterpart.

In the first example, the task of coordination was delegated to a single component. In the second example, it was delegated to the communications and responses among a plurality of autonomous components. Under a third type of arrangement coordination might be built as an automatic function into the larger system. This might be done by material arrangements, as the ramps of a clover leaf crossing guide the flows of traffic; or it might be done by interlocking habits of most of the components, as the workings of a competitive market—"the invisible hand" described by Adam Smith—force certain patterns of behavior on small businessmen who wish to stay in business, or as the balance of power between rival princes, according to Machiavelli, forces a certain behavior upon princes who wish to stay in power. We may call such arrangements *controlled by the super-system.*[12]

Human Decision Systems

The simplest way in which a decision system can be pictured from a communications viewpoint is to assume a message-receiving function (intake in Diagram 1) as part of a system which has stored memories somewhere internal to it.[13]

Diagram 1—A simple decision system:

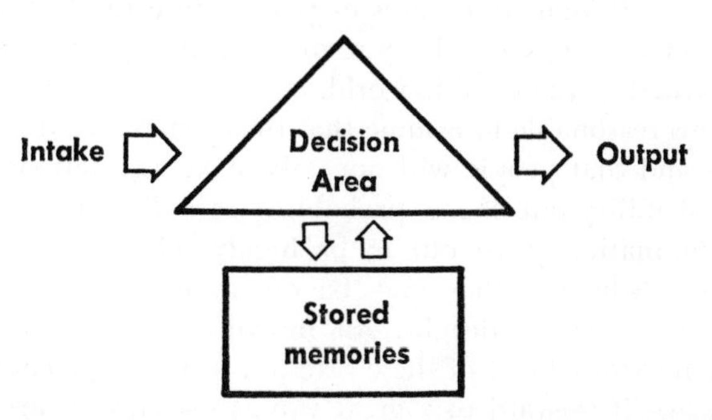

12. Cf. also the notions of sub-system dominance and super-system dominance in Morton Kaplan, *System and Process in International Politics* (New York: Wiley, 1957).

13. This, of course, is quite oversimplified. It is not intended to be a picture of an individual: it is intended to be a flow chart of functions. Cf. Karl W. Deutsch, *The Nerves of Government* (New York: The Free Press of Glencoe, 1963), pp. 258–61, for a more complete model of a decision system.

Instead of having the stimulus-response act of the experimental psychologist who is watching the twitching of the frog's legs, we are dealing with human beings who have vast and deep memories and who will therefore respond to most of the information intake primarily in terms of what is recalled from memory. A *decision area* may be pictured as one where incoming messages are combined with recalled memories for determining the output of the system. What a person will do cannot be predicted, therefore, from studying his intake of outside messages. What he remembers and what he will recall must be also investigated. This is the first caution against nineteenth century materialism. It must be realized that the memory of a human being is selective, dissociative, and combinatorial. The memory selects only a part of past messages, and it combines a selection of what we would like to remember with a selection of what our subconscious mind chooses to emphasize.[14]

In addition to selecting, memories dissociate. Men do not only remember a bird with wings; they remember the wings and the bird separately. And memories are combinatorial. In their minds, men put the wings of a bird on the shoulders of a man and imagined human flight thousands of years before the first airplane flew. Memories thus can be put together in new patterns that never existed in the outside world.

It seems reasonable to assume that the human memory is probabilistic and that people will not only make associations of very high probability but of low probability as well. If these improbable combinations turn out to be highly relevant and lead to significant behavior, they may be called inventions, strokes of genius, or flashes of insight. An individual may have subconsciously recognized one of these rare but promising combinations and pushed it forward to a great work in science or art or to a constructive solution or winning strategy in politics. Putting things together and estimating that a particular combination is worth developing is one of the processes behind all progress. It

14. Freud has demonstrated this selective remembering most convincingly. Cf. his *Psychopathology of Everyday Life* (London: Unwin, 1928)

results in outputs which somehow meet the needs of the situation better than before. In this sense, thought is innovating and creative, although it may prove to be miscalculated.

Any such creative effort or initiative may end up as a brilliant failure, for individuals, unfortunately, can think of combinations which fail. Nevertheless, win or lose, a memory has been employed that was not wholly determined by its current intake. One could predict with some probability what combinations would be likely to be selected, but this is a very different thing. It might turn out that some of the responses that were unlikely in the probability distribution of the environment would be the most probable in terms of the internal probability structure of the memory and decision system—the personality and character—of the particular individual.

"Mind" and "Group Mind": Memories and Decisions in Individuals and Groups

What has been said about individuals, applies also to some extent to groups. Pieces of information may be stored in the minds of different group members as well as in material facilities such as records, minutes, files, and libraries. Items of information from all these may be dissociated and stored, selectively recalled, communicated in the deliberation and decision process of the group, recombined into new patterns, and applied to current new information for autonomous group decisions about action.

In this sense, groups—from small committees to the decision-making bodies of whole cities or nations, or even to the entire politically relevant strata of the large political units—act like minds, drawing up ranges of memories and producing decisions different from those of any one of their individual members. *Thinking—that is, communicating, remembering, recalling, recombining, and decision-making—is, in this sense, a systems performance.* It is found in the rich communications system of brain, nerves, and blood within the body of each individual, but also in the larger, though simpler, interpersonal communications systems which we call groups, cultures, or social or political organizations.

In this view, it would be profitless to argue whether there is any such thing as a "group mind," or a "spirit of the times," or a "spirit of a people." But it seems more meaningful to ask what processes and proportions of selective memory storage and what probabilities of communication, recombination, and eventual application to behavior—as well as to new storage in memory—are involved in the individual and social processes of communication and decision to which these shorthand expressions or poetic names refer. With the help of this latter approach, the resources of systems analysis and content analysis can be a powerful aid to make an increasing part of these subtle processes amenable to verifiable research.

Memory

If social scientists observe the intake and the output of information of an individual and then attempt to correlate these two, they are operating at the level of the naive materialism of the nineteenth century. Memories would be ignored in such a naive research design, but memories are essential, although they are not directly observable. Some memories can be observed by examining literature, printed messages, mass communications, and so on, which go back into the memory of society, and by content analysis. On the whole the memories of individuals must be inferred. We can make the best use of opinion research, attitude research, and personal interviews (not only brief interviews but depth interviews such as the one conducted by Robert E. Lane with fifteen people at a housing project in New Haven in an attempt to find out what was the deep content of their memories, as these were relevant to their attitudes to politics).[15]

To some extent we must surmise as to what we think people

15. Robert A. Lane, *Political Ideology* (New York: The Free Press of Glencoe, 1963).

remember when we are dealing with foreign governments, as in the Berlin crisis, or with foreign leaders, such as Premier Khrushchev of the Soviet Union. One of the things we must try to estimate is: What do Russians remember about Germany? When the United States sends the Russians a message saying, (a) the Germans are only getting a small army and short-range atom bombs and (b) we are controlling them because they are in the North Atlantic Treaty Organization, we must be sure exactly what the Russian memories are in the light of which these messages are likely to be interpreted. And if Khrushchev says that he only wants to have Berlin a free city, as Khrushchev understands freedom, it would be good for him to think a little about what memories we have of the behavior of Russian Communists and how we are going to interpret his message. In a less emotional context, what were in January, 1963, the memories that were most often recalled by Britons when they considered entering the European Common Market, and what were the more salient memories of the leading political groups in France and Germany—and the most salient personal memories of such statesmen as Chancellor Konrad Adenauer of West Germany and President Charles de Gaulle of France—in considering the British request for admission to the Common Market under special transitional arrangements? The same would be true even when a municipal functional agreement is proposed. What are the memories which will be used to interpret this proposal and in what light will these policies appear to municipal officials?

A Second Look at Amalgamation and Pluralism

It is now possible to restate our earlier distinction between amalgamated and pluralistic systems of coordination and decision. Each such system, to have at least limited autonomy by itself, must have its own intake channels, its own memory storage facilities, its own decision area, its own output effectors, and its own external feedback circuits through information about the results of its past output that are returned to its subsequent input and thus may modify the system's further action.

Pluralistic systems, then, are those in which two or more sub-systems, each of them autonomous in the sense thus described, are so linked together that some output signals from one enter as part of the input signals into the other, but where the memories, decision areas, and main feedback circuits of the sub-systems—and thus their main decision-making facilities—remain distinct. This usually will require a series of autonomous decisions in both sub-systems in order to maintain coordination between them.

In the case of amalgamation, in contrast, some or all of the chief memory facilities, decision areas, and feedback circuits of the formerly autonomous subsystems have become merged. A decision produced by these major merged facilities most often is then automatically a decision for the rudimentary sub-systems, which may still have retained some minor or subsidiary autonomous functions. Such an overriding, or even directly effective, decision on the level of the higher system no longer requires any major decision on the sub-system level, except at most in regard to matters of implementation.[16]

Neither amalgamation nor pluralistic coordination may thus be cheap. In the case of amalgamation, the costs of coordination will have to be borne largely by the cost of creating and maintaining new, merged decision-making facilities. In the case of pluralism, the coordination will have to be met by the cost of retaining and, in fact, increasing the communicating and decision-making capabilities of the original components.

Some Implications for Study

One might then make studies of the degree to which pluralistic coordination of behavior may be practical, either in international communities or in metropolitan areas, when amalgamation might

16. Some current work by Fred Riggs at the University of Indiana deals with similar problems in administrative decentralization and delegation.

not be practical. Transaction flow, at the community perception level, must be examined as well as the institutional and systems arrangement, both amalgamated and pluralistic, which are available or which have been tried out. These two approaches might then come together. By looking at the demands that are likely to be made either of a pluralistic system or of an amalgamated system, by determining how much coordination and how many decisions of what quality may be demanded per unit of time, and by asking what will be the minimum responses acceptable to the needs of the people involved, it will be possible to gauge both the mutual relevance and the responsiveness of the system.

Mutual Relevance

Transaction flows first establish mutual relevance of actors. An actor with whom you have very much to do is relevant to you. This does not mean that the transactions are necessarily associated with rewards, that they are felt to be pleasant or beneficial, or that they are free of conflict. The one thing which is unlikely to accompany a high level of transaction is continued high tension and conflict, but it is quite possible to have high levels of transactions in certain fields combined with very elaborate social barriers. Nineteenth century middle-class families had domestic servants living in their homes, saw them face to face dozens of times a day, but erected very complicated social barriers to be quite sure that no human or social relationship should arise which might be interpreted as equality or human give and take.

A similar relationship exists in metropolitan or colonial situations. It is important to discover how relevant two territories are to each other. To what extent do they share compatible values? To what extent do they have interlocking roles? To what extent do they experience joint rewards? To what extent are they willing to set up common institutions? Perhaps most important, to what extent have they found each other and are now finding each other responsive to each other's messages and needs?

Metropolitan communities in the United States in particular have tried to combine a high income and high consumption economy in the professional and white collar services with a low wage economy in the unskilled service industries. As their own acculturated native or old immigrant labor supply moved into the high wage category, they found themselves scouring the world for the most illiterate, ignorant, and cheap sources of labor that could be discovered. When Italian workers, from their employers' point of view, became excessively literate and excessively prone to join labor unions and rise in the world, rural Negroes from Mississippi or former sugar workers from Puerto Rico were attracted into the low wage jobs which the older stocks had vacated. Pockets of low wage employment thus were maintained in many of the cities, resulting in economic complementarity of a high wage class of labor—professional managerial, white collar, and others—with a low wage class. Many of the jobs in the traditional low wage sector were not upgraded, making it necessary to find more and more primitive sources of labor supply. In the past a somewhat more homogeneous labor supply with a relatively high speed or moderate speed of acculturation existed, but now racial and color barriers have led to underpaid and incompletely acculturated colored urban cores of cities, abandoned by the predominantly higher income earners of the suburbs.

Economic complementarity based on inequality of wages may continue but at the price of increasing cultural alienation. There appears to be some cyclical process at work in today's large metropolitan areas. The trouble of metropolitan areas is not so much in race relations as in abandonment. High wage and high income groups moving out have abandoned the central city to its own fate by filling it with low wage sector people. The next step, urban redevelopment, may then bulldoze out the cheap housing and drive the low wage group in a wave into the first string of suburbs around the city. There, the first race riots occur as property value readjustments are feared or may have to be made. Then gradually some of the high income families move back into apartment skyscrapers in the city.

A way to understand the forces at work in a metropolis would be to study the multiplicity of transactions. The Puerto Rican who washes dishes in a cafeteria which is frequented before the theatre by commuting suburbanites has very little other transactions with this group. If it turns out that other bonds of communication arise and become multiple, one might obtain measures of acculturation, assimilation, and integration of immigrant groups by observing the multiplicity of bonds of communication that arise. If Boston's Irish, Pittsburgh's Slovaks, and Omaha's Czechs gradually become integrated with the rest of the population, the multiplicity of communications would tell a good part of the story.

Response

A second factor in this process of integration is the probability of response. *Responsiveness* can be measured as the probability of getting an adequate response within an acceptable limit of time. To use the Anglo-Irish example, when their union was concluded in 1801, one of the assumptions was that if the Irish would find themselves in need, the joint political system, the Parliament in Westminster, where English and Irish members of the House of Commons were sitting together, would provide the response needed. In the great famine of the 1840's, when hundreds of thousands of Irish lives were lost, Parliament showed itself incapable of providing famine relief large enough and soon enough to prevent this catastrophe. An ineradicable experience was gained by the surviving Irish; in their hour of need the English Parliament had not been responsive. Historians today have no doubt that if there had been as much starvation in London as there was in Ireland in 1846 and 1847, Parliament would have acted with considerably greater speed. It would have made the response on a considerably more generous scale and would have provided food that was considered edible by local standards of diet. When food was supplied to Ireland, too little and too late, it turned out to be American corn, which the Irish did not know how to prepare and were not in the habit of eating.

Sluggishness of response and niggardliness of relief thus were compounded by incompetence of selection. The net result was that in a crucial decision situation, responsiveness failed and the moderate reform movement for Irish participation in politics of the generation of O'Connor of the 1830's and 1840's was replaced by the extreme violence and terror movement of the Sinn Fein. Irish nationalism was never the same again. People cannot be left to starve and then be expected to regain faith in a parliamentary union under which this sort of thing could happen. In the 1920's Nicholas Mansergh, an English scholar, in interviews in Ireland, found that when asking Irish country people about grievances against England, the potato famine ranked highest.[17] It was remembered more vividly and more dramatically than Cromwell's massacres in the seventeenth century or the shootings during the Easter Rebellion in 1916.

Failure to respond to a group, a community, or individuals in situations which are crucial and highly salient to them would be one of the strongest ways of destroying a community. The capability of a governmental system for response is one of the most important variables to study. Response is the crucial part of the interactive process which makes any political decision system viable.

Capability vs. Level of Demand

A crucial variable in responsiveness is capability. It is not true that federations are promoted by the breakdown of component governments. There is a familiar image of the early American states as so incompetent and poorly equipped to handle their affairs under the Articles of Confederation that disgust with this bad state of affairs led to demands for federal union. On examination, this turns out to be for the most part a myth. Actu-

17. N. Mansergh, oral communication to the author, Princeton, 1953.

ally, the American states had greatly improved budgets, personnel procedures, legal powers, and patterns of government compared to what they had been in the colonial period. In the main, the federal Constitution followed not upon failures of the states but upon a great increase in state capabilities. In a similar way, the unification of Germany in the nineteenth century followed after a great increase in the competence and capabilities of the administration of the particular German principalities and states during the first half of the century. Unification of political systems for Germany followed improvement in component capabilities rather than degeneration of these capabilities.

Responsiveness is a function not only of the capabilities of the actors but of the level of demands made upon them. It is quite possible to destroy a joint institution which is functioning with undiminished efficiency simply by increasing the demands made upon it. If a telephone switchboard which gets a thousand calls a day gives good service, the probability of not getting through might be less than 1 per cent. If the same switchboard with the same operator gets 10,000 calls, it will be jammed most of the time and the probability of not getting through might become rather high. Even if switchboard operators were to be increased, the same thing will occur if the calls increase still more. What we are dealing with in government systems today is a race between two dynamic rates: the increase in capability of the common institutions or of the decision system of the community, and the increase in the burdens, the demands, the loads, or the claims made upon the system. What is needed for unification, either pluralistic or amalgamated, is a minimum margin by which capabilities manage to stay ahead of needs.

The growth in needs is not under the control of policy makers. The growth in needs is usually a byproduct of such developments as industrial, economic, and technological change; migrations; changes in consumer tastes; long-range secular dynamics of culture; and international challenges. The only variable with which policy makers usually can work is capability. Some of the elements for increased capabilities cannot be controlled or manipulated quickly, but others can. What remains is the ability of city planners, political scientists, statesmen, or the specialists of international organizations to discover and to suggest ways of organizing the existing elements of capabilities in such a way as to get a system whose performance will stay ahead of the needs and burdens with which it is confronted.[18]

Effects of Sovereignty: National vs. Local Authority to Make Decisions

In drawing these parallels between the metropolitan and national levels to measure capabilities, we must also consider the factor of sovereignty. We have experienced home-rule movements by localities in the United States, followed more recently by the phenomenon of partial shift of power to higher levels of government. It is the relationship of sovereignty to capability which determines whether governmental decision systems will be effective. In legal language, sovereignty is the ultimate right to make decisions, the right to make a decision from which there is no higher appeal. From a realistic political viewpoint, however, there is no such thing. There is no government in the world that can make decisions with ultimate finality, except either in short-range affairs or in the single limiting case where one government leader might decide to blow up the world and then do so. Short of blowing up the entire world, every major decision of a government is actually open to appeal to some agency, even though the latter may not be formally constituted. If the Polish government tomorrow should try to put dialectical materialism into Catholic religious instruction, Polish Catholics would have a way to appeal to world opinion, to the Vatican, and in general to all people interested in religious freedom. In some way, the Polish government would pay some price for the attempt to interfere with the content of religious instruction. The Polish government could

18. Cf. the analysis of Edward Banfield, "The Political Implications of Metropolitan Growth," *Daedalus* (Winter, 1961), pp. 61–79.

then choose to pay this price or not, but it is perfectly clear that the matter would not end with Poland.

Sovereignty in a political sense rather means the general competence to make decisions. When a government makes a decision on Topic 1, Topic 2, Topic 3, Topic 4, then it is sovereign as the probability goes up that it will also make decisions on Topic N. If the local government of a "dormitory suburb" or "bedroom community" is competent to say whether noise at night will be tolerated or not, it has power over one decision. However, such communities are never unifunctional. The bedroom community is also the "playpen community," the "kindergarten community," the "cocktail hour community," and the "wives' visiting community." It is actually multifunctional.

In a highly individualistic culture like the United States, we have gone further than any other country in almost deliberately trying to make every single function or district different from every other, so that the school district, the water district, the voting district, the job area, the shopping district, and the entertainment area are quite different from each other. This has led in the short run to functional satisfaction, since one often does not take active interest in these services as long as they are adequate. It has led to professional domination, since it is very hard for anybody to get excited about twenty different functional communities at the same time. It has made it convenient for the professional water engineers or the professional ward politicians to run their affairs without too much interference from the public, but it has also made it very difficult to get popular participation. If we have a functional community for function 1, a different community for function 2, and so forth, it is very difficult for any local government to assume the residual functions.

This is where the parallel between the nation-state and the local community breaks down. *The nation-state is the residual authority par excellence in the world today*. If something must be done and if no one else does it, the national government will. It will do everything from providing Salk polio vaccine for children and subsidizing performances of *West Side Story* in Moscow to buying intercontinental ballistic missiles and sending astronauts into space. The full-fledged nation-state is the one organization we have today that will do what people expect it to do—not with certainty, but with high probability. It will do whatever job the population urgently wants and which is not being done by any other unit. The United Nations still cannot be expected to do that, and ordinarily the local government is not expected to do it. In the Middle Ages it was the other way around: the city-state was expected to play this role. Even in the nineteenth century the state looked after the coinage, but the city aided the destitute. City hospitals had to take in the sick, and in Europe people were transported hundreds of miles to their communities of origin when they became destitute. Today in the United States no one would dream of shipping all the unemployed back to the Idaho or Mississippi towns where they happened to be born. This is no longer being done, and this is an indication that residual authority—and thus generalized authority—has migrated to the national government.

What are the prospects for any further migrations of this authority? How likely are specific functional authorities, and how likely is general or residual authority to shift upward from the nation-state to supra-national institutions on a regional or world-wide scale? And how likely is a similar shift of specific functional authorities, or of any general or residual authority, from the level of the single city to the level of inter-city institutions or of metropolitan area authorities? The communications and control approach may well be helpful as a guide toward research that might suggest answers to these questions.

III

Transaction Flows as Indicators of Political Cohesion

Continuing from the broad theoretical framework developed in the previous chapter, Karl Deutsch now concentrates on the prerequisite of any social science theory on integration: the development of meaningful, operational indices of political cohesion. Selecting transaction flows as quantitative indicators of social communication, he suggests several methods of investigation in developing these indices at both the international and metropolitan levels. Methods such as statistical analysis and content analysis are applied to mail flow, telephone traffic, and other measurable transactions to demonstrate the efficacy of the communications approach. Calling this technique "essentially a performance approach in the study of integration," he points out the utility of such empirical studies as independent checks on, and as guides to, institutional studies of governmental machinery and policies designed to facilitate political integration.

THE PRECEDING DISCUSSION HAS SUGGESTED THAT WE COULD IMPROVE our appraisal of the mutual relevance of political units to one another and of their potential cohesion by using as quantitative indicators the measurements of the flow of certain transactions between them. The use of some of these transaction flows as indicators deserves more detailed discussion, and the measurement of the flow of mail may serve as a convenient first example.

The Flow of Mail as an Example of Transactions

Almost four-fifths of postal correspondence in a modern country is written in a business context and about one-fifth is personal mail. In less developed countries there might be periods when a larger proportion of correspondence is personal, while in extremely underdeveloped countries most mail is limited to business and other public affairs. The range of first-class mail changes from less than one letter per capita per year to three hundred letters per capita per year in the United States. The rise of mail volume in a country can be used to indicate the degree to which people have become literate and are making use of their literacy.[1]

In 1929 in Nigeria, then a country of roughly 20 million people, about four million domestic letters a year were written. Nigeria, having a very adverse climate for non-Nigerians, has an extremely small white population, and it could be assumed that the large part of the one million letters in 1929 were written by the few white people and the other minorities, such as East Indian traders. About every nine years the number of letters in Nigeria doubled. By 1948 the domestic mail volume was approximately 32 million letters a year. Nigeria thus was not at all stagnant during this period; the figures indicate a rapid and continuing change in the country.

The second inference to be drawn from these mail figures is that 32 million letters a year clearly were not written by a small white minority. They mean that a good many Africans were entering the world of literacy and were writing and receiving letters. The white population of Nigeria had not strikingly increased compared to the rise in mail. A social mobilization of Nigerians was occurring, and mail flow data constitutes one of the quickest

1. Cf. Karl W. Deutsch, "Shifts in the Balance of International Communication Flows," *Public Opinion Quarterly*, Vol. 20 (Spring, 1956), 143–160.

ways of getting a measure of the speed and range of this development.

Furthermore, in 1929 almost one-half of the total mail went to foreign countries. By 1940 this proportion was changed. Almost three-quarters of the mail was domestic. One could infer from this reversal that there was a much more favorable set of conditions for demands for more independence, for a larger share of local self-government, if not for outright independence, among the population. If nationalist leaders or would-be leaders had started agitating in 1928, they would have got nowhere. By 1948, they would have had an excellent chance of finding a quite significant echo. In 1947–48 Nigeria went through its first great wave of strikes and unrest, the first great wave of demands for more active political participation on the part of the native population.

Milos Taborsky has done a study of Madagascar, where he found a similar rate of growth of mail, as well as an increasingly excellent market for nationalistic political action.[2] Between 1945 and 1948 domestic mail rates soared; 1948 was the year of extensive nationalistic uprisings in Madagascar. This does not mean that people rise in revolution whenever they write a lot of letters. It does mean that citizens who produce a large volume of letters and who communicate with each other in a fairly intense manner may require different forms of political treatment and administrative attention than a similar population at the low levels of communication of ten or twenty years ago. Additional studies of other nations show something fairly similar; mail data from Turkey and other countries show similar and fairly substantial increases and changes over the years.

Mail Flow as a Test of Functional Literacy

Mail flow statistics under some conditions may be a better indicator of social mobilization than literacy rates. For example,

2. Milos Taborsky, "Madagascar: Development and Social Mobilization," typescript, Political Science Department, Yale University, 1960.

a British census for India reports that at least part of the school children of India—of that minority that gets into school in the first place—then returns to villages where there is nothing to write about and no occasion to write. Some school-taught literacy disappears because these former pupils unlearn their knowledge. If they had the opportunity to keep writing and to receive letters from time to time, literacy would remain functional. Changes in mail volumes are, therefore, an excellent way for backstopping and cross-checking doubtful claims about literacy in a country.

Literacy that expresses itself in a high flow of letters is something different from literacy rates alone, for literacy may not be functional. If literacy were high and functional, one would expect a certain amount of mail flow. One could take the literacy figures for foreign countries from the *United Nations Yearbook,* as well as the letters per capita of these countries, and then graph them to see that, by holding literacy constant, rich countries or cultures are more likely to write more letters. If one holds letter writing constant and estimates the least literate society which will write a certain amount of letters per year, one can discover whether there is any general correlation.[3] Deviant cases will occur in plural societies where, for example, Armenians in Turkey might write far more than their quota of letters as compared to their Turkish neighbors. Still, a fairly good knowledge can be obtained of the relationship between these two factors.

What is of prime interest to political scientists is not merely to prove literacy statistics. What interests us in politics is the quantity of people in communication with each other. In the high communicating society, the high communicators have different aspirations, different images of the world (including politics), different plans, hopes, and aspirations for themselves and their families in life, different potentials, and different needs to be answered by government, politics, the society, and the economy. There exists

3. Cf. Bruce M. Russet *et al., World Handbook of Political and Social Indicators* (New Haven: Yale University Press, scheduled 1964) and forthcoming studies of the Yale Political Data Program.

a different potential for interest and for participation in politics.[4] A sharp increase in the high communicating sector of society usually signals an increase in the potentially politically influenced sector of society. And this is demonstrated convincingly by mail counts for such countries as Nigeria and Madagascar.

In theory, mail flow could decline. Yet it would be difficult for a long-term decline of mail to occur in any country in recent years. Short-term declines may occur because of wars or major dislocations. Presumably there may have been a decline in mail in Malaya in the early 1950's and a decline in domestic mail in Algeria until very recently. Universal Postal Union reports for 1952, 1955, 1958, and 1961 could be checked. One could then estimate the impact of the Algerian war and obtain a measure of the dislocation of the population.

There are, unfortunately, some gaps in the data available on mail flow. The worst of these gaps is United States–Canada data. The two countries simply treat each other as one postal unit. One could get this information by going to Washington and taking for a particular key year the 640 border crossing points in the postal service between the United States and Canada and add up the annual amount of mail processed. There is a similar problem between the United States and Britain. The two countries do not publish their mail volume, but the figures are available in Washington from the Post Office Department.

Shifts in Mail Flow

Several things can be said about the shift in the direction of mail. First, advanced countries tend to send out more mail than they receive. They are exporters of mail. This may involve partly the sending out of mail in which things are offered for sale. Advanced countries devote more of their resources to salesmanship, including sales promotion through the mails, than do backward

4. Cf. Rupert Emerson, *From Empire to Nation: The Rise to Self-Assertion of Asian and African Peoples* (Cambridge: Harvard University Press, 1960).

countries. Typically, the average ratio of incoming to outgoing mail in 1928 and 1938 was 0.8 for the United States, and similar ratios ranging between 0.52 and 0.83 can be found for France, West Germany, the United Kingdom, Japan, and other advanced countries. At the other extreme, countries which are underdevelopened but already have enough money to constitute good markets tend to receive three times as much mail as they send out. This was true, for instance, of Mexico.[5] By 1951, however, some of these imbalances decreased.

It seems that as a country becomes more advanced, it first ceases to be a net importer of mail, its mail flow becomes balanced, and then eventually it becomes a net exporter of mail. This, however, is not only a matter of general advancement but also a matter of diversified industries anxious for sales. For instance, Germany for many years has been sending much more mail to Scandinavia than Scandinavia has sent to Germany. Quite often the more aggressive and sales-conscious countries have excess mail going out.

A more interesting ratio is the ratio of foreign to domestic mail—D/F ratio—which is a striking indicator. Possibly the most important fact is that on the average for about fifty countries, the domestic to foreign mail ratio declined from 1880 to 1913 but has been climbing from 1913 on. This correlates well with many data available on trade and other transactions. In all these respects it seems that the world since 1913 has been getting more nationally minded and less internationally preoccupied.[5] This occurs despite the fact that a number of states have been settled by immigrants, resulting in the fact that much of the family correspondence that before their migration would have been domestic is now foreign. Nevertheless, the domestic mail is still growing faster.[6]

In international politics one may test the postal cohesion of the Soviet bloc. Here one might make an interesting discovery. Trade

5. Karl W. Deutsch, "Shifts in the Balance of International Communication Flows," *loc. cit.*, pp. 147–48.
6. *Ibid.*, pp. 151–56.

in the communist countries is subject to the wishes of government, making it quite easy to shift the mutual share of trade of the communist countries with each other from about 40 per cent to about 80 per cent between 1948 and 1950.[7] Mail, on the other hand, is directed mostly to relatives and friends and therefore follows the lines of human interest. This mail may have shifted much less, so that probably Poland today trades mainly with the Soviet bloc but corresponds still largely with the rest of the world in its foreign mail. On the other hand, Polish domestic mail probably has risen very substantially. In the Soviet Union, for which a longer series of data is available, the ratio of domestic to foreign mail has gone up from twenty-six to about ninety-six between 1926 and 1936, giving Russia perhaps the world record in postal self-preoccupation in the latter year—after which they ceased to publish these data.

On the metropolitan level, we can discover the ratio at which a metropolis corresponds with its hinterland. For instance, in New York in the 1950's, one-third of all letters ended up in New York, while two-thirds went to the rest of the country as domestic mail. The total domestic mail, both the internal New York and the rest of the country mail, was about nine times the volume of mail that went from New York to the rest of the world and that came from the rest of the world to New York.

American cities can be ranked by their ratios of domestic to foreign mail. In 1952, Washington, D.C., and New York stood at the bottom with an index of about nine and ten, respectively. Atlanta, Georgia, and Dallas, Texas, stood at the top with 121 and 95. This has interesting political implications. For instance, one might go to a community and ask officials whether in deciding about integration of schools or bus waiting rooms, were they also thinking of the impression they would be making in foreign countries in regard to race relations? Political leaders in a city like New York or Washington, D.C., where one-tenth of the mail goes

7. Cf. Zbigniew K. Brzezinski, *The Soviet Bloc: Unity and Conflict,* revised edition (New York: Praeger, 1961) and Frederic L. Pryor, *The Communist Foreign Trade System* (London: Allen & Unwin, 1963).

abroad, might be more interested in such a question than leaders in Southern cities which have one letter in 125 going abroad or coming from other countries. This issue, of course, reopens the question of leadership. It is clear that the mail flow does not determine whether integration in Washington will succeed. It merely tells something about the odds against a policy in one place or another, but it does not tell anything about the skill with which forces can be mobilized on either side.

Telephone Traffic: The Effects of Distance and Political or Social Boundaries

Another very simple measurement can be made by obtaining data on the number of telephone calls—long distance or toll calls—and the distance involved. This is fairly constant for the United States. By knowing the number of telephone calls between New York and Chicago, the volume of telephone calls between New York and Cleveland can be predicted very roughly by using the formula of $K = \frac{PQ}{D^2}$, where P and Q are the relevant populations, in this case perhaps registered telephones—the number of telephone subscribers—D is a measurement of distance, and K is a relevant constant.[8] If any such formula is applied, however, to telephone calls between New York and a city in Canada, there is a drop in the ratio. The volume of telephone calls is cut quite sharply by the effect of a national boundary, and the effect of the boundary may be measured by the size of the drop. These figures might then be further compared to the flow of telephone messages between New York and Quebec in order to discover if the barrier of the French language makes an additional difference. Canada could also be compared to Mexico to measure the effectiveness of different boundaries in cutting down the volume of

8. A more refined version of this appears in Karl W. Deutsch and Walter Isard, "A Note on a Generalized Concept of Effective Distance," *Behavioral Science*, Vol. 6 (October 1961) pp. 308–311.

telephone traffic.[9] Finally, the same principle may be applied to Harlem as compared to Brooklyn or the Bronx. A sample of Negro subscribers in Harlem might do a lot less telephoning with the rest of the United States, or else it might turn out by now that this is no longer true. Perhaps the Negro community has spread sufficiently beyond Harlem so that there is no recognizable difference in the distribution of telephone traffic from Harlem as it is from other places, but this is a question which can only be answered empirically.

Content Analysis: Indicators of Attention and Values

A third method of investigation is the use of content analysis of local communication. Content analysis can be employed to gauge the distribution of attention, as well as the distribution of favorable or unfavorable judgments and value patterns. These are two separate things, for it is quite possible for a community to have very favorable attitudes toward another community, based on ignorance of the values of the latter. For instance, when England and Russia were hostile to each other in the nineteenth century, Russians were pictured as barbarous, cruel, and treacherous, resembling bears that walk like men. When England and Russia made an alliance after 1907, the Russians were seen as profound, emotional, and inexhaustible; the English discovered the Russian soul between 1907 and 1917. When the alliance broke and Russia became Bolshevik, the Russians were back again to the level of shaggy, unwashed barbarians. The French, who had made an alliance with Russia in 1890, had a similar period of rapid reassessment.[10]

9. Cf. Deutsch and Isard, *op. cit.*, and Karl W. Deutsch, "Anatomy and Boundaries According to Communications Theory," in Roy R. Grinker (ed.), *Toward a Unified Theory of Human Behavior* (New York: Basic Books, 1956), pp. 278–297.

10. Cf. Dorothy Brewster, "The Russian Soul: An English Literary Pattern," *American Scholar*, Vol. 17 (1948), pp. 178–188; and Julius Braunthal, *The Paradox of Nationalism* (London: St. Botolph, 1946).

Similarly, in the United States, a white Southerner may say he loves his Negroes, who are so nice when they know their place. Actually the values of these Negroes may have changed, and a generation of young Negroes may have grown up who do not like their traditional place in Southern society, who express different values in their communications—where content analysis might reveal them—and who show a surprising propensity to sit at lunch counters and in front seats of buses. It is quite clear that the white man's attitude or values cannot be maintained unmodified. Either the white group will have to acquire a value for tolerance of the changed values of the Negroes, or they will have to revise their image of the happy darkies who love to live in their accustomed places in the South.

Using Several Indicators: Problems of Weighting and Aggregation

In terms of direct communication, mail is by far the predominant medium of communication between nations, with minor exceptions such as border crossing areas. The volume of mail is probably several hundred times the magnitude of telephone calls or personal contacts. In a metropolitan area telephone calls might equal mail in magnitude, if not in import, while direct personal crossing of sub-area boundaries might be as high as 50 per cent in some cases. This raises questions of attempts to weigh or to price the different media of communications. At the present time, however, only very rough estimates are possible. This has been done for self-preoccupation ratios, the ratio of domestic to international activities. Self-preoccupation in terms of mail tends to be much higher than self-preoccupation in terms of commodities. Human relations are thus far more nationally bounded than movements of goods.

Some scholars are now attempting to get a measure of aggregate transactions to construct a weighted index. The analysis of transactions suggested so far tries to do this also. This method asks whether interactions are going up or down, whether they are about as high or higher than they would be in a pair of comparable actors about whom greater past knowledge is known. This method asks: what is the trend of the times, and what is the comparison with levels of transactions that can be expected in this particular field? For mail it is high; but the method also asks about the movement of persons, telephone calls, and so forth. If a whole series of plus signs on every one of these indicators is discovered, one might expect to develop some over-all indicator for this process. However, the study of Bruce Russett on the collaboration between England and the United States has revealed a strikingly deviant case.[11] From 1890 to 1954 there was a sharp decline in the relative weight of Anglo-American economic transactions. In the 1890's England bought 50 per cent of American exports. Today England buys about 6 per cent of American exports, and we buy about 6 per cent of British exports. Although the mix of production has changed in those years, it seems clear that the two countries have drifted apart economically. The change in mix of production does not explain why more American exports are sold to Germany but not to England. On the other hand, in terms of military and political consultations and mutual exchange of news, America and England are as close together now as they were in 1890, if not more so.

In the metropolitan areas, just as in the international field, there might be a higher probability of error if only one index were used. On the metropolitan level, this would be true particularly when rather small and rapidly changing units in an area are studied. For example in the eleven-county Philadelphia area there are more than twice the number of local governmental entities as there are national political units in the whole world.

A start has been made on some types of indices,[12] but there are many difficulties still to be solved. In an article on indicators

11. Cf. Bruce M. Russett, *Community and Contention: Britain and America in the Twentieth Century* (Cambridge: M.I.T. Technology Press, 1963).

12. Karl W. Deutsch, "Towards an Inventory of Basic Trends and Patterns in Comparative and International Politics," *American Political Science Review*, Vol. 54 (March, 1960), pp. 34–57.

of basic trends, a question has been raised as to the relative importance of some measures of transactions. Perhaps the acquisition of necessary information needed to complete a national profile, a pattern analysis for a variety of units, would permit a system of controlled comparisons. After a large number of cases have been investigated and relative ranks assigned to certain variables, covariance could be analyzed.

One must also be careful to keep certain aspects separate. If a doctor examines a patient, it is not automatically helpful to reduce his findings about the skeleton, blood count, the red and white blood corpuscles, and the nervous system to a single number and call this a health rating. There are moments when an insurance company will do just that by placing people into A, B, or C classes of risks. Nevertheless, most of medicine avoids reducing a dozen different measurements to a single number. There are millions of possible configurations of human systems, but for many configurations the frequency with which people die at given ages is known, thus making possible the translation of symptom configurations, so-called syndromes, into life expectancies. Similarly, while an economist knows that there is a difference between lollipops and steel mills, he can nevertheless put them all together into a single national income figure. There are reasonably well-known and standardized procedures of national income accounting for doing this. When different measures are crammed into a single index number prematurely, however, there is a risk that every investigator will find another way of adding them up and another way of weighing them, giving as many answers as there are investigators. As long as the rise or decline of travel, telephone calls, and mail is measured separately, the results can be compared impersonally.

Some composite index numbers might be worth computing. Robert Angell has suggested one possible index for measuring the moral integration of a community, by dividing the crime rate by the community chest contributions. In a way this makes good sense since crimes are an obvious example of deviant behavior, and community chest contributions are an obvious example of sterling citizenship. By calculating the ratio between the two and by ranking many cities in terms of the results, the index should tell us something about cities.[13]

There is a variety of social processes by which different transactions are summed up and translated into attitudes of familiarity, of relevance, or of interest. Memories of transactions become associated with more or less favorable emotions, and finally they may even become associated with psychological role taking and identification. Unfortunately, the bookkeeping of this psychological process is not nearly so clearly understood as the bookkeeping of national income accounting. The time is not yet ripe for a single numerical index for transactions which would yield significantly more information than its components or which would at least yield the same information as its components with some degree of economy. Something similar has been attempted for social mobilization and for the entry from political isolation and conditions of low impersonal communication to high levels of impersonal communication and relatively high potential interest in politics.[14] Propositions about the covariance of various indicators, with the idea of setting up a joint indicator in mind, have also been made, using general rates of mobilization, composed of partial rates of mobilization—radio audiences, newspaper readers, and several others.

There is a real entity or state of affairs called wealth which can be measured by indicators ranging from tons of pig iron to yards of cloth to hours of leisure. In a similar way, it could be argued that mutual involvement of societies or of people is a real state of affairs measured more or less imperfectly by such indicators as communications and transactions that have been discussed. Measuring the investment of time or measuring mutual

13. Cf. Robert C. Angell, *The Integration of American Society* (New York: McGraw-Hill, 1941) and also his "The Social Integration of Selected American Cities," *American Journal of Sociology*, 47, 1941–42, pp. 575 ff. and "The Social Integration of American Cities of More Than 100,000 Population," *American Political Science Review*, Vol. 55 (September 1961) pp. 493–514.

14. Karl W. Deutsch, "Social Mobilization and Political Development," *American Political Science Review*, Vol. 55 (September 1961), pp. 493–514.

attention as a percentage of attention might be a way of bringing these indicators together.

Attention, however, may be emotionally neutral, or it may be hostile. If a single index for transactions is desired, it could possibly be done in terms of an attention percentage, which would be close to Richard Meier's concept of time investment.[15] A hypothetical guess about the total attention span of the actor is necessary, followed by asking how large a part of the span is taken by the partner, in all forms of transactions. The estimates and the computations would be exceptionally difficult. Four preliminary steps would be necessary: (1) obtain and rank single indicators or transactions for all the pairs of partners in which we are interested; (2) determine whether the levels and rank orders of different indicators vary together; (3) take a look at the deviant cases; and (4) also look at the critical thresholds. It is possible that certain indicators may vary together after a threshold but not before.

Thus far, we have assumed that all indicators will change in the same direction. In reality this would probably not be correct. If goods traffic should decline in the short run while mail flow goes up, this could be due to almost any kind of a fluctuation. For instance, there might be a shortage of goods or a change in manufacturing or a change in prices. If there were a long-run increase in mail, however, and a long-run decline in goods, such obvious developments might be occurring as an export of labor resulting in many more family ties. How should one appraise the potential for integration when two or more indicators move in opposite directions? A cross-pressure phenomenon would probably exist. Voting studies suggest that if a union member feels he should vote for his union leadership because he is a good unionist but also feels that he should vote against his union leadership because he is a good Catholic and the union leadership has been accused of Communism, the chances are that this voter will

15. Richard L. Meier, *A Communications Theory of Urban Growth* (Cambridge: M.I.T. Press, 1962).

stay home.[16] Ordinarily, if a cross-pressure relationship exists, integration will not make great strides. This hypothesis holds that integration will make substantial progress if, and only if, most major indicators pull in the same direction. Integration will decline, according to this view, if most indicators are pulling toward the decline, and it will tend to stagnate or fluctuate slightly if the indicators show cross-pressure.

The Meaning of Indicators: Some Difference between International and Metropolitan Communities

In the international field, if two countries grow apart in commodity trade, this development has an effect on the interest groups involved in trade, resulting in serious cross-pressure. On the municipal and metropolitan level perhaps movement of goods does not have this importance or these effects. The study of two communication maps of Nigeria concerned with movement of goods and movement of people demonstrates, that Nigerian voting behavior follows the movement of persons but not the movement of goods.[17] People's learning to perceive themselves as members of a community follows human communication a great deal more than commodity communication. It was one of the miscalculations of the South on the eve of the Civil War to think that King Cotton would bring Britain in on the Southern side in the Civil War. Not only was King Wheat on the other side but, what was probably more important in many ways, Britain's rewarding human communications were stronger with the North than with the South.

There are other differences between metropolitan and international integration. A very interesting question is whether there

16. Cf., for instance, Bernard Berelson, Paul Lazarsfeld, and William McPhee, *Voting* (Chicago: University of Chicago Press, 1954).

17. Udemezue Obi. Atuanya, "People, Politics and Nigerian Unity." An unpublished typescript, M.I.T. Cambridge, Massachusetts, 1956.

is more activity in the transactions that account for community integration within a controlled national environment than in the uncontrolled international environment. We would be closer to an understanding of "community" if we could get measures of such tendencies.

Intra-metropolitan Relations

In the metropolitan area, do suburbanites like downtown people, or do suburbanites want to see themselves as fundamentally different from downtown people? In point of fact, are downtown people, because of changes, settlement, and migration, becoming more different from suburbanites or less different? Are they becoming temporarily more different, while in another ten or twenty years they can be expected to be less different again?

It must be remembered that transactions increase saliency, which may be positive or negative. Perhaps the degree of distrust of the metropolitan center increases with the degree of interaction of the population and with the closeness to the metropolitan center, primarily because of the suburbanites' fear of annexation. Perhaps it is the adjacent suburbs which are most distrustful of the center city. The farther one goes out in the metropolitan area, the more one might meet indifference, as the transaction ratios decrease. These are questions capable of being answered empirically.

Is there increasing fear of the center of the city, the closer one lives to it, even on Saturday nights? Is this a peculiar American phenomenon or is this worldwide? For instance, there is a London County with a common government providing important services in many boroughs. Have studies of London shown that the suburbanites, either before or after the London County Council was constituted, showed great fear and dislike for London and that this was worse the closer they were to London? If the latter were the case, one would ask the question: what happened after they were brought under the London County Council? Did their resistance increase? A similar question could be asked for Toronto or Dade County in and around Miami, Florida, where federations of communities have been established. On the European Continent expansions of the metropolitan areas have been the rule. For New York the question could be asked for the 1890's, when Brooklyn was brought into greater New York. When and where do we find this pattern of suburban hostility against the center city? Is it universal or is it peculiar to particular times and places?

In some metropolitan areas of the United States, there appear to be concentric rings around cities with most hostility existing at the core. The geographic core is often also the area where the votes of the lower income groups carry relatively great weight. As a result, residence and relief policies are more permissive, zoning laws permit a settlement of poor people, welfare expenditures are high, and there is a fair amount of children and others who have to be educated at some expense even though at not very high levels of service. Around this area, the suburbs begin to spread out. Since these inner suburbs are still close to the city, most of their residents may not be very wealthy. These suburbs may be extremely hostile to the inner city because it is the city where they may become poor again. However, residents of the inner suburb are usually not hostile to the next fringe outside it but try to be friendly. They are trying to avoid the downward social mobility in the center city. They may be quite happy to think of upward social mobility moving by farther out. In the greater Boston area this seems to be a typical characteristic.

Economic Interests

There is another point involved here. One of the old arguments about political community contended that it was mainly a function of economic interest. In constructing the pure economic interest model of metropolitan areas, one could say: What are the economic interests that make for suburban resistance to the center city? The most obvious would be that every unit is trying to push the burden of the poor people and welfare cases off on some other city's budget. One solution is the enactment of suitable zoning laws and residence requirements, assuring a sufficient quantity of suburban voters from the middle income groups so that the poor people will never have a chance to capture the mayor's office, the Board of Selectmen, or the Welfare Office. The result is that poorer people will drift again and again to the central city where their votes will procure them more responsive welfare policies. On the other hand, in the central city there may be poorer housing and more crowded accommodation available at higher prices per acre, but at low prices per inhabitant, resulting in a slum pattern. There is a simple, clear-cut interest mechanism by which the suburbs act in such a way as to concentrate all the welfare burdens and all the social deficits of the metropolitan area in this center city.

According to this theory, metropolitan disintegration has become an adaptive mechanism to the welfare state. It is an escape hatch for the upper middle classes from the welfare state. Local autonomy is used as a device to keep the middle class from assuming many of the burdens of the welfare state in the sense of tax rates, but also in the sense of human burdens. The suburbanites do not want to hear the noise of the poorer neighbors' children or have their windows broken when these children play in the streets; they do not have to worry about delinquency, about low income adolescents, but only about delinquency of the middle income adolescents under these conditions. They have actually escaped many social costs.

This would be a theory of pure interest, and one could ask what prices are paid for it in dollars and cents. Probably suburban "sovereignty" means more expensive sewers, more expensive duplication of other public facilities, and inferior public transportation systems. The latter, however, at first matter little since the suburb is the location of the two-car family. But in the end it may mean clogged roads and bad traffic jams which are then frustrating even to the two-car family, which now may have two cars stuck in the jam instead of one. Nevertheless, the rising costs of commuting an hour each way might still seem a low price to pay in exchange for neighbors of the same income group, quiet suburban streets, a green lawn, relatively low tax rates, a relatively moderate real estate cost, and other amenities of the suburb.

This economic interest theory is one which requires the introduction of a theory of discriminating monopoly. By limiting transactions to certain acceptable fields such as commuting, employment, shopping, business, going to town for a few services, people are seen only in their roles as customers, as fellow employees, or as obstacles on the highway. They are not seen in their roles as laborers, as fellow members of the Parent-Teacher Association, as fellow voters, or as people for whom one has a responsibility in terms of public health. In this way a partial reduction of role complementarity results. A few roles are selected which are bound to be profitable or rewarding, while other roles are rejected.

Declining Transactions with the Center City

The direction in metropolitan areas today may be away from increasing transactions between the various communities. With the dispersion of industry as well as housing, communities may be able to become self-contained and to limit further the necessary transactions with the center city. If it is said that the suburban communities are becoming more self-contained, transaction flow measurements could confirm or modify this statement, preferably by a study of transactions over a longer period of time. One may ask how a certain community is more self-contained today than it was ten, twenty, or thirty years ago. Perhaps transaction patterns have changed and interactions no longer go only radially into the central city and out but also go around the city into other suburbs. This possibility also could be measured.

If suburb deals with suburb, there is no danger of a welfare burden. What would happen if practically all or most welfare and education expenditures were put on the state budgets? What would happen if the proportion between local, state, and federal financing of welfare and education expenditures were substantially shifted away from local expenditures? What would happen if the average level of per capita expenditures for a state were worked out and subsidies granted to local communities according to the proportion of the population with below average incomes and above average welfare needs? What would happen with an equalization of burdens established, so that no community could get much richer or much poorer by attracting people of one particular income group?

As an intellectual experiment, this could be done in the public finance sector. There is a question, of course, whether this would be desirable and whether the voters would like it. The rich would oppose it because it would increase their tax burden. Oddly enough, the poor might oppose it because it might diminish their chances to use their local voting strength to get additional local concessions in particular cities. The upper income groups in many states might be seen as engaged in a kind of Russian sleigh ride. Some of them manage to escape into the suburbs, and thus avoid some of the burdens of the remaining upper income group members who are forced to stay either by residence or big investments in downtown areas. This results in a differentiation in the upper income group, where part of this high income group has to pay a disproportionate share of the welfare and government burden for the poorer areas, while the other part pays a disproportionately low amount in the suburbs.

The suburbs might also be an escape mechanism for the people who would like to get into the upper income group but cannot afford to pay the city taxes and rise in society at the same time. If they manage to get into one of the suburban tax havens, one of those local communities where the taxes and welfare expenditures are less, they might be able to rise faster in living standards and social scale than they otherwise could.

If this phenomenon represents the desire for social differentiation, however, then perhaps adjacent towns of roughly the same social and economic levels might be able to pool their services. One could find out whether there are any functional agreements among cities with strikingly different percentages of high income families.

Out of this comes the question of whether there is differentiation among various kinds of functional agreements between different suburbs. Is it sensible to just throw all types of such agreements into a big bag and count them as one, or should one rather differentiate between types of agreements, treating, say, sewer agreement and school agreement as two quite different things? One theory might predict role differentiation both in transactions and in agreements. The opposite hypothesis would be the "spill-over" theory of Ernst Haas.[18] Under the spill-over effect, once any agreement is made, it enhances the propensity of the partners to make further agreements. According to the spill-over theory, people who ship coal and steel to each other eventually might be willing to die for each other. According to the role differentiation theory, sewer or police radio agreements may be easily entered into even in the face of sharp differences in the economic or cultural character of the neighboring suburbs, while school district agreements between them might be rejected. These are both empirically verifiable statements, and it might be interesting to find out when and where spill-over effects are found and when and where differentiation patterns predominate.[19]

Are there cases of emphatic acceptance of one functional merger together with emphatic rejection of merger in another function? Plausible arguments could be developed for either theory, spill-over or role differentiation. The level of satisfaction over agreements may be obtained by merely observing whether the agreement is still in force. In other words, despite grumbling, if an agreement is only grumbled about but kept in force, it is clearly not quite as unsatisfactory as if people were provoked into

18. Ernst Haas, *The Uniting of Europe* (Stanford: Stanford University Press, 1958).
19. Cf. Chapter 4.

ending it. Frequently agreements are entered into which are not easily broken. In fact there is a tendency for established agreements to be maintained. After some unpleasant experience in an agreement, however, there may be no further agreements between the same partners. This is the third plausible theory, that of disillusionment—giving us altogether three plausible theories: the differentiation theory, the spill-over theory, and the theory of disillusionment. The last two of these relate to a single function; the first pertains to the relationship of several functions.

The purpose of these various approaches would be to try to measure the probability of a class of pairs. If a hundred pairs of towns showed certain similarities in income, religion, political preference, education, or ethnic composition, then one might ask: "Given this characteristic, how frequent are agreements?" One then could make the computation not only for the pairs of towns that have agreements but for all pairs of adjacent towns.[20] Thus one would use the computer deliberately as an instrument for a fishing expedition. One would find out the correlations and then feed them back into the analysis. This is one of the roles of computers in social science, as partners in a discussion in which certain questions are raised and significant correlations between variables checked. Topography and the intervening rights of way also might be included as intervening variables in this work. However, these can be taken into account by reference to maps and legal documents. If after consideration of ten or twelve cultural and economic variables, a large number of pairs of cities which do not have agreements should remain unexplained, then it would be time to examine such topics as rights of way.

Similar problems occur in the analysis of transactions in international relations. In the world trade matrix of Deutsch & Savage[21] expectable trade among all countries to all countries is

20. Cf. Chapter 4.

21. Cf. Karl W. Deutsch and Richard I. Savage, "A Statistical Model of the Gross Analysis of Transaction Flows," *Econometrica*, Vol. 28, July, 1960, pp. 551–572; and *Regionalism, Trade and International Community*, forthcoming.

forecast by the use of a null model assuming free access. However, most colonies traded only with their mother country. The trade-distorting effects of colonialism stood out dramatically. Only when the intervening variable of colonialism was used could the model be used in explanation. Only when actual performance is compared to potential performance do structures, deviations, and patterns begin to stand out. Then, one could investigate whether colonies show a markedly greater distortion of their trade patterns from non-colonies. Research has shown the answer to be yes.[22] This outcome would be accomplished by tariffs, currency manipulation, by concentrating purchasing orders in the hands of colonial administration, by manipulating consumers' tastes, or by limiting credit to established channels of trade.

The next approximation would then be to investigate the nature of the economic and political controls and ties that stand behind these outcomes. The computer operation tells us certain facts for fifty colonies or emerging nations, checking quickly their relationship with each with one hundred potential trade partners. The basis has thus been established for fifty monographs on the economic policy of each emerging country. Once this background is obtained, anybody who wants to write a monograph on a particular country can first get a performance measurement. This research approach reverses the classical method of political science, where institutions by which people try to achieve an effect are first investigated. The technique outlined here attempts to find the size of the outcome before descriptive studies, which cannot tell the size of the outcome, have been written. Techniques for measuring outcomes are first developed and tested, and the results can then be fed back into the institutional studies of the machinery or the policies that may or may not have been designed to produce the outcome that has been found to have occurred in fact. This is essentially a performance approach in the study of integration, and it should produce some additional guidance for the study of the more promising instances of cooperation and conflict.

22. *Ibid.*

IV

Transaction Flow Analysis in Metropolitan Areas: Some Preliminary Explorations

Speculation about the impact of transaction flows on the political behavior of metropolitan communities, or between any set of political communities, often proceeds without a careful statement about whether there are in fact any significant differences in transactions. Employing a research strategy developed by Karl Deutsch in the previous chapter, James V. Toscano provides a variation on a statistical test for demonstrating whether differences in transaction flows—mail, telephone calls, work, migration, and the like—are more than those that can be explained by chance. A preliminary test is first employed for analysis of transactions within one set of political communities. The same type of test is then used on a somewhat different set of data—inter-governmental agreements in the Philadelphia metropolitan area—to determine whether the differences in type of agreement and number of agreements can be explained by chance or by some other factors. Additional variables are then added to increase the explanatory power of this technique.

Over the past fifty years or so population in the metropolitan areas of our nation has been spilling over municipal boundaries of the central cities into the surrounding countryside and into numerous other political subdivisions. With annexation virtually an impossibility in many areas, the center cities have had to adjust to these losses while the suburbs have experienced monumental growth and monumental difficulties in dealing with increased demands for services.

A high degree of social and economic interdependence in many areas has led some political scientists to predict that the areas would eventually become interdependent politically and would experience such high degrees of societal integration that some type of unified government for entire metropolitan regions would become politically possible. So far, however, this has not been the case, and political scientists have been turning their attention to other institutional arrangements ranging from federation to informal cooperation.

Insights from other Disciplines

Many students of metropolitan areas have stated that integration of peoples in the various political subdivisions is proceeding rapidly, but they have not been able to develop adequate theories and tools with which to measure the degree of this integration. Other disciplines, such as demography, ecology, sociology, regional science, and city planning, have been studied to see if there are any theoretical improvements which could be appropriated to understand political integration better in the metropolis. While these disciplines have been helpful, they have not yet been able to supply political scientists with adequate explanations and methodological tools to deal with political integration and intergovernmental relations. Some political scientists have looked to their sister discipline, international relations, which has borrowed so much from political science, for insights and have been encouraged by the explanatory potential of some concepts. As William T. R. Fox has written, "The only theory that can describe intergovernmental relations in a metropolitan community is a theory of international politics."[1]

Here, then, we will look to the study of international relations for concepts which may be useful in the study and analysis of the social characteristics which accompany political integration in metropolitan areas. We will concentrate on those concepts developed by Dr. Deutsch and applied to metropolitan area analysis in the preceding two chapters. The presumption here is that certain societal relationships enhance the potential for the formal, institutionalized integration of political functions. In other language, these societal conditions may be thought of as necessary, but not sufficient, conditions for political integration. Even with optimal societal conditions, there still remains the task of integrating governmental functions through the existing political leadership, a process which is analyzed in the succeeding chapter by William L. C. Wheaton.

The Study of Transaction Flows

As the study of international relations matures and becomes more sophisticated, the improved methodological tools available to this discipline have enabled scholars to measure more accurately the relationships between sovereign states. The study of transaction flows, a part of the communications and control approach developed by Dr. Deutsch,[2] appears to hold much promise for the study of political integration in metropolitan areas.

World trade matrices have been constructed by Deutsch and

1. See the *University of Pennsylvania Law Review,* Vol. 105 (Phila., 1957), 538.

2. Karl W. Deutsch, *Nationalism and Social Communication* (Cambridge: Technology Press, 1952) and Karl W. Deutsch *et al., Political Community and the North Atlantic Area* (Princeton: Princeton University Press, 1957).

Savage[3] which indicate trends in transaction flows in trade between sovereign states over the past sixty years or so. The technique used has been to plot the foreign trade of each state with every other state and to compare the various political, geographic, colonial, and time patterns that emerge. To modify this procedure, transaction flow matrices in metropolitan areas may be constructed using several variables to indicate trends in the direction of increased or decreased salience between the variables. These procedures are based on the following assumptions:

(1) The higher the transaction levels between two groups, the more salient each becomes to the other; however, salience may be positive or negative.

(2) The higher the levels of mutually indulging[4] transactions, the higher the positive salience; the higher the levels of mutually depriving transactions, the higher the negative salience.

(3) The higher the positive salience, the higher the probability for cooperation and integration; the higher the negative salience, the higher the probability for disintegration and conflict.

Therefore by studying transaction flows of a mutually rewarding type, or minimally of a type which would generally not lead to higher levels of negative salience, it may be possible to assess the potential for political integration and/or cooperation among various governments. Of course, some types of transactions produce both positive and negative salience. Therefore only the modal effect will be assumed for purposes here. It is recognized, however, that adjustments must be made in more complex models for increased scope. Contact between residents of the suburbs and residents of the city in certain areas is assumed to

3. Karl W. Deutsch and Richard I. Savage, "A Statistical Model of the Gross Analysis of Transaction Flows," *Econometrica,* Vol. 28, July, 1960, 551–572.

4. Indulging and depriving transactions are used in the sense of Harold Lasswell's Indulgences and Deprivations. See Harold D. Lasswell and Abraham Kaplan, *Power and Society* (New Haven: Yale University Press, 1950) especially pp. 61–62.

increase positive salience [i.e., the same way our *People to People* programs with the communist nations are assumed to increase mutual understanding] if there is mutual reward; however, there will be incidents of conflict or dislike upon contact. For example, some white suburbanites might be repelled by contact with residents of a Negro slum and go back to suburbia with the firm resolve never to let these people into their communities, their schools, their churches, or their homes.

Our assumption would be that some types of transactions are mutually rewarding. Indulging indices will be used here, but it must be remembered that depriving transactions will be just as useful in the study of potentials for disintegration and conflict. The assumption of unimodality of reaction imposes upon the researcher the necessity to decide whether a process is an indulgence or a deprivation. In future research the nature of a process can be typed better by survey research to determine its actual effects on a scientifically selected sample of a region's population or on a sample of the economy or polity where appropriate.

Preoccupation Ratios

A rough way to approximate the integration potential is to construct preoccupation ratios for all of the communities in an area. This preoccupation ratio (P.R.) would use some measure of communication, such as telephone calls, to gauge the insularity and/or interaction of communities. The formula for this ratio is:

$$\text{P.R.} = \frac{C_e}{C_i} \qquad (1.1)$$

where C_e is the number of communications from one community to another community in the area under study.
C_i is the number of intra-community communications.

P.R. indexes can be constructed for each community on such variables as mail flow, newspaper circulation, telephone calls, media audience, and so forth. Communities can then be grouped in various types ranging from completely extroverted to completely introverted. The potentials for integration would, of course, go up as the P.R. goes up. For example, a community with P.R.'s of .7 on all of the political integration and transaction indices used would have a higher potential for cooperation with its communicating neighbors than a community with P.R. indices all under .2.

Transaction Flow Matrices

In a second method to gauge transaction flows, place of residence for the millions in a metropolitan area might be compared to the place of birth to indicate the amount of mobility within the area included in the study. By tracing the main lines of mobility, one might be able to discover preliminary potentials for mutual understanding of problems between different areas in the

Table 3
An Index of Transaction Flow:
Place of Work & Place of Residence
Percentage of Total Work Force

	Place of Work						
	City A	City B	Suburb C	Suburb D	Suburb E	All other	Total
City A							
City B							
Suburb C							
Suburb D							
Suburb E							
All other							
Total							

metropolis. Place of residence might also be compared to such variables as place of work, place of entertainment, place of purchases, and place of major services for an indication of the interdependence of the various communities in the reward structure of the community. One matrix in this series might be exemplified by Table 3.

If the main diagonal from top left to bottom right is significantly larger than the other cells in percentage terms, we would find an insular metropolis. The writer would hypothesize that such an area would be without much hope of integration. If further comparisons using other variables bear out the findings in Table 3, then hopes for some type of voluntary cooperation would be significantly reduced. If, however, there is a considerable flow of people, services, and money from one community to another, or to many others, high levels of salience would result. Because salience is assumed to be a necessary condition for integration, it may be hypothesized that high transaction flows of this type between various communities would result in higher levels of positive salience, thereby enhancing the potential for integration.

Using a Null Model

While the indices previously mentioned might be of great use in indicating general trends in the region under study, they do not lend themselves to more precise measurement in present form. An additional procedure may be introduced to add greater analytic power to the measurement. Again the cue is taken from Deutsch's work.

By constructing a null matrix with expected values in each cell computed on the assumption of complete indifference and by then comparing these expected values to the actual values of each cell, an index of transactions can be constructed. Using the same basic matrix as in Table 3, each community's transactions with each other in the region under study can be charted and then compared to expected levels of transactions.

Expected values are determined by the indifference assumption according to the following formula:

$$PV_1 \times V_2 = EV_{1.2} \qquad (1.2)$$

where V_1 is the first variable (i.e. residence).
V_2 is the second variable (i.e. place of work).
PV_1 is the percentage of occurrence of V_1 in a sub-region of the area under study (i.e. residents of a center city in a metropolitan area).
$EV_{1.2}$ is the expected level of occurrence of V_1 and V_2 in a particular sub-area (i.e. people who both live and work in center city).

For example, using the residence and work comparison, the following hypothetical case can be analyzed. Table 4 shows the

TABLE 4

PLACE OF RESIDENCE AND PLACE OF WORK OF WORK FORCE IN HYPOTHETICAL METROPOLITAN AREA

	Work Force			
	Residence		Place of Work	
	Place of Residence V1	% of Region's Total Work Force	Place of Work V2	% of Region's Total Work Force
Center City	400,000	40	500,000	50
Satellite City	200,000	20	250,000	25
Suburb A	150,000	15	80,000	8
Suburb B	100,000	10	100,000	10
Suburb C	50,000	5	20,000	2
All others in Region	100,000	10	50,000	5
Region Total	1,000,000	100	1,000,000	100

hypothetical number and per cent of the work force by place of work and by place of residence.

To find the "expected levels" of residents and workers in each area, the previous formula (1.2) is used and the value computed for each cell of the matrix as seen in the upper left diagonal of each cell in Table 5. The figure in the lower right hand corner of each cell is the "actual" number of persons in our hypothetical case.

For example, if 40 per cent of the region's work force resides in Center City and if place of residence makes no difference in

TABLE 5

EXPECTED AND ACTUAL NUMBERS OF PEOPLE LIVING AND WORKING IN HYPOTHETICAL METROPOLITAN AREA—IN THOUSANDS

Place of Residence	Place of Work: City Center	Satellite City	Suburb A	Suburb B	Suburb C	All Others	Total
Center City	200 250	100 63	32 10	40 57	8 9	20 11	400
Satellite City	100 100	50 67	16 5	20 2	4 2	10 4	200
Suburb A	75 45	37.5 50	12 33	15 14	3 2	7.5 6	150
Suburb B	50 35	25 35	8 5	10 16	2 1	5 8	100
Suburb C	25 15	12.5 15	4 7	5 2	1 1	25 10	50
All Others	50 35	25 20	8 20	10 9	2 5	5 11	100
Total	500	250	80	100	20	50	1000

place of work, one would expect that 40 per cent of the labor force of each sub-regional unit would be composed of residents of Center City. Or if 10 per cent of the region's work force resides in Suburb B, given the same assumptions of no difference, one would expect that 10 per cent of the labor force of each sub-regional unit would be composed of residents of Suburb B.

Transaction Indices

By then obtaining the actual sub-totals for residence and place of work, comparisons can be made and a transaction index constructed according to the following formula.

$$\text{T.I.} = \frac{A - E}{E} \quad (1.3)$$

where:

- A is the actual value for each cell.
- E is the expected value for each cell according to the indifference theory.
- T.I. is the transaction index, indicating either positive or negative levels of transaction.

The T.I. has been computed for the hypothetical case in Table 6.[5]

5. Because $-1 \leq \text{T.I.} \leq \infty$, we must interpret positive and negative T.I. scores differently. Following Deutsch and Savage, *op. cit.*, we can compute a critical ratio using the basic formula:

$$\text{C.R.} = \frac{A - E}{\sqrt{V(A)}}$$

where C.R. = critical ratio
A = actual number
V = variance
E = expected number

to obtain significance. The reader is referred to the above-cited article for an elaboration of this point. Cf. also a report on the Chicago SMSA by S. J. Brams (Northwestern University, 1963), which employs the technique spelled out here.

From Table 6 the pattern of transactions in the region is made meaningful and more useful for analysis. For instance, it can be observed that 20 out of 36 cells are negative, indicating a lack of strong interdependence in the region as a whole. Probably region-wide programs calling for such things as aid to commuters to center city and requiring the approval of all units will not do well if we can take this table as a prediction of behavior.

TABLE 6

TRANSACTION INDEX

	Center City	Satellite City	Suburb A	Suburb B	Suburb C	All Others
Center City	.25	—.37	—.69	.43	.13	—.45
Satellite City	.20	.34	—.69	—.90	—.50	—.60
Suburb A	—.40	.33	1.75	—.07	—.33	—.20
Suburb B	—.30	.40	—.38	.60	—.50	.60
Suburb C	—.40	.20	.75	—.60	0	—.60
All Others	—.30	—.20	1.5	—.10	1.5	1.2

However, sub-regional patterns become more clear. While most communities have favorable internal transaction ratios, Suburb A is by far the most insular, employing 175 per cent more of its own residents than expected by complete indifference. Suburb A does have a favorable T.I. with Satellite City, but the reciprocal is not true. In fact, there are no reciprocals which are both positive, again indicating little potential for area-wide integration.

By the use of time series, the increases and decreases in the T.I. can be charted, enabling the researcher to observe trends toward greater or lesser potentials for integration. While only two variables, residence and place of work, have been studied, it is desirable to chart numerous other indicators over time for a better and more complete picture.

A Case Study of the Wilmington, Delaware, Standard Metropolitan Statistical Area (SMSA)

In order to check the implications of our hypothetical case, we attempted to apply these procedures to an actual area to determine the measure's validity. Because of the limitations of the data available, a modified matrix had to be constructed which considered only three areas in the Wilmington, Del., SMSA and which omitted all transaction information outside this area under study.

For the Wilmington, Del., SMSA, the information in Table 7 was obtained from the 1960 Census tracts.[6]

TABLE 7

WORK FORCE

Place	Place of Residence	% of Total SMSA Residents	Place of Work	% of Total SMSA Workers
Wilmington, Del.	32,493	28	54,534	46
Rest of New Castle County, Del.	67,421	57	45,315	39
Salem County, N.J.	17,698	15	17,763	15
Total	117,612	100	117,612	100

The expected values, assuming complete indifference, were tabulated according to Formula 1.2 and compared to the actual totals. See Table 8 where the expected values are in the upper left diagonal of each cell and the actual figures are in the lower right diagonal of each cell. Only actual totals are given.

On the basis of Table 8, the Transaction Index for residence and work was computed according to Formula 1.3. The results are strikingly parallel to our hypothetical case and demonstrate

6. Bureau of the Census, *Wilmington, Del.–N.J., Standard Metropolitan Statistical Area,* Final Report PHC (1)-173 (1960) Table P-3, p. 42.

TABLE 8

PLACE OF WORK

Residence	Wilmington Del.	Rest of New Castle Cty. Del.	Salem Cty. N.J.	Total Residence
Wilmington, Del.	15,270 26,999	12,688 5,309	4,975 185	32,493
Rest of New Castle County, Del.	31,084 26,916	25,830 39,415	10,124 1,090	67,421
Salem County, N.J.	8,180 619	6,797 591	2,664 16,488	17,698
Total, Place of Work	54,534	45,315	17,763	117,612

the potentials for integration in this metropolitan area. Table 9 below shows that, for political integration purposes, as measured by only one test case, there are no mutually positive transactions. Salem County, N.J., which is not only separated from the rest of the SMSA by a state boundary but also by the Delaware River,

TABLE 9

TRANSACTION INDICES

WILMINGTON, DEL.—N.J. SMSA

	Place of Work		
Residence	Wilmington Del.	Rest of New Castle County, Del.	Salem County N.J.
Wilmington, Del.	.77	—.58	—.93
Rest of New Castle County, Del.	—.13	.53	—.89
Salem County, N.J.	—.92	—.91	5.19

appears completely divorced from Wilmington and the rest of New Castle County, Delaware, and it presents a good picture of an insular sub-area of the somewhat arbitrarily determined SMSA.

Each sub-area only has positive T.I.'s with itself, with Salem County actually employing more than 500 per cent more of its own residents than could be expected by our indifference assumption. Further work is needed on this area, but on the basis of this one test it may be hypothesized that the potentials for political integration of any kind between the various sub-areas will not be very good, especially for Salem County, N.J., where insularity is reinforced by formal state boundaries.

Transaction Flows and Agreements

Another relevant measure of transaction flow is that of functional agreements between various communities in a metropolitan area. Agreements to send children to regional schools or to establish joint sewer authorities are indicators of directions of transactions in a metropolis. In the so-called Penjerdel region (the eleven-county area in the Delaware Valley encompassing the cities of Wilmington, Philadelphia, and Trenton) there are 377 units of local government. By constructing a matrix matching each community against all other communities in this area, the direction of major transaction flows can be charted for the region. Using a computer routine, this matrix would utilize approximately 140,000 cells and, for present purposes, would be both unwieldy and wasteful.

Instead of this large matrix, a beginning can be made by constructing a partial matrix which could match each community with each of its neighbors. Preliminary sampling in the Philadelphia area has already indicated that an overwhelming amount of functional agreements are made by contiguous governmental bodies. Because of the contiguous nature of most agreements, the more important transaction patterns are caught, while the number

DIAGRAM 2

Communities:

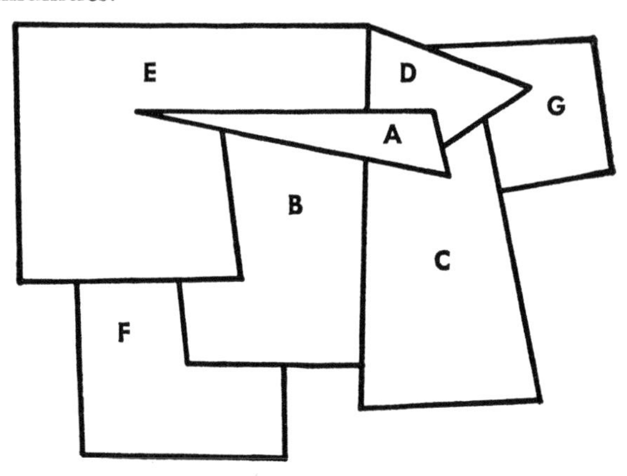

of cells for the Penjerdel area is reduced to a more manageable figure of approximately 2,000. Of course, in a multi-member pact on a functional service, only neighbors appear as agreeing while two communities which are separated by an intervening neighbor but are nevertheless both members of the pact and much closer to each other, do not appear in this preliminary attempt to chart the transaction flows. The method in constructing the partial matrix would be as shown on the map in Diagram 2 which extracts a partial area in the larger region.

The pairs of communities which would appear on the partial matrix would be AB, AC, AD, AE, BC, BE, BF, CD, CG, DE, DG, and EF, while such pairs as AG, AF, BD, BG, DF, EG, and FG would not appear.

By then listing all the possible contiguous pairs and noting functional agreements between pairs, the major transactions can be charted and the pairs rank ordered from high agreers to low agreers. Correlating this ranking with other social, political, and demographic variables might lead to significant insights into the process of integration in such an area. For example, if high agreers are closer together on social rank than low agreers, significant generalizations about social and political differentiation can be formulated.[7]

It may be hypothesized that communities closer to each other in social rank are more likely to agree with each other. Social rank can be measured by the Shevky-Bell method which is based on occupational and educational levels in a community.[8] In this indicator of social rank, the percentages of citizens over twenty-five years old with certain levels of education and certain occupations of the male work force are obtained from census materials, standardized, and weighted equally in a combined index to give a measure of a community's social homogeneity. As a measure of closeness, the mean of absolute differences between social rank scores of communities having more than one agreement will be employed. By using the mean of absolute differences, communities all along the social scale would count equally, with the absolute difference between the pair the only variable under study. This would make it possible to obtain a comparative measure. Pairs low on the social scale but close to each other would figure equally with cooperating pairs close to each other and high on the social rank scale. It is further hypothesized that the position on the social rank scale does not significantly affect a community's decision to enter into a functional agreement, but it does affect the choice of the partner. Because only neighbors are being studied a certain homogeneity of area does enter in; however, when the possible pairs are examined it is predicted that the two closest in social rank to each other are more likely to cooperate with each other in the provision of some service. Besides social rank score, other variables may be investigated to discover regularities in cooperation among pairs of communities in a metropolitan area. Such other variables as school costs, taxes, assessments, dominant political party, and ethnic and religious

7. See the paper by Oliver Williams *et al.*, "Urban Differentiation and Political Integration," delivered at the American Political Science Association Annual meeting, September 5–8, 1962.

8. See Eshref Shevky and Wendell Bell, *Social Area Analysis* (Stanford: Stanford University Press, 1955).

divisions readily come to mind. For example, pairs of communities with the same political party in power might differ significantly in their over-all co-operation levels from others where different political parties are in power in each of the units of the pair.

Testing the Spill-Over Hypothesis: A Second Case Study

Another related transaction flow index would be to test the utility of theories developed in the study of international integration, such as the spill-over hypothesis formulated by Ernst Haas in his study of the uniting of Europe.[9] Spill-over, as previously explained, means that favorable agreements in specific areas lead to other agreements between the parties to the favorable agreement. On the metropolitan level, we can test all the logical possibilities by incorporating agreements between the contiguous pairs mentioned in the preceding section into a transaction flow matrix which itself is based on testing various theories of political integration. The null hypothesis would be that a second agreement between contiguous pairs of communities occurs by chance.

The logical possibilities of such a matrix are summarized statistically in Table 10.

In the Philadelphia area, for example, up-to-date records on the type and kind of functional agreements have been collected by Oliver Williams and his associates at the Fels Institute of Local and State Government of the University of Pennsylvania. Using three types of agreement—police radio pacts, school districts, and sewer authorities—a null model can be constructed with expected levels of agreements computed on the basis of our hypothesis of the preceding section and then compared to the actual level of agreements. A ratio can be obtained between the

9. Ernst Haas, *The Uniting of Europe* (Stanford: Stanford University Press, 1958).

TABLE 10
POSSIBLE EXPLANATIONS FOR AGREEMENT PATTERNS OR LACK OF THEM

Explanation	Number of additional agreements between pairs of communities with one agreement
Spill-over Theory	Statistically significant higher level of occurrence than by chance
Indifference Theory	Null model dictated by pure chance
Disillusionment Theory	Statistically significant lower level of occurrence than that by chance

actual and expected values and the statistical significance calculated. The ratio, similar to the transaction index, can be calculated by the following formula:

$$R = \frac{A - E}{E} \qquad (1.4)$$

where

R is the agreement ratio on two functions by contiguous pairs.
A is the actual agreement level.
E is the expected level computed according to the null hypothesis.

To calculate the expected levels based on the assumption of pure chance, the separate probability of each agreement of the two agreements between the pairs of communities is calculated. Taking education as an example:

$$P_e = \frac{A_e}{N_t} \qquad (1.5)$$

where

P_e is the probability of education agreements.
A_e is the total number of agreements on education.
N_t is the total number of pairs of communities.

To get the expected number of agreements on education and, say, police, by contiguous pairs of communities, each separate probability is multiplied to get the combined probability and then this probability is multiplied by the total number of pairs.

$$P_p \cdot P_e = P_{p.e} \tag{1.6}$$

where

P_p is the probability of police agreements.
P_e is the probability of education agreements.
$P_{p.e}$ is the probability of having both agreements.

and

$$P_{p.e} \times N_t = E_{p.e} \tag{1.7}$$

where

$E_{p.e}$ is the expected number of agreements based on indifference.

Using this procedure over the whole range of possible combinations, the following results in Table 11 were obtained in a pilot study of the five-county area in and around Philadelphia.

Table 11 demonstrates the added complexity of the situation in metropolitan areas. When agreements are kept distinct by subject covered, it becomes readily apparent that there are vari-

TABLE 11

Agreement Pairs	Actual Number of Community Pairs having Agreements	Expected Number of Community Pairs having Agreements	$\frac{A-E}{E}$	Sig. Level of χ^2
Police Radio Pact and Sewer Agreement	47	27	.74	>.001
Police Radio Pact and School Consolidation	43	46	—.07	>.50
School Consolidation and Sewer Agreement	22	47	—.53	>.001

ous degrees of cooperation in the area, and that *the sequential probability of agreements does depend upon function.* Each of the three possible explanations, spillover, indifference, and disillusionment, are supported in turn by the various pairs listed in Table 11. Police radio-sewer agreements appear to be easily attained while school-sewer agreements are much harder to achieve. This latter type of agreement is reached between statistically significant fewer pairs than would be expected by chance occurrence.

Intervening variables, not included in this elementary scheme, probably account for some of the variations. Factors such as topography for sewer agreements, community size for school agreements, and low budget costs for police radio do have an importance in determining which agreements are entered into for communities. However, an examination of Table 12 does show that there is a relationship between social rank and agreement patterns. When the mean absolute difference between Social Rank[10] scores of each community in the agreeing pairs is examined, a clear substantive finding emerges: *the "more difficult" it is to agree,* i.e. the less probable a pair of agreements according to Table 11, *the closer the communities are in social rank.* Where agreements are least likely to occur between pairs of communities, i.e. school-sewer agreements here, the factor of social homogeneity, as measured by the difference in social rank scores of each unit in the pair, seems to make a difference in raising the probability of agreement. That is, on the sewer-school agreements which occur at significantly lower levels than would be expected by chance, the pairs of communities which *do in fact have agreements* are much closer to each other in Social Rank scores than those pairs of communities having "easier" agreements. The variance in the absolute difference in Social Rank of communities which have come to an "easy" agreement, i.e. police radio and sewers, is more than three times that of those who had to agree on a "difficult" arrangement.

10. The Social Rank scores, calculated for each community using the Shevky-Bell method, were supplied to the author by the Fels Institute of Local and State Government at the University of Pennsylvania.

TABLE 12

Agreement Pairs	Mean of Absolute Differences between Social Rank Scores of each Pair with Agreements	S^2	S
Police Radio Pact and Sewer Agreement	11.5	538.2	23.2
Police Radio Pact and School Consolidation	8.7	374.8	19.4
School Consolidation and Sewer Agreement	7.2	158.0	12.6

While we cannot yet establish which theory of agreements might hold true in the long run, we can, by using time series analysis, establish the most recent trends for regions and thereby be in a better position to assess future potentials for integration.

PROSPECTS FOR FUTURE RESEARCH

Procedures to measure integration, such as those outlined, will enable students of metropolitan areas to get a better view of the processes which are already changing the face of America and which are developing political problems as they continue. By being aware of the trends and by assessing the integration potential, not only for the area as a whole but for every sub-section of the area, political scientists may be in a better position to gain understanding of the dynamics of integration and disintegration, and to build up a reliable body of knowledge with which to help predict future trends.

The adaptation of theories of international integration to the study of metropolitan integration using concepts and operations originated by Deutsch and his associates enables the student of local government to use meaningful quantitative measures which are comparable for all areas within and between the various Standard Metropolitan Statistical Areas in the United States. By using actual political behavior in areas as independent checks, such as the governmental integration in Dade County, Florida, or Toronto, Canada, the efficacy of these measures can be checked. For the Philadelphia region, the preliminary test case on agreements does point to certain societal attributes as enhancing the stability of some types of functional integration, but the whole question of larger area-wide governmental integration still remains. The concepts and techniques outlined here offer one procedure for furthering research in this area and show some promise of helping students of metropolitan areas to understand better the extent of political integration. What is now needed is research using these techniques on the various SMSA's in the United States, such as was attempted here for the Wilmington and part of the Philadelphia SMSA's.

Further research on the utility of the procedures contained herein and further improvements in the techniques are still needed if the dynamics of change in megalopolitan America are to be understood. The analysis of societal shifts which precede political integration should be improved so that reliable indicators can be developed, and, more important, so that social science can develop better insight into the process of change.

It is only through such further research on political integration at the metropolitan level and improvement in our techniques that we will be able, hopefully, to contribute some meaningful theory on political integration to the literature on political behavior.

V

Integration at the Urban Level: Political Influence and the Decision Process

Despite the apparent chaotic pattern of political communities in American metropolitan areas, coordinated efforts between and within political communities are not uncommon. William L. C. Wheaton takes a critical look at research on the process of political coordination and concludes that recent community power and influence studies are of little help in understanding the forces at work in local government in metropolitan areas. He offers instead a set of propositions explaining inter- and intra-community coordination in terms of "networks of influence." Such networks develop from convergences of interests within and across political boundaries. Avoiding the assumption that for every coordinated set of activities there first must be stable, institutionalized coordination, he suggests that metropolitan institutions will emerge from changes in the existing networks of influence, changes which can be aided by deliberate public policy.

Issues of Concern in Metropolitan Political Integration

THE POSSIBILITIES FOR POLITICAL INTEGRATION OR COORDINATION IN metropolitan areas, the characteristic form of twentieth century urbanism, rest upon hypotheses as yet unstated in the literature of political science or upon premises which are apparently false or at least unproved. We will review here the issues as they have appeared in recent literature and action programs and ultimately suggest some promising lines of inquiry. That metropolitan areas have become the characteristic form of civilization has been adequately documented. The economic, social, and political interdependence of such areas is attested by Gulick, Robson, Wood, Vernon, and officially in the United States by the Commission on Intergovernmental Relations, in Great Britain by the recent Royal Commission on London Government.

This awareness and concern and the accompanying recognition that urban government has a critical role to play in providing an integrated set of services, as well as common standards of service for metropolitan populations, have not been matched by any comparable expansion of our knowledge of the nature of the forces at work in local government in metropolitan areas. The old reformist solution, "metropolitan government," has been rejected by the electorate in the United States (with two exceptions); plans for voluntary cooperation have proved incapable of facing major issues; and only state assumption of financial responsibility and standard-setting in critical areas like education and highways has kept the creaky machinery of local government functioning at minimal levels. Old ideological patrons of metropolitan government have almost abandoned their hopes.[1] Young supporters of the dream concede its fragility.[2] Some "new thinkers," in an attempt to close the gap between reformers' hopes and political realities, have concluded that the reformers are wrong after all, that the market for government services, like all other markets, fattens some and starves others and must therefore optimize some social Darwinian function in the absence of revolt.[3]

1. Luther H. Gulick, *The Metropolitan Problem and American Ideas* (New York: Knopf, 1962).

2. Robert C. Wood, *Suburbia, Its People and Their Politics* (Boston: Houghton Mifflin, 1958). See also John C. Bollens, (Ed.), *Exploring the Metropolitan Community* (Berkeley: University of California Press, 1961).

3. Edward G. Banfield, and Morton Grodzins, *Government and Housing in Metropolitan Areas* (New York: McGraw-Hill, 1958).

Recent political research and theory contributes but little to a joining of these issues. The lively controversy between the power-elite theorists following Hunter and the process-pluralist theorists of the Dahl-Banfield-Sayre persuasion has produced a revival of academic interest in local government, a host of case studies, and a few "comparative" studies. The methods of the "reputationalists" have been demolished in theory by Dahl, Wolfinger, and others as having little relevance to the problems of government or political decision making.[4] It is clear that scientifically rigorous methods may be used in a variety of circumstances to demonstrate that informed people believe that a power elite exists and that it makes or can influence many community decisions. It also appears that in some communities, some of the time, some such elite groups do influence some decisions but not race relations in Atlanta or steel wages in Pittsburgh. On the other hand, the preponderance of evidence now clearly demonstrates that in most communities most of the time, power and influence are dispersed among numerous groups and that no elite exists which can regularly make or influence decisions on a broad range of public policy issues. Rossi has proposed to classify communities as pyramidal, caucus rule, polylith, or amorphous in recognition of these distinctions of reputation.[5] This generalization requires qualification with respect to its decision-matter referents as is suggested below.

The pluralist or process theories of power hold that no such elite exists, that power is dispersed among various groups having particular or narrow interests, that decisions result from agreement, competition, conflict, or bargaining among such groups

4. Floyd Hunter, *Community Power Structure* (Chapel Hill: University of North Carolina Press, 1953.) For a summary of the opposite viewpoint cf. Robert A. Dahl, "The Analysis of Political Influence" in Charles R. Adrian, (Ed.), *Social Science and Community Action* (East Lansing: Michigan State Continuing Education Service, 1961). Cf. also his "A Critique of the Ruling Elite Model," *American Political Science Review,* Vol. 52, (June, 1958) and Raymond E. Wolfinger, "Reputation and Reality in the Study of Community Power," *American Sociological Review,* Vol. 25, (October 1960).

5. Peter H. Rossi, "Power and Community Structure," *Midwest Journal of Political Science,* Vol. 4, No. 4, November, 1960, and works there cited.

and that "public policy" is the aggregate of such decisions.[6] These theories also remain unproved, even as they apply to single municipal jurisdictions. The multiplication of case studies of individual public policy decisions or groups of them indicate that some groups do exercise relatively great influence in some subject matter areas, while other groups exercise influence in other areas.

This is a necessary but not a sufficient demonstration of power diffusion. Proof would require the presentation of a matrix of *all* public policy decisions together with an analysis of who was influential on each in some jurisdiction and for some time period. Some of the case studies move in this direction, but none purport to deal with more than a handful of decisions.[7] Proof would require a demonstration that those groups which appeared to be influential in large numbers of cases did not consult each other, did not have agreed goals or bargain, or in other ways concert their policies to achieve collective ends. This might well be proved, but the history of antitrust cases suggests that conspiracy is difficult to demonstrate even in quite limited areas. Since people of affairs and influence tend to meet frequently on public and private business, even though they may have very different political positions or views on public issues, the existence of a functioning power elite cannot be proved merely by association.

Finally, and most important, it should be noted that the preponderance of power studies and case studies relate to single municipal governments rather than to metropolitan areas. Within such jurisdictions elite groups and powerful political machines may be expected to be more common and bargaining arrangements between machines and their competitors to be fre-

6. Cf. Robert A. Dahl, *Who Governs?* (New Haven: Yale University Press, 1961); Edward C. Banfield, *Political Influence.* (New York: The Free Press of Glencoe, 1961); Wallace S. Sayre, and Herbert Kaufman, *Governing New York City* (New York: Russell Sage Foundation, 1961.)

7. e.g., Banfield, "Political Influence," *op. cit.* and Robert J. Mowitz. For comparative studies see Morris Janowitz, and Heinz Eulau, *Community Political Systems* (New York: The Free Press of Glencoe, 1960).

quent. When jurisdictional lines are crossed, however, even these systems of influence collapse or lose most of their force. The case study material plentifully illustrates that, at this point, the processes of decision making become amorphous, to use Rossi's classification, and county, state, or federal influences come into play. The powers of higher levels of government are usually weak, however, require local cooperation or consent, and are sensitive to highly particular local pressures. The highway cases are particularly relevant.[8]

Networks of Influence

In an attempt to clarify these issues as they bear upon the political integration of metropolitan areas, it is essential that the power-influence theories be modified and restated, that they be related to metropolitan areas and that they then be further related to the demographic and economic circumstances that produce changes in the system. The following propositions are an attempt in these directions. Methods of testing them are suggested where appropriate.

1. Political influence is distributed among groups of persons or institutions, each of which comprises a constellation or network of communication or influence. Illustration 1 is an attempt to portray some of these networks in a typical central city of a metropolitan area. Each constellation is characterized by relatively higher rates of communication or influence among its members as opposed to comparable rates of communication or influence with others. The members of such a constellation will tend to see each other more frequently, to do business more frequently or in larger volume, and probably to share similar views

8. Cf. Robert Daland, "Realignment of Route 22" (Westchester County) and Deil Wright, "Harper Woods" (Detroit), manuscript cases to be published by the Inter-University Case Program, and Robert J. Mowitz and Edward Banfield, *op. cit.* for illustrations. The Banfield cases are of particular interest because of the frequency of appeals to higher levels of government in Illinois in a variety of subject matter fields.

ILLUSTRATION 1

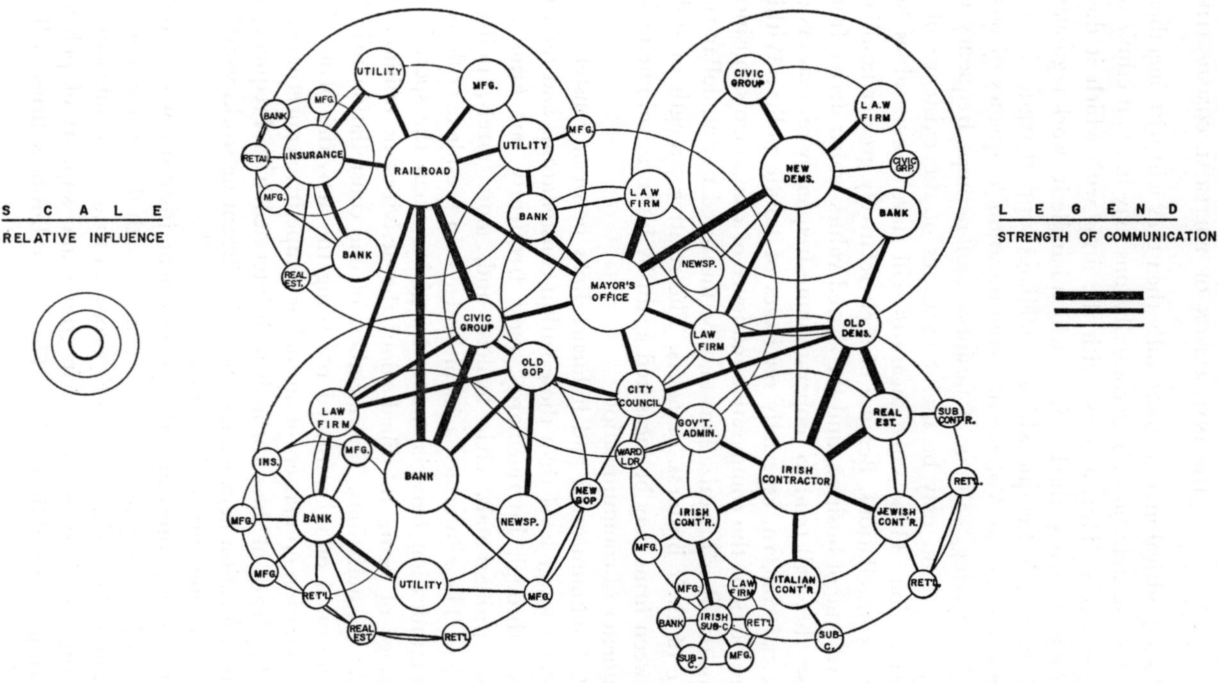

COMMUNICATION AND INFLUENCE STRUCTURE IN CITY DEVELOPMENT DECISIONS

on local political matters more fully then they will with members of other constellations. The constellations may have an ethnic or religious core. Thus a bank, with the firms with which it does business regularly, the law firms which handlc its work regularly, and the political clique which its affiliates support regularly may be a constellation. Volume of communication, frequency of face-to-face meeting, volume of business, and perhaps frequency of similar opinion may be useful measures of the existence of a constellation. These same measures will have lower values between constellations. Because of their relatively greater familiarity, volume of business, and the shared values which derive from these, they will tend to cooperate more frequently on matters of external concern, especially on issues of public policy. Within constellations the comparative influence of components, business firms or other organizations may be measured by the dollar volume of their business, or assets. The relative strength of links between firms may be measured again by business volume or by frequency of communication.

2. Communication and influence links between constellations are at a lower level than those within constellations and tend to occur through intermediaries, most frequently law firms and other professionals, civic leaders, and, more rarely, political leaders. These intermediaries or bridge men preside over flows of communication between networks, giving them the special advantage of being informed about the activities or opinions of other constellations. The members of one constellation may be uninformed or misinformed regarding the activities of another constellation on matters of mutual or competitive concern, except as they learn of these through such intermediaries. Frequency of communication between members of different networks would be a feasible measure of this function.

3. Constellations and their component institutions or groups have widely varying degrees of concern with different subjects of public policy. They express this concern through membership in or support of specialized civic groups and support of political machines or public officials. Thus most business firms will be

concerned about property tax rates, but few about recreation. Civic groups dealing with tax issues will draw heavier support from constellations having a major stake in tax rates, and those dealing with recreation will find less support. Civic groups, however, like political machines, become intermediaries in the fields of their specialization. They learn who will support or oppose measures of interest to them. Illustration 2 depicts these relationships. It also illustrates the fact that some subjects are more completely "covered," i.e. subjects of interest than others and that the field of public policy is "loose," to use Dahl's phrase, or open to active intervention if new or existing groups take an interest in some particular subject or field. The scope and degree of interest of any group or constellation may be measurable by the identification of the subjects with which it deals and the number of actions, messages, resolutions, etc., which it devotes to each.

4. Most constellations have a geographic locus, often the central city, within which they have interests, are informed, or may be influential. This is of primary importance to metropolitan issues. For the typical central city, constellation will have only tenuous links with counterpart constellations in the suburbs. Illustration 3 presents a simplified version of these relationships. While individual business firms may have branch plants, stores, or offices, in the suburbs, other components of any constellation may not. Since the central city constellation has a central locus, components with business outside the constellation's locus must take a subsidiary position in another suburban constellation to become part of that system. To the extent that suburban constellations tend to be dominated by local businessmen and linked to local political machines and local civic groups, branch representatives of central firms with a more metropolitan orientation and high mobility may be excluded or admitted only marginally to full participation in the suburban network of communication and influence. The relationships between central city and suburban political machines are often weak and sometimes

Illustration 2

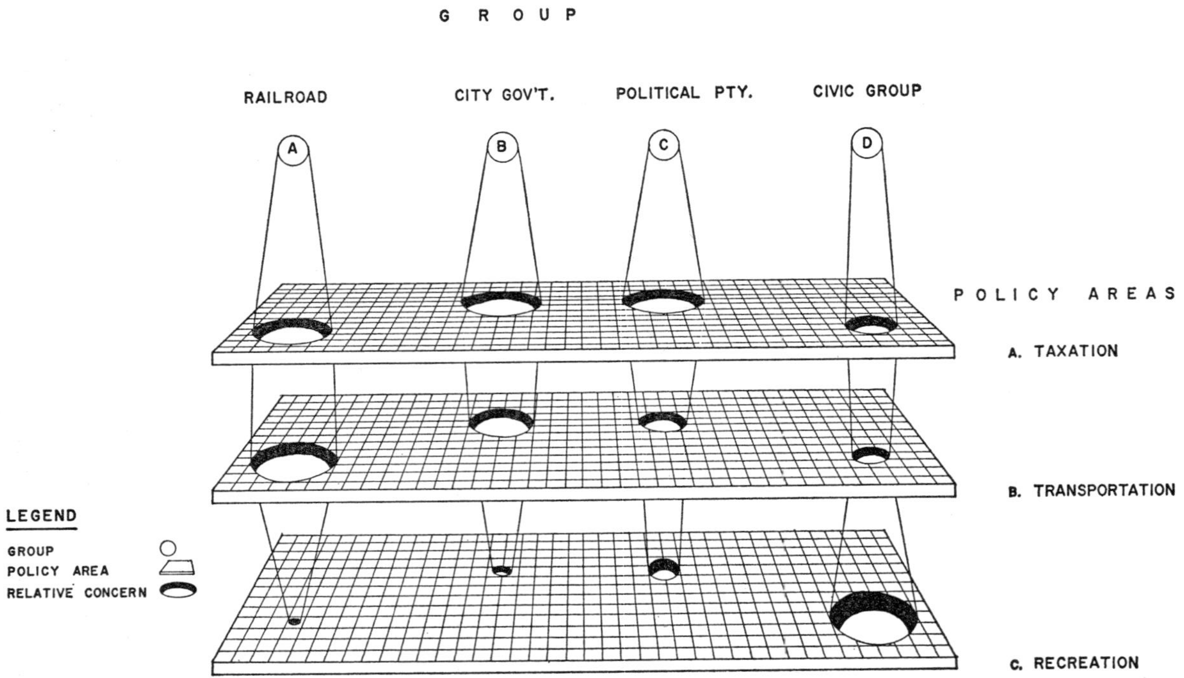

RELATIVE CONCERN OF GROUPS IN DIFFERENT AREAS OF INTEREST

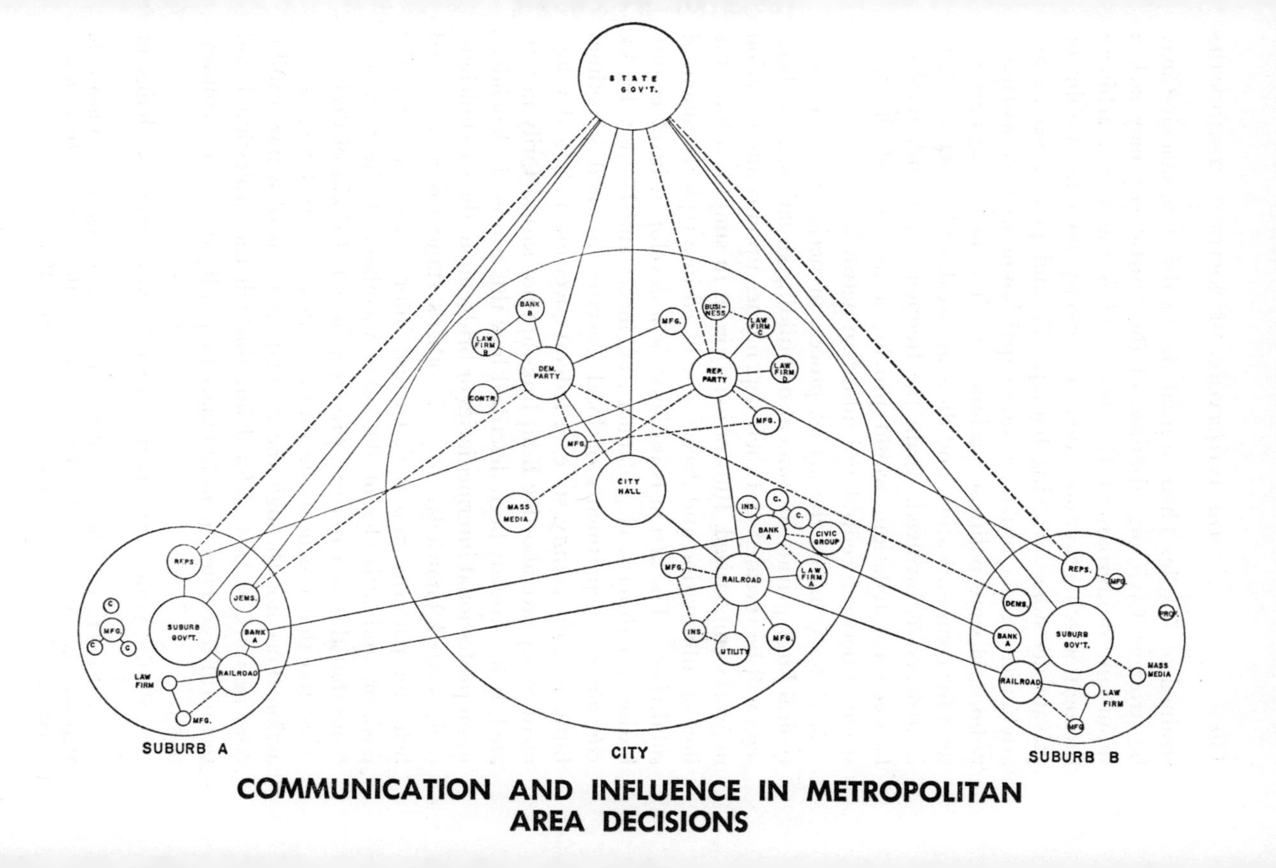

COMMUNICATION AND INFLUENCE IN METROPOLITAN AREA DECISIONS

strained or hostile. Their mutual ties to the state machine may be stronger. Civic organizations of the central city may lack a suburban counterpart or vice versa. Thus the very machinery through which communications commonly flow for public or private decisions involving both public and private agents are attenuated, if not broken at municipal boundaries. Newspapers, radio, and state political machines may be almost the only systems for communication, and these are weak or ineffectual where controversy is involved. Again the frequency of communication between constellations would provide a measure of the link-strength between central and suburban networks.

5. If we examine the actual process of decision-making in a typical large private investment or building situation, these linkages will be revealed and their dependence upon communication networks emphasized. Illustration 4 traces in simplified form the flow of information and decision involved in a typical residential subdivision. The action is initiated by a developer, involves professional architects, city planners, engineers and lawyers, banks, contractors, departments of local government, and sometimes bureaus of the county, state, or federal government. The development will prove abortive if all links are not satisfactorily negotiated. It has already been described how this process is dependent upon professional intermediaries or bridge men, their technicians, their shared knowledge of each other's standards and normal behavior patterns, and their current information regarding the position and attitudes of the other members of the network.[9] Note that this is a *routine, privately initiated* chain of decision. Note too that much of the information necessary for successful action flows not through the normal channels of a power-influence network as here defined but through the professional and technical associates of individuals in public or private employment.

6. Public policy actions involve far more complex chains of

9. William L. C. Wheaton, "Public and Private Agents of Change in Metropolitan Development," *Conference on Metropolitan Development* (Washington: Housing and Home Finance Agency, 1963).

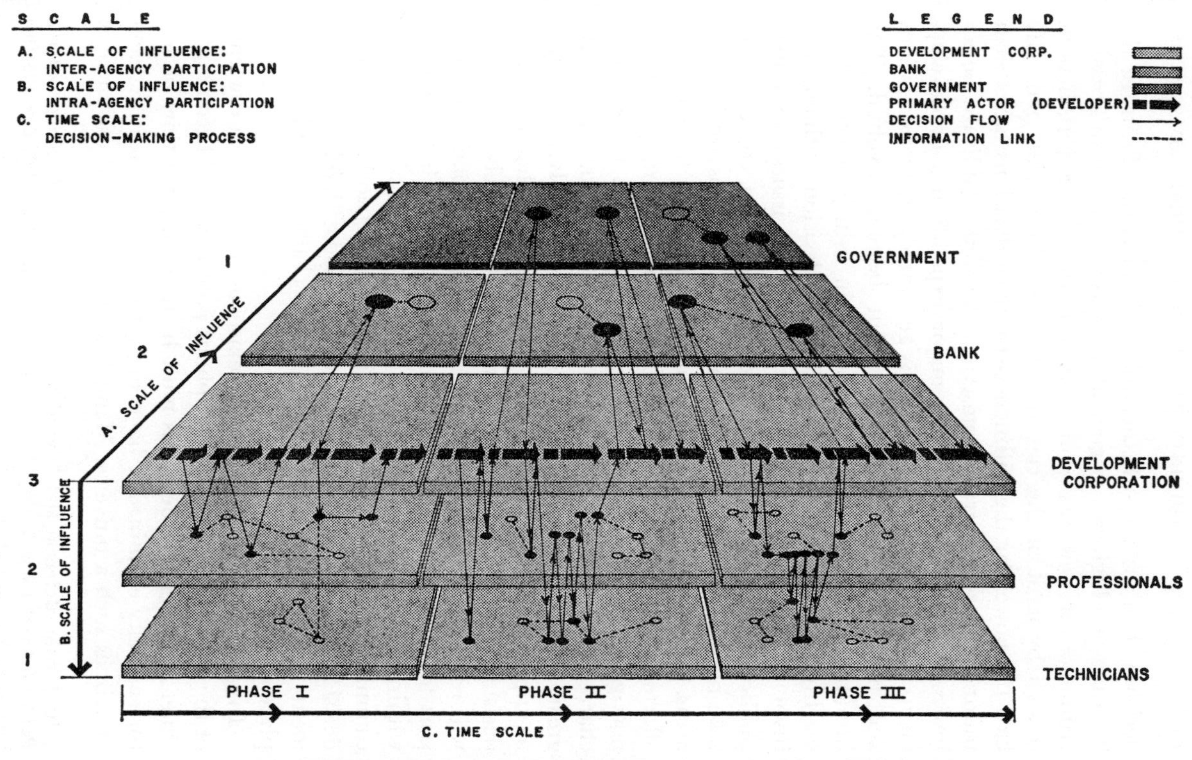

FLOW OF COMMUNICATION IN A DEVELOPMENT DECISION PROCESS

decision than private, whether the decision is specific, as in the building of a highway, or general, as in the adoption of a zoning ordinance or new tax policy. Within the single jurisdictions treated by most of the case materials, public officials generally lack the power, or the willingness to make decisions other than routine ones which are circumscribed by well established policy limits. Where new policies or major expenditures or developments are concerned, controversy is generated, and constellations and networks outside of government become involved. The literature is almost barren of cases in which governmental machinery works smoothly to obtain a decision without such involvement. Characteristically, proposals or issues are raised, public officials and private agencies consider them, constellations take positions in areas of concern to them and abstain in other areas. Often new groups are formed among those most directly affected, either favorably or adversely, by any proposal. These new groups may be highly local, particular, and transitory in character, but their momentary power to stop action is very great.[10] Public officials delay decisions interminably, attempting to appraise the balance of power pro and con. They may defer decision indefinitely if the balance is approximately equal, and will reach decisions only when there is clearly preponderant support for one position. Often decisions are reached by bargaining within the power network, through specially appointed citizens committees which are representative of the network. Frequently decisions may be referred to experts or to other levels of government so that local public officials can evade responsibility or place it elsewhere.

In this connection, tests of the existence and relative efficiency of the so-called pyramidal-amorphous power systems become possible. A universe of decisions must be selected for a time period for each city examined. I have suggested an investment decision matrix as such a universe. Mann has suggested land use changes

10. Martin Meyerson and Edward C. Banfield, *Politics, Planning and the Public Interest* (New York: The Free Press of Glencoe, 1955), describe this process with great clarity.

for these purposes.[11] The existence of an elite power group would be measured by the frequency of referral of decisions to that group for advice or recommendation and the frequency of action in accordance with the choice of the elite group. High values on both scores would affirm the existence of an effective power center of wide interests, while low values in either would tend to affirm the pluralist view, as would distinct segregation of classes of cases referred. If pyramidal power systems do exist they should produce distinct differences in procedure in the time necessary to reach a decision of given type and size and in the proportion of issues posed which are decided at all. If both pyramidal and polylith systems follow similar procedures of referral, consultation, debate, delay, bargaining, and use of experts; if time from inception to decision is similar; and if the proportion of issues resolved is similar, then the "power" described would be a mirage, unless the benefits were invariably favorable to the elite in the one instance and dispersed in the other.

7. Metropolitan public policy decisions are a special class of cases. They arise most frequently in connection with highways, airports, and regional recreation, hospital, and utility systems. The relative autonomy historically granted to local governments, the attenuation of influence networks across municipal boundaries, the rapid emergence of state and federal aids as means for overcoming local fiscal inadequacies and for obtaining minimal standards of service, all combine to make these cases in which state or federal agents appear in crucial roles. (Banfield's *Political Influence* is particularly revealing in its indication of the dependence of Chicago on state decision processes.) Once these officials become involved, the network of influence extends enormously, since any local decision can be "appealed" by those adversely affected to the state or federal agencies. Some major metropolitan highway locations have been in debate for decades,

11. Wheaton, *op. cit.;* Lawrence D. Mann, "Sources and Processes of Urban Environmental Change," *Research Previews,* Vol. 10, No. 3, May, 1963. (Chapel Hill: University of North Carolina.)

because of the inability of local governments to accept an alignment which would adversely affect a comparative handful of their residents and of the inability of state officials to resist these veto pressures. The frequent necessity for unanimity between federal, state, and local officials gives each level an additional veto. On the other hand, in these cases, the role of the expert, the engineer, armed with grant-in-aid money, is sharply outlined. A common escape for local officials, trapped between conflicting pressures after intially considering an issue "political," is the public pronouncement that the issue is, after all, technical and financial and that it has therefore been decided (over local protest, of course) by these experts. In such instances close *professional* cooperation between experts at different levels may provide the only means for finding the optimum political solution and implementing it. Where central cities and suburban areas are in conflict in such metropolitan cases, the relatively more proficient professional staff of the central city may be a distinct advantage in dealing with most suburban and many state agencies. Education, particularly because of state financial aids, standards, and the professionalization of school administration, provides another lucrative field for case studies. These two fields then provide opportunities for tests of the roles of influence networks, professionals, and procedures in decision making.

8. In the absence of change or innovation both the systems of influence which we have been discussing and the products of those systems, i.e. local government policies, would remain in equilibrium and would not themselves change materially through time. March and Simon have noted that most important innovations in administrative systems are externally motivated.[12] Certainly the rapid growth of urban areas, the high degree of mobility within them, and the consequent expansions in demand for public services are among the most important causes of change in service demands; these demands in turn generate conflict over the scope of government and ultimately changes in

12. James G. March and Herbert A. Simon, *Organizations* (New York: Wiley, 1958.)

the networks of influence affecting government.[13] Most of the case materials on local decision making demonstrate these points, since in large degree they deal with controversies arising from changes of the classes described.[14]

Mann distinguishes problem-oriented changes from opportunity-oriented changes and suggests that public policy changes may be commonly of the former type and private changes of the latter.[15] But it should be noted that the networks of influence which we have described are mixed enterprises, consisting largely of private components. Thus the opportunity-oriented changes initiated by private home builders, let us say, generate demand for use of the influence network to solve problem-oriented public policy issues. On the other hand, the influence network may regard some inadequate public facility or service (an airport or convention hall) as an opportunity, thus generating a problem for the network of securing change in public policy. The recognition of the need for changes in public policies may arise at any point in the network. Staff members of civic or public agencies who are employed to perform these functions and political and business leaders all appear as initiators of decision-sequences. A systematic statistical analysis of the case studies might well be conducted to shed light on this point. Often a problem or an opportunity, accompanied by proposals, may be generated more or less simultaneously at several points in the network, become a subject of private discussion, and gradually emerge to the stage of public discussion or formal proposal for action. Some subjects of possible action are proposed and lie dormant for months or years until interest in them emerges or

13. Cf. Gladys M. Kemmerer, and others, *The Urban Political Community*. (New York: Houghton Mifflin Co., 1963), particularly pp. 198 ff. On the controversies generated by changes in scope cf. Robert E. Aggar, "Comparative Experimental Study of Educational Decision Making in the Community." (Institute for Community Studies, University of Oregon, Eugene: 1962) mimeo.

14. Mann, *op. cit.*

15. Mann, *op. cit.*

pressures build up sufficiently to create active issues for the network.

The case studies throw little light upon the relationships between social and economic changes and the responsiveness of the influence network and political system to them. They begin, descriptively, at the point where the system recognizes a problem or an opportunity. Yet measures might readily be devised to test the responsiveness of various types of networks, their components, and public officials. The time lag between the growth of school age population and the initiation of action toward a school expansion program illustrates the type of measure involved. In larger local jurisdiction these facts may be recognized and forecast regularly by staff but not accepted by public officials or influence networks as problems. In smaller communities even the facts may be lacking. One measure of the efficiency of the system is its arrangements, formal or informal, for having data available.

Local Integration and Metropolitan Fragmentation

For our purposes, dealing with local government, we may define integration as that minimal consensus which permits the maintenance of social order, the functioning of a system of public and private institutions for the production and distribution of services regarded as essential, recognition of minimal rights of all groups in the population, enforcement of those obligations necessary to maintain the system, and the provision of those services necessary to maintain the system and permit its normal growth and change. This crude definition recognizes that a society of ample resources, dedicated to individual well-being, can tolerate very wide differences of individual behavior or welfare and wide differences of individual or group values but must provide certain minimum levels of service and enforce those minimum standards of behavior necessary for its collective welfare. No considerable number of people can be permitted to starve, be illiterate, or contaminate the water needed by others for drinking. So viewed, our urban governments are of primary importance to the maintenance of society because they provide most of the essential services, police, fire, health, sanitation, transportation, and education necessary for such maintenance. In addition they must provide many services which, while not essential to system maintenance, have such a high marginal return to the local society as a whole as to justify their public support, i.e. convention halls in Atlantic City or subways in New York City.

The local government decision processes which we have attempted to describe work tolerably well to meet these minimum standards of service and to provide or enforce some minimum standard of integration in the restricted sense in which we use the term. In addition the processes themselves tend to maintain consensus on the scope of government and the fundamental "fairness" of society because they require participation, consultation and consent at so many points. In this sense these processes prevent alienation, hostility, and disintegration.[16] These processes perform their integrative function at considerable price. They provide extraordinary protection to small fractions of the population against adverse consequences of public action. A few score homeowners, if organized and articulate, can prevent the construction of a school or playground fronting upon their properties even when it would serve thousands of others in the same neighborhood. As a consequence, the system of local decision making involves long delays in reaching conclusions and probably frequently results in lost opportunities, higher costs, or lower standards of service than those which might otherwise prevail. In short, if it were possible to calculate welfare with greater precision, we might discover that our local decision processes paid a very high price for consensus.

In dealing with metropolitan area problems, however, the same types of decision processes do not appear to function with tolerable efficiency either to produce services or to produce the processes that result in metropolitan consensus. Here the delays in

16. Cf. Aggar, *op. cit.*

reaching decisions appear to be even longer, and the proportion of issues resolved by some affirmative action appears to be lower. Whereas in the single city, one duly constituted and representative official or group of officials must ultimately be subject to conflicting pressures and weigh the welfare of different groups, in metropolitan decisions no such situation exists. A state highway official may have to consider the welfare losses of home owners, for whom he has little concern, against the welfare benefits of automobile riders, with whose problems he is fully familiar. Further, within the metropolitan area, minimum standards of service may vary over extraordinary ranges, and the costs may be shifted to groups or communities receiving no benefits. Or benefits may be derived by groups contributing nothing to costs. The confrontation of issues within the influence network may never occur, so that the consensual effects presumed may never arise.

Two illustrations may serve to emphasize these points. A state highway department has planned a five-mile bypass expressway serving the metropolitan area and running through a section of a small suburban area. Two hundred residents of that community, whose homes will be taken at an average value of $20,000, aroused and organized, persuade their local government to oppose the highway and withhold the required local consent. As a result there is a ten-year delay in the construction of the highway and its eventual costs rise from $5 million to $10 million. During the ten years, ten million riders per year, driving an average of five miles, lose in extra mileage, travel costs, and travel time $10 million in benefits which they might otherwise reap.[17] The losses of welfare (costs) over a ten-year period aggregate $15 million and are borne by citizens of the whole metropolitan area who might use the facility and who would happily pay in user taxes and tolls for its cost. The beneficiaries of delay are 200 home owners, 75 per cent of whom will have moved during the ten year period and been replaced by others.

17. We are here drawing upon, and simplifying, an unpublished case by Paul Davidoff, "The Blue Route Controversy," (University of Pennsylvania, Department of City Planning, 1962). Similar cases in New York, Detroit, and other areas do not present cost-benefit calculations.

Confronted with this situation, in a single jurisdiction, the influence network would have produced pressures from automobile riders to oppose pressure from home owners (represented at least by their city councilman), provided ample hearings, and reached a decision in the community interest, at some psychic cost to the home owners. In fact, however, the central city network is powerless in the suburb and weak in the state highway department vis-a-vis local officials with a high motivation to obstruct. The local network serves local interests and contains no representatives of metropolitan interests. An economically advantageous solution might have required an average payment of 50 per cent more than the value of the homes (extra cost $2 million) in order to secure agreement from the opponents and a net gain in welfare to the community of $13 million.

Even more serious consequences arise in the field of education. Despite so-called equalization payments, expenditures per child in typical metropolitan areas may vary from $300 to over $1,000 in different municipalities in the same metropolitan area in Northern states. Assuming educational benefits to be roughly equal to costs, a family with two children of school age may increase its real income by $1,400 per year by the simple expedient of moving from the low to the high expenditure district.[18] While tax, transportation cost, and housing cost differentials will reduce the benefit gain slightly, state aid differentials tend to enhance the gain, so that strictly economic incentives for migration become quite large, to say nothing of social or other less measurable incentives. Migrating families not only obtain a gain in real income but also avoid making an effective contribution to the costs of educating other children wherever state taxes levied in a jurisdiction exceed aggregate state aids to the jurisdiction, the common case in central cities.

Banfield and Grodzins argue that these circumstances create a socially useful market for municipal services and locations, but

18. We are here drawing on an unpublished paper, Robert Conley, "Five Families Choose a School District" (Department of City Planning, University of Pennsylvania, 1962).

the argument holds only where all costs derive from local taxes and cannot be shifted to other jurisdictions.[19] Such forces appear to operate to reinforce the separation of metropolitan areas. Where migration is selective and motivated by a desire to escape problems or to gain benefits without corresponding assumption of responsibility for costs, the local political consequences may be to intensify localism and to strengthen the local suburban communication and influence network.[20] The functional interdependence of the metropolitan area may also be increased by such selective migration, but this interdependence has as yet not generated corresponding influence-network systems. In the longer run, of course, migration generates problems and necessitates adjustment in the growing local suburban area, and it will also increase the problems of state and federal officials, but without increasing their capacity to handle problems in any corresponding degree or rate.

In the face of these problems and emerging issues it will certainly be necessary for the formal institutions of government to adapt and change to meet new demands. But since these changes are likely to emerge as a result of the actions of existing networks of influence, it follows that their ability to accept and handle metropolitan problems must be enhanced prior to governmental reorganization. If our hypothesis is correct, their influence is greater upon state and federal policies than upon suburban; it also follows that solutions to problems of metropolitan integration may take more probably the form of increasing state and federal responsibility, enlarged grant-in-aid programs, and relative reductions in local power and responsibility, an extension of the trends of the last fifteen years.

Improvements in the efficiency and capacity of influence networks may take several forms. First, the area of interest of existing networks and components can be broadened. The establish-

19. Banfield and Grodzins, *op. cit.*

20. Cf. Scott Greer, *Governing the Metropolis.* (New York: Wiley, 1962) and Robert C. Wood, *Suburbia, op. cit.* and *1400 Governments.* (Cambridge: Harvard University Press, 1961.)

ment of metropolitan data systems and planning agencies which expand our knowledge of the facts, particularly those dealing with the economic interdependence of metropolitan areas, would provide better information for the system. Such information would be utilized by the system for private opportunity-oriented adaptations and changes, leading to the utilization of the same networks for solving the public problem initiated issues that result. Since information is channeled and interpreted in the system by professionals, staff members of civic agencies, the bridge men of the system, strengthening of their roles will tend to enlarge system capacity for change. Similarly, local, state, and federal bureaucracies, functioning as experts, may be expected to face increasing problems. The further professionalization of these groups and the development of their informal systems of professional communication and cooperation will facilitate the more regular and rapid invention of solutions which relieve the weaker parts of the system of responsibility for decisions they are unable to make. One consequence of such trends would be increasing functional specialization on the part of components and networks as well as in governmental decision making. Since such functional specialization makes difficult any comprehensive weighing of competing welfares, in the long run networks must overcome their geographic localism, if it exists, and become metropolitan in the scope of their interests and activities. The initiative for such expansion of locus must come from central city networks whose members are metropolitan and have metropolitan business or other interests.

To summarize, we have sought to examine some of the main arguments of recent studies of political power and influence in metropolitan areas. We have stressed the role played by informal networks of communication and influence which handle both private and public business. A number of propositions regarding these networks have been made, together with suggestions for means of testing them. As our knowledge of these phenomena expands, it may prove possible to utilize these systems more effectively to achieve metropolitan integration. The rapid changes occurring in metropolitan areas will necessitate changes in both informal and formal institutions, but the former are likely to be a condition precedent to the latter. For this reason, the solution to many current urban problems may well be influenced by our research in these areas.

VI

The Price of Integration

In this chapter, Karl Deutsch seeks to determine the conditions that create maximum probability for integration. A central concern is the extent to which governmental performance meets people's needs and demands. The distribution of economic, educational, social, and cultural benefits is held to be a basic correlate of governmental effectiveness and hence an important factor affecting integrative behavior at both the international and metropolitan levels. Central to this analysis is a communications theory assumption of feedback—that social values help determine the distribution of resources in a society and that this very distribution reinforces the existent social values. Neither completely materialistic, yet employing the concepts of joint reward and joint deprivation, nor completely idealistic, yet suggesting ways to develop more effective policy, he attempts to answer the question, "What price integration?"

INTEGRATION DOES HAVE A PRICE, ONE WHICH MUST BE MET BY government and is, in part, set by those who are governed. In fact it is the capabilities and performances of governments that provide the key to integration and cohesion in societies. By their very nature, governments have the means to establish and maintain certain standards of well-being for their populations which are basic conditions for integration. How can indicators of governmental performance be obtained? At present levels of knowledge and data collection, how can reliable indicators be found to evaluate this performance?

Survival as a Measure of Performance

One of the simplest ways to check the performance of a government is to assay its ability to keep populations alive. Life has ranked high, often even before liberty and the pursuit of happiness, among basic political values.[1] The distribution of this value may tell us something about the performance of different governments. This can be accomplished by checking mortality figures.

For another indication of the difference of living standards among races, life expectancies or death rates are quite useful. In the United States, for instance, the life expectancy for white males in 1959 was 67.3 years, while for male Negroes it was 60.9. For women the spread between races in the United States was almost eight years; that is, in 1959 it cost eight years to be colored in America if you were a woman and six years if you were a man.[2] Child mortality figures account for some of this difference. On the international side, the crude mortality is 5.5 per 1,000 for whites and 32.2 per 1,000 for Negroes in Northern Rhodesia. The frequency of death is thus six times as great for the colored group as for the white.[3] These very crude measures for the conditions of life and the degree of public health protection show their use in this sense.

Other useful indices are the number of inhabitants per physician and the number of inhabitants per hospital bed. One can

1. Karl W. Deutsch, "Social Mobilization and Political Development," *American Political Science Review,* Vol. 55, September, 1961, especially 507–514.

2. U.S. Department of Commerce, Bureau of the Census, *Statistical Abstract of the U.S., 1962* (Washington: Government Printing Office, 1963), p. 61. Figures cited are for 1959.

3. United Nations, *Compendium of Social Statistics, 1963* (New York, 1963) p. 96.

begin to correlate the survival rate of two countries if they have the same level of medical care or physicians per population, or if they have the same number of hospital beds. Taking only those four figures together, we could correlate them with national per capita income to answer the question, "How much life expectancy does a given level of income buy?"[4] Life expectancy is quite strongly correlated to income, but the deviant cases are also interesting. The per capita income of Belgium and Sweden was fairly similar in 1957—about $1,200 and $1,380 respectively—but the Swedes had a higher life expectancy for the same income than the Belgians—75 against 67 years at birth—even though some Belgians might argue that they enjoy life more.

Standards of Well-Being

The actual performance of governments should also be measured in terms of economic, educational, cultural, and other standards of well-being for each country. For instance, literacy figures range from 99 per cent to between 1 and 5 per cent from Sweden to Ethiopia. Ordinarily there is no exact and undimensional correlation between literacy levels and differences in income. In Ethiopia, $54 per capita income is correlated with between 1 per cent and 5 per cent literacy, while in Burma, a similar income of $54 is correlated with 48 per cent literacy.[5] Burma is in some ways an entirely atypical country. It is far too literate for the income it has. A high level of aspiration can be expected, yet there exists little or no economic ability to fulfill

4. An early correlation of this type was presented by Otto Neurath in the form of pictograph or isotype symbols in *Gesellschaft und Wirtschaft* (Leipzig: Brockhaus, 1930).

5. United Nations, *Demographic Yearbook* (New York, 1960), pp. 504–507, and Research in Economic Development and Culture Change, University of Chicago, "The Role of Foreign Aid in the Development of Other Countries," in U.S. Senate, 85th Congress, 1st Session, Senate Document 52, *Foreign Aid Program: Compilation of Studies and Surveys* (Washington: Government Printing Office, 1957), p. 240.

it in any near future. A very high level of political instability can thus be expected. The recent history of Burmese independence is replete with a variety of *coups* and a long drawn-out civil war. Burma is about as unstable as a country can be.[6] Similarly, in India the most literate state is one of the poorest—Kerala, with 46 per cent literacy in 1961—and it is the one state which elected a Communist government at one time.[7] A highly educated but poor population is a security risk for the established governments. Some people are too educated, if not for their own good, at least for the comfort of their rulers.

Redistribution of Wealth as a Price of Integration

In addition to maintaining the general level of well-being, it is necessary to assure wide distribution of benefits throughout the population. General acceptance of some redistribution of wealth among regional or social groups, combined with actual governmental ability to redistribute this wealth, usually accompanies high levels of integration among politically active populations. Where wealth distributions are so skewed that only a small percentage of the population receives a large percentage of the nation's wealth, social conflict and disintegrative tendencies also usually exist. More than a century ago, Benjamin Disraeli caught the essence of this argument when he referred to the two nations, "the 'rich' and the 'poor.' "

The highly integrated, richer nations of the noncommunist world accept more wide sharing of wealth by government than do poorer, less integrated nations. Moreover, governmental capability in these highly integrated nations far surpasses that of

6. Lucian Pye, *The Spirit of Burmese Politics* (Cambridge: Center for International Studies, M.I.T., 1959) and *Politics, Personality and Nation Building* (New Haven: Yale University Press, 1962).

7. Government of India, Ministry of Information and Broadcasting, *India: A Reference Annual, 1962* (New Delhi, 1962) 1.78 and Ministry of Education, *Review of Education in India, 1947–61* (New Delhi, 1961), pp. 327–28.

governments in the less integrated countries. The price of "community" clearly indicates acceptance of governmental redistribution policies for the well-being of the entire nation.

The Government's Share of Income

A high ratio of government revenue to total income of the society usually correlates with a high level of integration. Taking general government revenue as a per cent of gross national product, the ranges go from 9.6 per cent for the lowest country, India, to 36.4 per cent for the highest noncommunist country, West Germany. These are total government sector incomes—national, state, and local. These income percentages are approximately: 25.3 for the United States, 26.7 for England, 32.5 for Sweden, 33.7 for Austria, 12.7 for Pakistan, and 9.6 for India. In countries with a per capita income of less than $100, the government sector thus seems to amount to 8–13 per cent while in countries with a per capita income of over $900, the government sector amounts usually to more than 25 per cent.[8]

On the metropolitan level, using income estimates for communities and individual municipal budgets, a measure of the municipal budget as a percentage of community income could be obtained. It has been discovered that, although higher income communities have higher expenditure levels than lower income communities, the proportion of local tax effort, the proportion of local taxes to total presumed income (as measured by per capita values on the tax assessments), is lower for high-income areas than they are for lower-income areas. In other words, richer communities have a higher level of public services with less effort than poorer communities. This may contrast to some extent with the situation described above with respect to the rising percentage of public expenditures with rising income levels among nations.

8. Political Data Program, Yale University, *Basic Data for Cross-National Comparisons, Provisional Profiles*, Research Monograph #1, Table 20.

In the United States the per capita national income in 1959 was $2,720 and the average proportion spent in 1960 by all sectors of the government was about 28 per cent or about $750. The national government accounted for about 20 per cent, or $540 and the local state governments shared the remaining 8 per cent, which were divided roughly in a ratio of 2:1 between them, leaving an average of about $140 per capita to be spent by local governments and $70 by states.

However the richest 10 per cent of local communities might have per capita income in the $4000–$5000 ranges. For example, Swarthmore, Pennsylvania, had 46 per cent of the household units earning more than $5000 a year in 1950. Communities with high per capita incomes do not spend 6 per cent of this high income but usually less. Actually they may spend 5 per cent, giving them the opportunity to spend on additional local services. The result is better and well supplied local services at a lesser tax burden. The difference between the nation-state and the local unit is that the richer national state cannot shed its responsibilities. It must spend more; the richer it gets, the more its people expect from it. On the other hand, the richer municipalities in the United States can and do shed a large part of their responsibilities on neighboring communities or on the state or federal government. In this respect, Switzerland is something like a suburban community of Western Europe. One-fifth of the Swiss labor force are foreigners. This practice shifts the dependency burden—the cost of caring for their children, women, and the aged—from the Swiss economy to the German, Italian, and Austrian economies.

Apart from such exceptions, however, it may turn out that the impact of taxation is progressive within nation-states and within municipalities but that it is regressive on the international and on the intermunicipal levels. That is to say, within the nation-state and within the local community there holds ordinarily a presumption of solidarity. Citizens accept a considerable measure of responsibility for helping one another in case of need and for doing so in some proportion to their ability to pay. This principle also applies to the bulk of municipal taxes. Even though property in land and buildings often has become by now a very imperfect measure of the ability to pay, the incidence of an equal municipal tax rate upon the unequal assessed values of real estate results in a progressive distribution of the tax burden, in comparison to what it would be in a flat per capita apportionment of burden, such as in a poll tax. Within the nation and within the city, the rich are thus taxed to some extent to help the poor, and this practice—as Gunnar Myrdal has pointed out—is made legitimate in each case by the presumption of the existence of a more or less closely knit community and thus by the habitual acceptance of a high level of political integration.[9]

Resistance to Redistributive Economic Policies

This intra-national acceptance of a high level of integration and this presumption of community are absent between nations and between municipalities. Traditionally, rich nations have rejoiced in their good fortune and have refused to accept any major responsibility for the populations of poorer and more crowded lands. Neo-Malthusian theories have sometimes been cited to justify this stand when it began to be felt that this rejection of responsibility might require some justification. The poorer nations—so some recent arguments have run—are so improvident and irresponsible in having children that only poverty, illness, and starvation have slowed down the reckless growth of their populations. Any economic improvement in their lot would only increase their population, until new millions at new levels of overcrowding in these countries would reduce everybody to the old levels of misery. Putting any substantial burdens upon the

9. For the acceptance of some redistributive taxation as an operational test of political integration, particularly of the nation-state, Gunnar Myrdal, *An International Economy* (New York: Harper, 1957), pp. 29–31. Cf. also, his *Beyond the Welfare State* (New Haven: Yale University Press, 1960) pp. 30–42, 159–199.

richer countries in order to increase economic aid to the poor and improvident nations, according to this theory, would be worse than useless, and in the long run it would not reduce the misery and desperation of these poorer peoples but only increase the numbers of the desperate.

Although this argument recently has been applied more frequently to international relations, it has its origin in domestic politics. Economists may recognize in it the old and long discredited "iron law of wages" by David Ricardo, according to which any wage increase would only lead to more reckless breeding among English workers and to a higher rate of survival of their children, until the larger number of workers competing for an unchanged or less rapidly expanding number of jobs would once again depress real wages to the old level of minimum subsistence. Long buried in labor economics by the criticism of theorists and by the successful practice of labor unions and high wage policies in the advanced countries, the argument has been revived once more at inter-municipal and intra-municipal levels. Once again it is argued that local expenditures on social services and welfare will merely encourage reckless breeding and that all efforts at lasting economic and social improvement will be wiped out by a rising tide of population. Often this theory was elaborated further by ascribing particularly dangerous levels of irresponsible fertility to the poorest urban minority groups of the period. Thus in the United States in the mid-nineteenth century it was the Irish, in the late nineteenth century the Italians and East Europeans, in the mid-twentieth century the Puerto Ricans and the Negroes, who were expected to respond with a rising flood of babies to any substantial improvement in their lot.

Despite their variety in detail and their exaggeration and distortion of reality, all these theories expressed a common attitude: the well-off did not want to pay. Where they could avoid paying for aiding at least some of the poor, they preferred to restrict as much as possible the circle of persons for whose well-being they had accepted some share of responsibility. And the poorer members of their communities ordinarily showed little desire to encourage the entry or inclusion of any large number of additional poor claimants and competitors for jobs and social services.

On the international level, these attitudes have led to economic nationalism and the drastic curtailment of international migrations. On the inter-municipal level somewhat similar attitudes have led to the psychological secession and the continuing legal and fiscal separation of the suburbs from the central cities upon whose employment opportunities and services they still depend. Between nations and between cities, regressive patterns of taxation still predominate. In the international community, as well as in the inter-municipal community of metropolitan areas, relatively little has been done by the political system to reduce the distance between the average economic levels of the richest and the poorest units. On the international level, this gap between the richest and the poorest countries appears to have increased in recent decades. On the inter-municipal level in the United States, the gap between the poorest and the richest municipalities, on the contrary, may have somewhat declined, but this narrowing of the gap has not been accomplished by any political institutions of the metropolitan areas themselves.

In the absence of any effective political attitudes and institutions of a metropolitan community, the function of mitigating extreme economic differences between municipalities in the United States has been left chiefly to the federal government and to a lesser degree to the states. This function has been accomplished through various forms of transfer payments because the poorer rural areas receive government subsidies from the urban communities which are relatively richer. Amply documented records of transfer payments between states through the U.S. treasury exist. The people of the State of New York pay thirty cents out of every one of their federal tax dollars to support services in such poorer states as Arkansas, Missouri and Louisiana. This amounts to a transfer of perhaps 6 per cent of their income to other states in the name of national union. The same process operates on a state level. To analyze local burdens, transfer payments of all sorts would have to be eliminated. For an analysis of an aggregate of the differential political power of different areas—of rural areas in farm states particularly—transfer payments would have to be considered to see to what extent these communities have used their political power to tap resources outside their own jurisdiction.[10]

This raises another question. To what extent are transfer payments mainly an expression of political power of the recipients? In the international scene, to what extent is the American economic aid payment to Afghanistan or Pakistan an expression of the political power of those regimes? To what extent, on the contrary, is it an expression of their weakness and of the power and self-interest of the United States?[11] To what extent is it in the interests of New York to pay taxes to see to it that Missouri and Arkansas do not produce too many illiterates who might then come and make the New York suburbs or downtown New York dangerous? If one part of the United States became an incubator for unemployment, under conditions of mobility, it would be reflected in various industrial and commercial centers of the country with a delay of five, ten, or twenty years. In similar cases, Congress is told that we pay Burma money, not because Burma is powerful and we pay tribute to them, but because it is in our interest that Burma not get too poor. It is now argued that once in a while, it is in the interest of the wealthier states to subsidize some poorer area, and this argument is heard increasingly not only within federal nation-states but also on the international scene.

The need for the reduction of extreme economic inequalities, by means of some redistributive taxation, or other forms of transfer payments, is thus being accepted gradually both on the international and the inter-municipal levels. On the international level, it is largely done by the decision of sovereign states in regard to their relations to other nation-states, that is, to units on

10. Cf. U.S. Department of Commerce, Bureau of the Census, *Statistical Abstract of the U.S., 1962* (Washington: Government Printing Office, 1963) p. 426.

11. Cf., for example, George Liska, *The New Statecraft* (Chicago: University of Chicago Press, 1960) and John D. Montgomery, *The Politics of Foreign Aid* (New York: Praeger, 1962).

the same system level. The share of organizations at higher system levels, such as regional or international federations or organizations[12] in bringing out such redistributive transfer payments has been relatively minor. For Western Europeans in 1962 it was less than 1 per cent of the budget of the six governments involved. On the inter-municipal level, by contrast, almost all transfer payments are brought about by organizations at higher systems levels. There are very few effective agencies at the metropolitan area levels serving this purpose in the United States, although such organizations as the Metropolitan Transport Authority (MTA) for Greater Boston, or Dade County for Miami, may be counted among the possible exceptions. The chief instruments for transfer payments between municipal areas in the United States are the federal and state authorities—and sometimes the counties—and the redistributive effects of the various federal and state taxes and grants-in-aid still offer an important field for study.

Inequality, Redistribution, and Political Stability

All of these methods are various ways of approaching the question of political stability. How much does the regressive impact of economic burdens have to be modified in order to hold the national community together or knit a metropolitan area more closely? How much does the wealthier part have to pay for whatever value there may be in the cohesiveness of the entire region? Intra-nationally, some progressive imposition of burdens seems to work well. But does a progressive principle apply between nations? Thinking of each individual unit in reference to their responsibility to the rest of the world, do nation-states behave very much as wealthy New York or Connecticut does in

12. Such organizations include the European Common Market (ECM), the Organization of American States (OAS), the North Atlantic Treaty Organization (NATO), the Organization for Economic Cooperation and Development (OECD), in the non-Communist world; COMECON among the Soviet Bloc countries; and the United Nations at the most general level.

regard to the rest of the United States? States really do not want to pay any more than they have to for other states; what they do have to pay is determined by the organization and cohesiveness of their communities. How much does the United States pay for aid to India, Brazil, Burma? How much is it willing to modify what is in effect its international regressiveness so as to contribute to cohesiveness of its friends, both allies and neutrals?

One aspect that might reward further study would be the willingness and ability of elites to accept demands for some redistributive taxation and the willingness and capability of the lower strata of the population to press demands of this nature. Modern national states with private enterprise economies tax themselves more for domestic purposes because in these countries there are usually by now relatively strong private elites with ample funds. The richer the country, the greater these elites; and the larger their income, the larger their financial contribution to the government, which they may use in part for social redistribution.

As reported in the 1961 United Nations *Report on the World Social Situation* the top 10 per cent of the income receivers in two well-to-do countries, the United States and the United Kingdom, received 31 and 30 per cent, respectively, of the national income before taxes, but retained only 28 and 26 per cent, respectively, after taxes, thus surrendering respectively 3 and 4 per cent of national income or 10 and 13 per cent of their own pre-tax shares to redistributive taxation. In a poor but reasonably well-governed country, India, the share of the richest one-tenth of the population was 34 per cent of the national income before taxes, and still 33 per cent after taxes, surrendering only 1 per cent of national income, or 3 per cent of their own pre-tax share, to national redistribution.[13] The concentration of much of national income in the hands of the top strata in much of Asia is similar to that in India. The bottom 80 per cent of Asian in-

13. United Nations, ECOSOC, *Report on the World Social Situation* (New York, 1961) p. 147, Table 8.

come receivers are estimated by U.N. officials to have on the average only 55 per cent of the national income of their respective countries; and in Latin America inequality is still sharper, with the bottom 80 per cent receiving on the average only about 40 per cent of the national income in their particular countries and the elites conspicuously unwilling to accept any significant amount of redistributive taxation.[14] Not surprisingly, several Latin American countries are among the politically most unstable in the world.

In general—and with the important exception of parts of Latin America—economic inequality and political instability within nations have tended to decline somewhat, once a high level of national income has been achieved, other things being equal. Generally, as the country gets richer, the rich become more generous. Since they see less destitution around them, their defensive reactions become weaker. Also, as the country becomes richer, marginal utility of money declines, and the rich may be more willing to pay more taxes although there are limits to this declining marginal utility.

The crucial variable consists in the political capabilities of the poorer income group. When a country gets richer, its poorer citizens usually become more skillful at organization, more insistent and demanding for the vote, and once they obtain it, more skillful in the use of the vote. If the record of the last one hundred years is a guide, they are more likely to threaten revolution if they do not get the vote. In rich countries, the poor populations are politically relevant. In order to set up some pluralistic compromise among the different interests, the compromise level for the strongest among the poorer groups gets stabilized at higher and higher shares of the national income.

Where the poorer population resides permanently in a country and cannot be ignored, it becomes politically relevant. The Swiss have succeeded in avoiding this problem, at least partly, by getting some waiters and road builders from Southern Italy and

14. *Ibid.*, p. 147.

sending them home when the summer season is over. Wages for Swiss labor and social security benefits remain high, but there are specific prohibitions against the Italians bringing their families. The wives and children must stay where they will not bother the Swiss taxpayers. Very similar arrangements exist in many other countries. Even the United States has an arrangement with Mexico for the import of some Mexican seasonal workers. On the other hand, Puerto Ricans come freely to the United States mainland with their dependents who have the same claim for social services as dependents of natives there; and Puerto Ricans are becoming increasingly important in our metropolitan politics. Earlier, at the end of the 1930's, migratory workers in Californian agriculture began to obtain an increasing—but still low—share of civil rights and welfare services at the places of their seasonal employment.

Empire and Colony: Case Study of Governmental Performance

The whole issue of the price which must be paid for integration, in terms of distributing well-being throughout the area of government, has been faced clearly and decisively in the experience of empires.

According to the defenders of colonial systems, colonial status brings large benefits to the benighted natives since the white man, selflessly shouldering his "burden," brings them hospitals, medical care, and all the rest—literacy, income, and production.[15] According to the African or Asian nationalist, the precise opposite is true. Colonialism is nothing but exploitation. The colonialist, in this view, chiefly plunders, enslaves, and impoverishes the population. With the help of empirical data, it is fairly easy to have a look and see which of these two statements, both of

15. Cf. Sir Alan Burns, *In Defense of Colonies* (London: Allen and Unwin, 1957).

which sound plausible, is nearer to the truth. Among the world's most illiterate and medically, as well as economically, neglected, countries of the world are two sovereign states—Ethiopia and Liberia. However, in their immediate levels of literacy and public health, there are between six and ten countries, all under long colonial administration, which are administered by European governments at Ethiopian and Liberian levels of honesty and efficiency. On the other hand, quite a number of African and Asian countries that are not under foreign rule do better than certain colonies. Therefore, there is no very good statistical evidence either for a blanket claim that colonialism stands for exploitation or that colonialism stands for improvement in income or health.

Colonialism undoubtedly makes some people richer in the metropolitan countries, while there is no evidence that it makes most people richer in the colonies. On the other hand, there is no very firm evidence that it makes most people there much poorer. However, one should remember that the sovereign countries—Liberia and Ethiopia—are situated on the two most unpromising pieces of real estate remaining in Africa. Generally, the more desirable the resources and equipment of an African territory have been, the greater the probability that it would be seized by some Western power in the days of European military superiority in the nineteenth century. Making allowances for such things as the resource endowment and accessibility of the different countries, colonialism seems to have tended slightly to make countries somewhat poorer than they otherwise might be.

In a comparison of Thailand with Burma, two Southeast Asian irrigation countries with rice as a major crop and with Buddhist culture but with Burma having had seventy years of the benefit of British colonial administration, it turns out that Burma in 1955 had about $52 in per capita income at the time that Thailand had $100 and that the literacy figures which were 48 as against 69 per cent, and the mortality levels—35 against only 9 per 1000—all were substantially more favorable in Thailand. Thailand, in all these respects, seems to be distinctly better off than Burma; although Thailand never had the supposed benefits of foreign rule.[16] Possibly the European challenge was beneficial in the cases of Japan and Turkey as well as in Thailand, but in these three relatively successful countries this foreign influence remained indirect. In other countries, direct foreign administration has been quite often a very mixed blessing, if not a disadvantage. If one agrees with John Dickinson of Pennsylvania who wrote in 1773 that a fool can put on his own shirt better than wise men can do it for him,[17] then the general argument that colonial nationalists are stupid in demanding self-government, since this flies supposedly in the face of their own obvious economic advantage, is not borne out by the facts. The sacrifice of cultural or national political values, which is normally bound up with the acceptance of foreign colonial rule, usually finds no compensating economic reward.

In the area of Spanish speech and culture, Puerto Rico is well ahead of Cuba and might be an exception to our previous hypothesis. On a per capita basis, Puerto Rico is ahead of such countries as Columbia but well behind Venezuela; however, Venezuela has resource equipment of a very considerable nature. The difficulty in Puerto Rico is compounded, of course, by the fact that Puerto Rico has exported a very large part of its population. If a comparable part of Latin America exported a third of its population to New York and other places, while keeping the same amount of capital and resources, the per capita income of the remaining population might also be higher. Nevertheless, since actual connection with the metropolitan country in Puerto Rico has included this opportunity for massive emigration, the net result has been a very favorable arrangement. Electoral figures in 1960 showed approximately 65 per cent of Puerto Ricans

16. This takes the approximate midpoint of Burma's estimated literacy rate of 45–50 in 1950. See footnote 6 above for full citation of sources.

17. Cf. his accompanying arguments in John Dickinson, *The Political Writings* (Wilmington: Bonsal and Niles, 1801), 2 Vols., and Henry Steele Commager and Richard B. Morris, (Eds.), *The Spirit of 'Seventy-Six* (Indianapolis and New York: Bobbs-Merrill, 1958) for supplementary documentation.

preferring the present arrangement, another 32 per cent wanting statehood, and only 3 per cent desiring secession, indicating that the Puerto Ricans have a pretty good idea which side their bread is buttered on, as well as where their political and cultural life is free to develop.[18]

The corollary to our hypothesis has three parts in Puerto Rico: (1) mass emigration, (2) substantial tax privileges to induce inflow of capital and managerial talent, and (3) a unique political arrangement involving the ingenious constitutional or rather extra-constitutional compromise giving Puerto Rico a Commonwealth status, for which no provision has been made in the American Constitution. This is one of the most valuable of the constitutional innovations which the American political system has produced in the last decades. Under this arrangement, Puerto Rico is not under direct administration but has two of the essential aspects of sovereignty. It has direct internal administration by its own personnel, and it has the explicit right, accorded to its people by an act of Congress, to vote their island out of the U.S. political system if they want to. Whether Congress will be enthusiastic if Puerto Rico ever does so is an open question, but the fact is that Puerto Rico has this right. Therefore, in making policy decisions, in passing laws in Congress, this possibility of Puerto Rico's choosing to abandon its status at any time is taken into account. Colonialism might be what Puerto Rico has now—or at least it is not fully sovereign—but its actual situation is very different, being similar to the status of a British Dominion or of an associate community.

The Bases of Economic Dependency

Other indicators of the effects of colonialism may be derived from the use of a sovereignty code. We might simply dichotomize

18. Based on election of Resident Commissioner in 1960. Cf. *Statistics of the Presidential and Congressional Election of November 8, 1960* (Washington: Government Printing Office, 1961), p. 49.

data for a large number of countries on the question of sovereignty. If a country is not sovereign, what is the paramount power? Where does direct political control lie? To get at economic colonialism, we might measure foreign ownership among the principal industries. Another method might be to measure the ratio of GDP to GNP (gross domestic product to gross national product). In many of the cases where gross domestic product is sufficiently less than gross national product, there might be a *prima facie* presumption that colonialism exists.

Of course, the availability of capital, which is a basic factor in indigenous economic growth, depends to a large extent on the willingness of foreign countries to buy into the industry of the country. Such a measure would show the United States under British economic "imperialism" in the middle of the nineteenth century, when as a matter of fact it was precisely the flow of British capital into the United States that assisted the launching of some of our own industries. Actually such colonialism, which imports capital and skill, may prove to be either non-damaging or even beneficial. It is a possibility that this comparison will simply show that a heavy inflow of foreign capital is correlated with generally desirable indicators, such as high income, longer life expectancy, high literacy—or at least rapid improvement in all these. According to the classical Leninist theory of imperialism, the opposite correlation should turn up.

Capital import alone is not economic colonialism. Economic colonialism is involved if ownership of capital import remains geographically or socially insulated from the bulk of the population of the country. One obvious way is the buying of land by subsidiaries of foreign corporations. In this sense, insofar as the East India Company had trade privileges in America, American colonies did perceive it as an alien corporation. The denial to natives of the right to buy into such a foreign company is usually a sign of this insulation. Canadians, for instance, complain that they have no opportunity of buying into the ownership of certain American corporations operating on Canadian soil.

Colony vs. Mother Country: Social Barriers to Diffusion of Wealth and Opportunity

The next question is: Do the foreign owners of such capital facilities and their managers move their centers and managerial decision units into the country? Do they, having moved into the country, mingle with the natives in activities ranging from poker playing to church attendance to intermarriage, as the British in the nineteenth century regularly did in the United States? Or, do they insulate themselves from the natives as did the British in Buenos Aires for three generations? Or, as the German executives and personnel insulated themselves socially from non-Germans in most of Eastern Europe?

Economics here must be translated into sociology. This translation can be made because sociological barriers against intermarriage could be thought of as a probability function in regard to the diffusion of property and income. Let us assume that a minority of foreign capital owners with an average income of about 1000 units come into a region at some time when the natives of that region have an average income of 100 and that the two groups intermarry freely. (This would be a rare event with such an income difference.) One could say in this case there would be a measurable probability that within fifty years or so the income differences would become much less because the mechanics of inheritance and of family preferences in business partnerships, employment, and promotions would have spread the wealth over a larger group of persons. The wealthy of the larger native population now will be related to the newcomers. If, on the other hand, the newcomers have a cultural bar, as the British had against the Argentines—or a color bar as the English people had against the Indians in India—most of the property and income differences would remain; and they might even grow if the newcomers should prosper. If the market mechanism tends to give to those who have and to take away from those who have not, and if the mechanism of human attraction—intermarriage—does not work to counteract this tendency at least to some extent, then a sharpening of social cleavages is very likely to result.

The degree of control exercised by the foreign owners of capital over economic public policy can also be measured. If, for instance, there is discriminatory legislation against aliens, one would presume that the interests of the foreign capital would be to get rid of this legislation or to block it in the first place. In some cases, they might be successful where there are pressures which they could mobilize. The facts concerning such a situation can be checked in various ways. If there were laws protecting nationals as landholders comparable to the California legislation in the nineteenth century, which made it difficult for the Japanese and other aliens to acquire land in California, one might discover what per cent of land of a given quality (since the quality of the land is an important consideration) is protected by national laws. Second, quite apart from theoretical protection, how large a per cent of land is, in fact, in the hands of nationals or in the hands of the national majority group? Complications do arise. For instance, some American citizens owned large plantations in Cuba. Other Americans became Cuban citizens but remained culturally and socially members of the American and not Cuban community, while still other Americans began to intermarry with Cubans and became members of the Cuban community. When all three cases arise, a problem in coding occurs for the social scientists, but it can be overcome.

One has to be extraordinarily careful in taking into account the working of informal processes. For instance, licenses for certain economic functions might be obtained only by nationals with various special exemptions. Those exemptions might be briskly issued under the counter to any foreigner who knows how to bribe the right men among the native administrative personnel. Or it might work in another way. Theoretically every ethnic minority might have exactly the same rights for getting import licenses, but, by a very strange coincidence, Armenians have had at some periods an extraordinarily difficult time getting licenses from Turkish officials. Again the informal processes are those which have to be studied, since the actual situations may be very different from what the statutes prescribe.

Center vs. Suburb: The Distribution of Benefits and the Patterns of Mobility

Are there any similar problems among municipalities? What is the benefit of the suburb to the central city, and vice versa? We can measure benefits for a colony, but what about a suburb? We can find out whether the colony has a higher income or a more favorable average life expectancy than a comparable territory in culture, geography, and climate that has not had a colonial administration or does not have one now.

On the international level, we know, for example, that the difference in measurable levels of well-being between two territories is the more significant the fewer the people that shift back and forth between them. Between England and India in the days of the British Empire, far less than 1 per cent of the population born in the one country would be found living in the other at any time. By contrast, the degree to which populations are actually intermingled behind a single tariff in a successful federation could be measured in terms of probability functions for the out-of-state residence of Americans who are free to move around in their country. This has been part of the answer of the American frontier problem both before and after the closing of land frontiers in 1890. For the last one hundred years since the Census of 1850, roughly 30 per cent of the Americans have lived in states other than the one in which they were born. This high American ratio contrasts with the low ratio for Bavaria in 1880 which had only 5 per cent of its residents born in the rest of Germany outside its borders. From the middle of the nineteenth century on, Bavarians were free to move anywhere in Germany, and other Germans were free to settle in Bavaria. The actual use made of the right, however, was much less than the use that was made of it in America.

Other figures show how the level of mobility gradually became higher in Switzerland. The Swiss intra-national mobility ratio of the people living in another canton than that of their birth was 7 per cent in 1850 and 33 per cent in 1950. During the same period, the ratio of foreigners living in Switzerland—and hence the international mobility ratio—remained much lower and grew much less, from 3 per cent in 1850 to only 6 per cent a century later. In 1850, the average ratio of extra-cantonal Swiss nationals to foreigners was roughly 2 to 1, while in 1950 it was more than 5 to 1.[19]

On the metropolitan level, the actual degree to which suburb and center city are separate could be measured by the number of people born in the one that are now living in the other. For example, the population in the Philadelphia Standard Metropolitan Statistical Area can be placed in a thirty-six box matrix based on current residence and place of birth, employing the following six categories: Center City, Inner Belt, Rest of State, Rest of the U.S., Puerto Rico, Foreign. (Table 13)

The question to ask is: Who is where? for certain boxes might be empty. Which zone exports people to which other zone? By finding the proportion of the people in the main diagonal cells, the ones who do not move as against those who move, we would begin to discover to what extent dependents are transferred through the mechanism of moving. Another diagram could differentiate between residence and work. A third one could compare the transfer of payments. Charles Kindleberger once claimed that the United States became a single financial market, integrated in this sense, only in the 1920's. Kindleberger's and Gunnar Myrdal's definition at one time stated that countries constitute a single market if, and only if, the prices of the main factors of

19. From data in *Eidgenössiche Volkszählung,* 1. December 1950, Vol. 24, Bern, 1956, p. 35.

TABLE 13

Now Living

Born	Center City	Inner Belt	Rest of State	Rest of U.S.	Puerto Rico	Foreign
Center City						
Inner Belt						
Rest of State						
Rest of U.S.						
Puerto Rico						
Foreign						

production are the same, or very nearly so, throughout their territory.[20] The most obvious measures are capital and credit. From the end of the Civil War until the 1930's the costs of credit in Mississippi were always much higher than in the North. This is true even if the element of business risk is held constant.

Similarly, mobility studies show that workers ordinarily do not move for a wage difference that is less than 20 per cent. Textile workers from Rhode Island do not go to other areas as long as the wage difference is below 20 per cent.[21] A few foot-loose youngsters would move sooner, and a few very steady characters would not go even at 25 per cent; but apparently the cut-off is somewhere near 20 per cent.

Something similar might apply to metropolitan areas. If the average wage for a charwoman in downtown Philadelphia is so

20. Oral communication, M.I.T., 1957. Cf. C. P. Kindleberger, *Foreign Trade and the National Economy* (New Haven: Yale, 1962), p. 236, n. 17. Cf. Gunnar Myrdal, *International Economics* (New York: Harper, 1956), p. 11.

21. W. Rupert Maclaurin and Charles A. Myers, *Movement of Factory Workers* (New York: Wiley, 1943).

much and the average wage farther out is so much higher or lower, the difference might be accounted for by streetcar fare, and so forth. Land values, credit costs, wages, possibly standard services, could be used as other indicators of the extent of market differences.

For purposes of investigation, one might make an imaginary experiment. Take an area that is far enough from the metropolitan core so that it clearly is not metropolitan, open up a new road—turnpike, suburban railroad line—making it part of the metropolitan area, and observe what happens under different conditions. If a fence could be put around the whole area, would the area as a whole gain or lose? What would happen to the probability of the average individual's staying there if he could no longer commute to work freely or if the supply of certain goods or services from the outside became more costly to secure? We might then try to identify those individuals who would clearly gain or keep gaining and those individuals who would lose or keep losing, as well as try to strike a balance for the area as a whole. Of course, where actual roads or railroad lines have been opened or closed, data can be gathered in the real world to verify or modify the results of the experiments we made in our imagination.

Cultural Preferences and the Appraisal of Government Performance

Some scholars point out that in measuring gains or losses, in terms of categories like this, there is a built-in ideological premise in favor of some kind of welfare for populations. They contend that it is possible that there may be an ideological factor which the government does in fact control. Taking Spain, for example, this factor might lower its position in terms of certain categories, such as the average level of food, housing, or education enjoyed by the people, but it is claimed that this outcome is intentional and that the people want it. (However, if the present regime in Spain were mainly built on the peculiar traditions of the Spanish people, it would not have needed so many Moors, Italians, and Germans to put Franco in power in the 1930's.)

The difference in national income is usually a measurement which cuts across cultural differences. National income may be spent on a bull fight, a fast automobile, French cooking, or a cathedral, according to cultural tastes, but if glass and stones for the cathedral, or the bulls and the arena, or the leisure time are not available, then you cannot have either the cathedral, bulls, or the car. Also, the facilities for each of these types of expenditure exchange in markets can be measured to a large extent in money.

Finally, life expectancy is to some extent a cross-cultural value, for if you are not alive, you do not enjoy any of these other values. In fact, surveys show that mothers across the world in a restricted but cross-cultural preference favor the survival of their children. There is no major operating government that says, out loud, proudly: "We like child mortality; we think it is unimportant compared to national pride." It may be conceded that the Nazis may have approached this position, especially for the child mortality rates of other people, but not even they went before the German public and said: "We do not mind German children dying like flies or like Egyptian babies; we think it is fine for the self-respect of the survivors." In the second half of the twentieth century, no government could stay in power and avow publicly that it disdained or opposed the survival of children. Similarly, there is no government in the world today that dares to say: "We like being poor." And it further turns out that poverty and child mortality are highly and positively correlated.[22]

People could possibly be interested in maintaining their original culture pattern in the face of possible increases of income which accompany industrialization. This also happens in suburban sections of metropolitan areas. However, let us count gaining

22. See, for example, Fig. 12.2 in C. P. Kindleberger, *Economic Development* (New York: McGraw-Hill, 1958), p. 207.

or losing in terms of life expectancy, income, and various other amenities such as educational service. Let us count these as material gains, then count against them a cost factor which can be called habit change. Conceptually there is very little doubt that both for populations and for individuals the change of habits usually carries a fairly high and specific disutility. Peripheral habits are changed easily; but deep-seated habits have a high cost factor, and coordinating habits involving personality structure may have a cost higher than the rate of survival. Involved in the latter is pathological learning, the acquiring of habit patterns which are suicidally expensive to change; race discrimination sometimes approaches such a type of habit pattern. A person may come to feel that he is losing his virility and everything that makes life worth living if he no longer can feel superior to another race. Once a man has thus learned to stake his self-respect on his pigmentation, or his lack of it, rather than on anything else, he is in a dangerous position, since new evidence or the pressure of the national government for interracial integration of the schools will threaten to destroy his main basis for self-respect. In Algeria, South Africa, Kenya, the Rhodesias, or the former Belgian Congo, settler responses sometimes have approached this potentially suicidal pattern, and milder but not wholly dissimilar reactions have occurred in parts of the South in the United States.

In the metropolitan areas, the resistance to change is usually less intense. In the natural history of a suburb, the people who stand to gain—landowners—often resist change until the price gets higher. At $500 per acre landowners want to keep it a nice rural community. At $5,000 per acre, very few people do. A curve of price at which different classes of landowners are found willing to sell, even though they originally dominated the community, sought to maintain their dominance, and resisted change, can be plotted to demonstrate their respective thresholds of cave-in.

Buyers of land may act differently. Migrant former non-landowners who seek a rural image for their homes often are indifferent to change during the time that the first few developments come in. Their expectations are largely being fulfilled. At some point, however, the inundation of the once countrified landscape by other people like themselves becomes intolerable, because it is defeating the image that they sought. They will then spend time and effort—but not much money—to organize political movements for slum clearance or zoning to keep poorer people out.

The Acceptance Price of Integration

Whether political integration can be priced in a similar way that the sale of land for suburban subdivision is priced is an empirical question. However, in the international area complications arise. There may be a suicidal pattern where no price is high enough. Integration between whites and blacks in South Africa may not have a price tag. In another context, we do not know whether there would have been a price at which 51 per cent of the U.S. Southern slave owners in 1860 would have sold out, because no credible and substantial offer was ever made to them on the eve of the Civil War. There was some talk in Congress about compensating slave owners for the emancipation of the slaves on a federal basis, but the Southern senators voted against it. They would not admit the principle of the slaves being for sale before the right price was mentioned, and they realized that on a federal basis they and their own commerce might have been taxed by the majority to buy their own property. If the North had offered the South two-thirds of whatever the Civil War ultimately cost as a compensation price for their slaves—and if they had offered to make this payment from revenues raised in the North and not again reimposed directly as a burden on the economy of the South—this might have been a different story.

Furthermore, we do not know how Algerian *colons* would have behaved if the United Nations had offered them, or if France had offered them, $5,000 per capita or $20,000 per family of four for resettlement on the French Riviera. Since the French were spending $3 million a day on the war in Algeria, they were spending roughly $1,000 a year per Algerian French settler. If these rates held in earlier years, they may have spent $7,000 per Algerian settler already during the seven years of war. For what the French had already spent on the war in Algeria, they could have transformed a sizable part of France. This would have been economically feasible. It was being done during the same decade in Germany where the repatriated East German minorities are now more prosperous than ever. In the end, the French public accepted Algerian independence only in 1962, after more than four years of gradual persuasion by General de Gaulle and by pressure of events after even more wealth had been dissipated in the war.

When a minority culture becomes unpopular in a competitive society, no one thinks there is a reason to compensate this minority. Hardly any historical case where the right price was offered exists, except one—the Anglo-Scottish union of 1707. The English Parliament appropriated more than a million pounds to compensate all the stockholders in Scottish public companies on condition that the Scottish Parliament would ratify the Anglo-Scottish Union. Whether this was wise compensation or shameless bribery is difficult to decide. Practically everybody in the Scottish elite had money in the Darien Company which had just lost everything in an unsuccessful colonial venture. Now Parliament was offering to compensate them. The union went over rather promptly and has remained in operation to this day.

In theory, this could be done also in metropolitan areas, but in most suburbs nobody offers to pay anything for a change in settled local mores. Suppose a state like New York or Texas declared the following: "It is public policy to carry through local racial integration in our communities. We shall define residential integration as a situation in which the average race mixture in any community will be close to the national average—let us say 10 or 12 per cent. We will, therefore, declare that everybody living in a local community in which the minority is at least 10 per cent but not more than 30 per cent of the local population will get a 20 per cent rebate on all state taxes." Or, the federal government, rather than the state of Texas, perhaps would grant subsidies to all those communities in which these conditions were met. This may sound utopian. It would mean, however, that the community that carries the burden of integration and acculturation of Negroes or Puerto Ricans would be recognized as performing a service for the whole country rather than just for itself; and it would then rightly claim a subsidy from the whole country for this service.

The Economic Rewards of Separate Suburbs

To find out whether segregation habits do or do not have a price, the economics of the situation will have to be known. If in an all-white suburb, in the absence of a federal integration subsidy, a higher ground rent and higher costs for transportation still are accompanied by a higher resale value of houses, the community will probably remain white. But if the suburb stays white and property depreciates under these conditions, some integration may follow. It is obviously true that most people make decisions about almost anything without very complicated rational calculations. Anthropologists report that if a tribe has become habituated to catch fish on a full moon in the second bay to the left, and there is never any fish there, the tribal habit is likely to fall into disuse. If, on the other hand, almost every time they go fishing there, they do catch fish, the tribal beliefs and the words of the command of the great spirit will be followed. Anthropologists call this a "prosperity policy." Does it matter how accidentally intuitive or fortuitous the formulation of the decision is? If the decision tends to be reinforced by rewards, it is likely to be repeated.[23]

The suburbs reward their residents because they are not troubled with city welfare and police costs. The tax investments of suburbanites in their sovereign municipalities return a high level of services which they do use, such as education. Per capita local government expenses reflect this variegated pricing mecha-

23. Cf. George P. Murdock, "Ethnocentrism," *Encyclopedia of the Social Sciences*, Vol. 5 (New York: Macmillan, 1937), pp. 613–614.

nism. Per capita expenditure is more a function of income than it is of density. However, there is a direct relationship between density and local government per capita expenditures. The higher the density, the higher the local government expenditures. A people-acre dollar index can be constructed by dividing the average amount of local taxes received in a community by the average number of people on an acre. It might reach its maximum value in thinly settled suburbs of rich people. How would this index correlate with local government expenditures? It is probably a direct ratio. The higher the index, the higher the dollar expenditure on municipal services per capita. However, it might be bi-modal because of the disproportionate amount spent in the suburbs for education. In the central city there are only medium expenditures for education but a lot of other costs that suburban governments do not carry at all. The central city traffic, hospitals, and welfare expenditures tend to equal or exceed educational expenditures.

Education expenditures are, to some extent, an investment since they come back in the earning capacity of the next generation. On the other hand, less wanted expenditures from the upper-income taxpayer's viewpoint, such as municipal expenditures on traffic, hospitals, and social welfare, have next to no investment function. They do not add appreciably to his future wealth, or to that of his children. If one separates "productive" government expenditure on the "investment" service side from government expenditure on welfare, etc., then, as one moves out into the suburbs, tax dollars come back in higher frequencies. They are returned to a large degree in the earning capacity of its children. In this sense, the all-white suburb *might* be economically rewarding. However, one must be sure what economic reward is. A man might live in a white suburb at an economic sacrifice for reasons of preference or prejudice, but if it turns out that he is really saving more money because he is putting it into the education of his children in good quality schools, then he would actually be rewarded. It is a well-known fact that prejudices that become associated with the experience of an economic reward tend to be reinforced by it; and it is also well known that during the period 1930–1955, by any measure, amenity, cost per capita, outlay for housing and government services, and transportation, the American suburb was an enormous bargain for its residents.

If the suburb is still a tremendous bargain from this simple economic viewpoint, then it might be in the economic interest of the suburbanites to turn down the small bargain of a common transport authority or of a metropolitan district or county in order not to endanger the big bargain of the separate suburban government. It is important, as in all politics, to know if one is dealing mainly with a cultural mechanism which is keeping two countries or municipalities from merging or from federating in spite of economic advantages in making it a federation. Or is one dealing chiefly with an economic mechanism which rewards separateness and penalizes federation, at least for one of the partners, quite apart from cultural considerations? Or, finally, is one dealing with the most intractable combination of the two—a cultural prejudice steadily reinforced by economic rewards—genuine prejudices which are used to defend the institutional setup which will perpetuate the rewards?

Motives for Integration: Economies or New Rewards?

In international studies there is no case on record in which two countries have merged simply on the grounds that this merger would save money by eliminating needless duplication of governmental services. Economy of services has never been an effective motive in uniting two countries. On the other hand, there are quite a number of cases where the prospect of getting something new as additional reward was quite effective. For instance, the American states did not federate in the hope that this would reduce the machinery of state government. On the contrary, the state governments were greatly strengthened in the period before the Articles of Confederation. Integration into a federal union did promise, however, a very effective way of opening up and settling the western lands, thus inaugurating the greatest real estate operation of all time. The stake was a continent to be had, if only the colonies on its eastern fringe had the wits to cooperate in settling it. They did by federating, and they got the continent with the Louisiana Purchase and all that followed from it.

Joint loss can also be conceptualized. Being united in an empire that was just big enough to get into war on Germany's side in 1914 was disastrous for the Habsburgs. If Austria-Hungary had been small and insignificant, they would have been left alone. Their heterogeneous population responded to defeat by dissolving the Empire and making no serious effort to reconstitute it to this day. The populations of Germany, Italy, and Japan, by contrast, responded to military defeat in two World Wars by giving every indication of a continuing desire to stay together.

A new operation which is expected to be very rewarding is very effective as a motive for integration. The first example was that of the American continent and the western lands. The second would be the Italian railroads. The prospect of a national Italian railroad network on the eve of Italian unification set off an exaggerated set of hopes for the rewards that would follow from such a project. The third case is the German customs area in the Industrial Revolution that came after the *Zollverein,* which also worked. The fourth is the transatlantic tobacco trade for the Union of England and Scotland. Economy of scale is, then, not thc inducement toward metropolitan government or toward municipal merger in any major sense. Nevertheless, there are a number of functional mergers—smaller mergers, not of metropolitan government but of others. Perhaps they lend themselves to the analysis of metropolitan areas, but it is difficult to measure exactly what is at work here, economy of previous types of expenditure or anticipation of new services or joint rewards.

A Possible Test of the Theory at the Metropolitan Level

A beginning in the study of joint reward in a metropolitan area might be made by listing all pairs of adjacent communities in the area and listing all the services for which there is a good technical reason to hope for some economies of scale. A probability function could be computed which might indicate the potentials for some forms of integration in that area. Because of the importance of leadership in the study of integration, one might calculate the frequency with which leaders take the initiative in proposing certain policies. One might then calculate the frequency of acceptance. This will demonstrate who the leaders are and how well they organize. Assuming that joint rewards are important and that mere economy in ongoing operations is much less effective, what are any major functional mergers among local government units that would promise such substantial joint rewards? In other words, if it is perfectly clear that the suburb is a bargain, or has been a bargain until quite recently, are there many joint rewards to gain, or major and imminent joint penalties that can be averted, through functional mergers? Where would mergers pay, and where would they not pay? One might also inquire who is to be rewarded and how widespread the later rewards would be.

Of course, there is a presumption of democracy in this argument, a presumption that the government is intended to serve the median or the average person. Low-income situations in fact may be highly rewarding to people who control government. Our assumption is not that governments ought to do anything in particular but merely that we now live in a period where the bulk of the population cannot be neglected. It is quite possible that the income distribution of Laos was very rewarding to highly placed Laotian government personnel. The Laotian peasants, however, also began to count for something. In the civil war that was fought against the Communist guerillas, it turned out that the guerrillas fought with a certain amount of motivation, while the Royal Laotian Army at times seemed to be engaging in a sit-down strike. The ratio of surrenders and desertions to casualties formed an attrition ratio which became the equivalent of a plebiscite. The election returns for a neutralist compromise were obtained on the battlefield.

On the whole, given a minimum competence of ruling personnel, it becomes clear that if a government has control of about one-third of a national income of say $1,000 per capita to play around with, it would have to be uniquely incompetent to make all factory workers truly disgruntled communists. It could be done, but the rulers would have to work at it. Ordinarily, it seems much more likely that minimal social adjustments would be carried through successfully. If the country is poor but honest, with the per capita average of national income at $200, the government would be likely to control only about one-fifth of that, and it would have to be very skillful and well-organized to spread a small amount of welfare sufficiently around to maintain social peace. Even with $500 per capita income, such as in Israel, a very elaborate institutional setup is needed to maintain a high level of concord. Yet, as Israel shows, there are cases where a low but widely distributed level of reward contributes sufficiently to political stability.

Whether we are thinking in terms of the restiveness of suburban communities or of their self-satisfaction with their separateness, or their readiness to form some other attachment, or whether we are thinking of the same thing in international terms, a very important element to check in each case will be the degree to which the rewards are widely distributed as against the degree to which the new plan—whatever it might be—would increase the unevenness of distribution. One can measure the spread, for instance, by taking the income of the top 5 or 10 per cent of the income receivers as a percentage of the total. There are estimates of that kind in the United Nations' *Economic Survey of Europe*. For example, in England it was about 40 per cent in the 1930's, and it was doubtless 35 per cent in the '50's.

Ideally, what is wanted is to get the whole income profiled on a Lorenz curve to see just how uneven the income distribution is for each group in the country for each level of income.[24] David Potter in his study, *People of Plenty,* makes the point that traditionally Americans have been much less interested in making the slices of the national cake equal than in making the cake bigger.[25] Very typically, one cannot move an American electoral meeting by speaking about social justice, but one could feel the emotional response going through the room should someone say, *soziale Gerechtigkeit*—social justice—to a popular audience in Germany. There is an entirely different cultural and emotional context in the two countries.

Studies have demonstrated that evenness of income distribution and high average wealth are positively correlated with each other and with a high degree of political stability. If a trend line of per capita income is drawn, it can be used as a crude indicator of stability. On this trend line there is a threshold below which there is a very good chance of frequent overthrows of governments. Of eight countries in which the per capita income was under $100 in 1955, six had violent overthrow of government since 1945. The chances are better than 75 per cent for such governments to get into trouble. On the other hand, of a dozen governments over $900 per capita income, only one had such a change of government. The chance of getting overthrown goes down to 10 per cent.[26]

This may be a highly materialistic outlook, but there is one difference. A materialist would call the income distribution a cause and stop there. He would call the income distribution a prime mover or an uncaused cause. An idealist would say that the income distribution is clearly a symptom of underlying values

24. Bruce M. Russett and Hayward R. Alker, Jr., "On Measuring Inequality" (Mimeo.: Yale University, 1963). Forthcoming.

25. David M. Potter, *People of Plenty* (Chicago: University of Chicago Press, 1954).

26. Cf. Karl W. Deutsch, "Toward an Inventory of Basic Trends and Patterns in Comparative and International Politics," Vol. LIV, *American Political Science Review,* March 1960, p. 57.

held by rich and poor in the society. An empirical social scientist would probably say that the values feed into the distribution and the distribution reinforces these values. Calculations can be made to discover at what stage of this feedback cycle one may obtain the most leverage to bring about most change.

VII

Integration and the Social System: Implications of Functional Analysis

Beginning with a broad restatement of Parsonian functional analysis for more extensive interpretation of political data, Karl Deutsch applies general systems theory to the study of political integration. Employing Parsons' four "functional imperatives" for any social system—pattern maintenance, adaptation, goal attainment, and integration—Dr. Deutsch analyzes several categories of exchange or interaction between them with particular focus on the government or goal system. Although each of the four sub-systems may function to either facilitate or inhibit integration of the total system, the interchanges between the pattern maintenance and the adaptive systems are held to be especially critical to inquiry into the process of political integration.

WHAT WILL BE ATTEMPTED HERE IS TO POINT OUT THOSE IDEAS OF Talcott Parsons that are particularly relevant to the understanding of the political process and, in particular, to the behavior of political systems.[1] I cannot hope to give in one brief chapter a

1. The major works of Talcott Parsons include *The Structure of Social Action* (New York: The Free Press of Glencoe, 1949); *Essays in Sociological Theory, Pure and Applied* (New York: The Free Press of Glencoe, 1949); *The Social System* (New York: The Free Press of Glencoe, 1951); *Structure and*

balanced view of a major intellectual effort presented in hundreds of pages. I can only present here a few aspects as they have appeared to me and as I have found them useful in my work.

For this purpose, Parsons' ideas must be seen in context. His work has been criticized often for things which he really has not attempted to do. What others say Parsons is supposedly doing and what he actually is attempting to do are often two different things. Parsons has sometimes been criticized for having produced a great many matrices and conceptual schemes into which all sorts of empirical data could be put, rather than giving substantive empirical data. Even if he had done no more than this, it would be no mean achievement. For anyone who has once had his desk piled high with miscellaneous correspondence would appreciate the services of a good filing system. If it were possible for a single comprehensive system to bring order into the variegated facts that are known or believed to be known about social and political behavior, a major contribution would have been rendered. The fact that there might be alternative filing systems does not preclude the great desirability of having one, especially one that assists in systematically ordering information and provides for rapid retrieval in an efficient way. But Parsons has done more. An efficient conceptual scheme, like any truly efficient system of organizing information, highlights relevant connections and plays down less relevant ones. The question is whether Parsons' system is not only comprehensive and consistent, but also whether it tends to highlight interesting dimensions, variables, and relevant correlations, and whether it suggests fruitful questions and possible discoveries. It seems to me that it does all these things.

Once a classification scheme or theoretical system is used to highlight particular correlations, the social scientist is already making predictions, at least in probabilistic terms. He is predicting

---

Process in Modern Societies (New York: The Free Press of Glencoe, 1960); with Edward A. Shils and others, *Toward A General Theory of Action* (Cambridge: Harvard University Press, 1951); and with Neil J. Smelser, *Economy and Society* (New York: The Free Press of Glencoe, 1956). See also Parsons, "An Outline of the Social System," in Parsons *et al.* (Eds.), *Theories of Society*, Vol. 1 (New York: The Free Press of Glencoe, 1961), pp. 30–79.

that certain correlations are either critically high or low and that certain relationships will be significantly correlated with others. Furthermore, within this general system, empirical facts show that certain variables tend to be distributed around certain medians or mean values with specific variations. Since the system might suggest that the correlation of Variable A with Variable B is very high, and Variable A can be empirically determined, knowledge of Variable A and the correlation predicted or suggested by the Parsonian system ought to permit some degree of prediction of expected levels for Variable B. In this sense, what looked like a purely formalistic system turns out to be a system that contains predictive implications when put to actual use. The system for the efficient selection, storage, and retrieval of information thus turns into a guide to relevance and an engine for the production of new knowledge. Efforts are only now being made to place actual data into some of these boxes to find out what happens to this classificatory and intellectual filing system and to its output.

The second criticism is that the system is nonempirical, but this is only a criticism of an early stage in the historical development of many theories. One way of theory building is to collect empirical facts and assume that they will somehow speak for themselves, that an obvious classificatory scheme will emerge from their gross and conspicuous aspects.[2] More often it turns out that either the facts by themselves do not suggest an obvious classificatory scheme, or if they do, that the obvious scheme is not very good. A better way is to develop on intellectual grounds what might be a good scheme, try it out and see what happens when empirical data are used. This is Parsons' approach.

Fundamental Requirements of Social Systems

Parsons has proposed thinking of all social systems as fulfilling a minimum of four basic functional requirements. One can ask

2. This view was suggested early in the twentieth century by the biologist, Karl Pearson. For a critique of its weaknesses, see James B. Conant, *Science and Common Sense* (New Haven: Yale, 1951), pp. 7–8, 42–50.

what does a system do, or what ordinarily does a system have to do in order to continue as a system? The general concept here is that a system is a set of parts or sub-systems which interact in such a way that the components tend to change so slowly that they can be treated temporarily as constant. These slow-changing parts can be called *structures.* Their interactions and transactions in relations with each other are such that their basic structural characteristics persist; if these transactions turn out to be conducive to maintaining or reproducing the system, they are then called *functions.* (A communications engineer would be inclined to say then that many of these functions will turn out to be feedback cycles with homeostatic properties.)

Parsons finds four broad classes of functions which every system has to fulfill. These are the four functional imperatives. The first is the function of *pattern maintenance* (PM) sometimes called latency (L) (See Diagram 3). The system must do something or behave in such a way that basic patterns whether overt or hidden are maintained, reproduced, or preserved.

In the second place, the system must in some way succeed in adapting itself to changes in environment; this is the function of *adaptation* (A).

The third function in most systems serves goals other than its own maintenance. Most systems tend to be in substantial internal disequilibrium unless they reach some particular state or relation with respect to the outside world at which the internal disequilibrium is lessened. When a person's blood sugar level is very low there may be disequilibrium; very specific chemical and neurological messenger processes are triggered and hunger is the result. Eating produces somewhat higher blood sugar levels, restoring internal equilibrium. The goal in this case—obtaining blood sugar—involves some specific relationship toward the environment outside of the body—getting food and eating it. The goal, therefore, is always a situation or relationship between a system and its environment, such that some internal disequilibrium of the system is significantly or markedly lower than it would be with other relationships. This distinguishes goal relationships from non-goal relationships. Every system tends to fulfill some function or require some facility for moving toward goal relationships or *goal attainment* (G.A.). The particular goal of one system may be different from that of another: a commercial association may seek money; a school may promote education. Quite often a system will have a multiplicity of goals. The goal attaining facilities of systems are thus not necessarily limited to a single goal but to the class of all those goal situations relevant to the acting system.

When a system is functioning to maintain its own fundamental patterns by adapting itself to various changes in environment and pursuing one or several goals, problems arise concerning the integration and coordination of the various messages and the allocation of facilities or functions inside the system. This is the *integration* (I) function which requires that something be done to prevent the different operations of the system from interfering with each other in a frustrating or destructive way. The maintenance of compatibility and the shift from mutual inhibition to mutual facilitation of the fundamental efforts are all tasks of an integrative system. As we go up the ladder of organic evolution, integrative problems increase in importance and complexity. Relatively simple integrative functions can be served by means of patterns that are transmitted by processes of genetics. Genes and chromosomes themselves have a good deal to do with certain aspects of pattern maintenance and a good many other aspects of the physical makeup. The earthworm will have to maintain various ways of adapting itself to cold or heat; he may at times be in certain relationships where he is seeking goals. The earthworm may be looking for a female earthworm or may be seeking a supply of food, and in the very simple nervous system of the earthworm, his integrative problems are relatively easy. But merely by going from an earthworm to a bird, integration problems become more complicated, for a bird's crucial homeostatic problems include maintenance of body temperature. Integration problems become enormously complicated in the human being, and the probability of psychic and functional conflict is quite high. While birds do not usually experience psychic conflict because one pattern of behavior is clearly dominant or clearly subordinated at any one moment, human beings can be intellectually and emotionally torn between two courses of action.[3]

These four general functions are meaningful in the analysis of group behavior and in examining group needs. They can be applied to the analysis of political integration and disintegration. If a particular community attempts to resist change and to preserve itself, to what extent is the insistence on *suburban* sovereignty or on *national* sovereignty mainly a matter of *pattern maintenance*? Citizens are used to the community and want it to continue. To what extent does suburban or national sovereignty serve the *attainment of a variety of goals*? The goal of buying better education for less money might be a significant reason for middle-class families to move to suburbs. To what extent do suburbs *adapt* in response to congestion, to wear and tear on land, to air pollution? To what extent do suburbs attempt to serve *integration functions* in order to escape from the anonymity of the tenement house or the big city block apartments, to get into a neighborhood where neighbors are few and far enough so as not to get on each other's nerves, yet near enough for socialization of families?

This is the Parsonian approach to *general* systems theory, and it has wide applicability. It could conceivably hold in analyzing such things as automatic guided missiles as well as particular organisms. The Parsonian system, however, is not merely an analogy. It is a step toward a *general* systems theory. When a physicist says that all heavy bodies fall to the ground, he is not talking about analogies. He is taking a generalized view of the whole system, of all objects on earth and indeed of all objects with mass—a view that can be verified to a significant extent by observation. In other words, analogies are limited. It is perfectly clear that certain objects, such as a feather, will fall very differently from other objects in mass such as a piece of lead, when they are not in a vacuum. Nevertheless, to speak of the physicist's concept

3. Cf. Julian Huxley, *Man Stands Alone* (New York: Harper, 1941), pp. 1–33.

of mass as being an analogy between a feather and a piece of lead is to miss the intellectual concept of mass.[4] One of the most typical defenses of people against unproved theories is to say they are just analogies. This is a good defense mechanism and deserves its honorable place in some appropriate footnote in Freud's works. Defense mechanisms slow down the impact of new ideas to a rate acceptable to the mass of unprepared readers.

However, if certain analogies verifiable by observation have potentials for predictive power, then it is more helpful to think of them as analogous *properties*. If certain analogous properties are found to be reliable and relevant, then classification begins. In this sense, time is not just an analogy among different things that change—or rather between rates of change—and masses are not just analogies among different things that either fall to the ground or take energy to stop when they have been moving. If Parsons asserts—and he may be wrong on empirical grounds—that all observable systems will turn out to have some facilities that devote part of their resources and part of their operations to activities of one or more of these four basic types, then they already become classifiable and analyzable in terms of the Parsonian four functional characteristics which possess greater generality than many other characteristics one might see in systems.

Any action may be analyzed in terms of the functions it fulfills for the system to which it is related. A given action may serve one or more of the four functions. For example, if one owned a ship one could repaint it to protect it from rust. This would be a change involving pattern maintenance. Or the ship could be adapted for a cruise in the arctic by altering the keel. This involves both pattern maintenance and adaptation. Or the ship could be redesigned and altered to win a race by increasing the sailing surface or strengthening the engine. This would primarily involve goal attainment. Finally, if the ship were sluggish in steering and information from the lookout and the radar were

4. For a good, brief discussion of the concept of "analogy," see George Polya, *How to Solve It* (Princeton: Princeton University Press, 1944).

transmitted too slowly for the helmsman to reduce the risk of collision, something would have to be done to increase both mechanical integration of the ship and the ship's communication system, that is, to serve the integration function.

The functions of a system are not only complementary but may also be competitive. For instance, an adaptive response may require a sacrifice in pattern maintenance. Adaptation itself is not possible merely by pattern maintenance, for an adaptive response may require a sacrifice in pattern maintenance. If the oceans are reduced from constituting most of the earth's surface to only three-fifths of the earth's surface, resulting in a number of shallow stagnant pools, fish, by mutation, may learn to breathe air. They would give up pattern maintenance by their tried and trusted gills, making an adaptive response to the changed environment by becoming amphibious. Under such circumstances complete pattern maintenance would be non-adaptive. Biologists have found that eleven of every twelve species known to science have died out. Throughout world history biological species usually end up with heavy pressures toward pattern maintenance, and pattern maintenance turns out to be non-adaptive in about 92 per cent of the cases.[5] As a further example of competitive functions, an automobile engine can be designed mainly for speed or mainly for safety; within an intermediate range of design criteria the two are compatible, but an automobile can be built with a speed capacity which is so high that the rate of safety falls to zero. In the long run it is not even speedy because it becomes scrap iron in a very short time.

Using the four essential functions for analysis implies a quantitative aspect. None of the four can be completely sacrificed, but, beyond the minimum of each function, there is a range where the functions are competitive with each other, while still remaining compatible. (The reduction of any one of the functions to zero would be as invalid as the famous abstract concept of geometrical lines with length but no width.)

5. Cf. Julian Huxley, *Evolution, the Modern Synthesis* (New York: Harper, 1942).

The Distinction Between Function and Structure

Functions, we said, are processes that change quickly, or they are repetitions of such processes. Their results, however, may preserve structures which are processes which change slowly. No quick process can occur unless it occurs between others that are slower or more stable in their repetitions. Thus all functions imply structures among which they occur. Thus the blood flows quickly through slow-changing veins, sustaining a body which is not immortal. From this point of view, the distinction between structures and functions appears relative.

Diagram 3

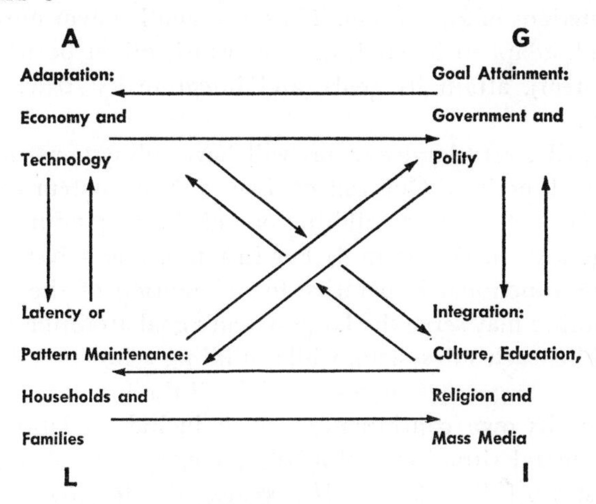

There is a second distinction between the two, however. Ordinarily a particular function occurs only among a particular set of structures; my blood sustains me by flowing through my veins and no others. Only each *class* of functions is general: there is a circulation of the blood in many bodies, serving the same specific biological function in each, as well as the same general function of pattern maintenance. The latter concept is a class of classes.

A particular structure, on the contrary, can serve many functions. One peg can be used to hang many hats; one circulatory system can receive many blood transfusions.

The Relationships of Sub-systems

Since Parsons sets out a general proposition for general systems, it follows that the four functions ought to be observable or identifiable in systems of any level or size of generality. What does this imply for large systems which have smaller sub-systems? Usually each sub-system only serves certain functions of the larger system; but it must simultaneously *for itself* fulfill all four of the basic functions of any system. Thus, the small system must maintain itself, adapt to its environment (which might be within the large system), attain its goals, and integrate its structures and activities.

Ordinarily, very large systems will have sub-systems that serve particular functions. One can envisage a large system composed of four sub-systems each fulfilling one of the major functions for the large system. (Diagram 4) For instance, one sub-system may fulfill the functional imperative for adaptation of the large system. Another may serve the large system's goal-attaining function. Meanwhile, each sub-system, while fulfilling a functional requirement of the larger system, must satisfy all the functional requirements for its own continuance (which includes adapting to its environmental situation within the larger system). A sub-system that is successfully adaptive is a system which pursues its own specific functions while promoting the functional goal or requirement of the larger system.

Parsons suggests that to study the relationships of the great sub-systems in modern societies, one might use the actual social structures and social systems found in contemporary institutions. These institutions usually perform more than one function, but they do tend, nevertheless, to serve one function more than another. For conceptual purposes they can be thought of as a first approximation, as being particularly dedicated to one function.

The economy might then be considered as the adaptive subsystem which deals with getting whatever is needed out of the physical environment as well as out of the intellectual capacities of the population to adapt to all the various needs. Parsons suggests that the family and its household can be considered as the pattern-maintaining system which reproduces the species and maintains the culture.

DIAGRAM 4

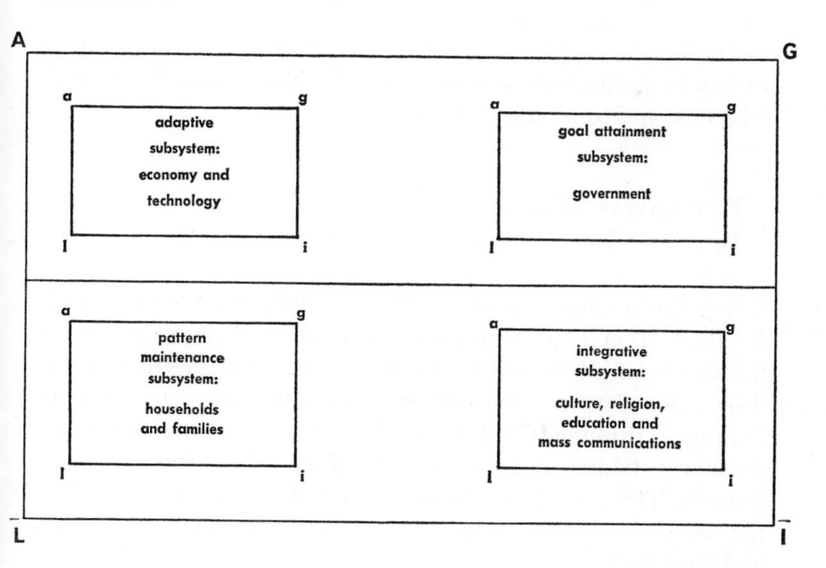

The goal-attaining system in the society in Parsons' view would be the government, for government and politics tend primarily to be related in a modern industrial society to goal-attaining. In a traditional society which has as its main goal nothing else but the maintenance of patterns, where the government has no other task but to maintain public tranquility and protect vested interests, the goal attainment function of the government merely serves pattern maintenance. If, on the other hand, the goal of a society is an increase in material well-being, an increase in education, an increase in freedom, or an increase in the likelihood of individuals to reach their individual goals, then particular demands will be made on the government, and it will have the function of facilitating the movement of the society in the direction of these goals. Also, if the society has as its main goal a desire for conquest of its neighboring societies, as in a warrior state or culture, then the government will be primarily the agent for serving the attainment of this particular goal. When it becomes the goal of the United States to put a man on the moon, then the federal government has to do this.

Finally, the integrative sub-systems can be found in great variety in a pluralistic society, especially those related to cultural, religious, and legal institutions.

Functional Interchanges Between Economy and Society

In fulfilling these functions the particular systems do not act in isolation from each other, but each serves the greater society through working in intimate cooperation. The interplay or the transactions between the different functional sub-systems can be envisaged through the idea of interchanges. Interchanges are constantly taking place between the four sub-systems. (See Diagram 5). The interchange between A and G, economy and society, has been discussed at length in *Economy and Society* by Parsons and Neil Smelser.[6]

The interchange between the household and the economy is a good starting point in the entire interchange pattern. Classical economics has already described a double flow in this interchange pattern. Households put labor into the economy. Breadwinners will sail forth each morning to catch the 7:45 or 8:15 and go to work somewhere in the economy. The economy in return pays

6. See note 1 above.

Diagram 5

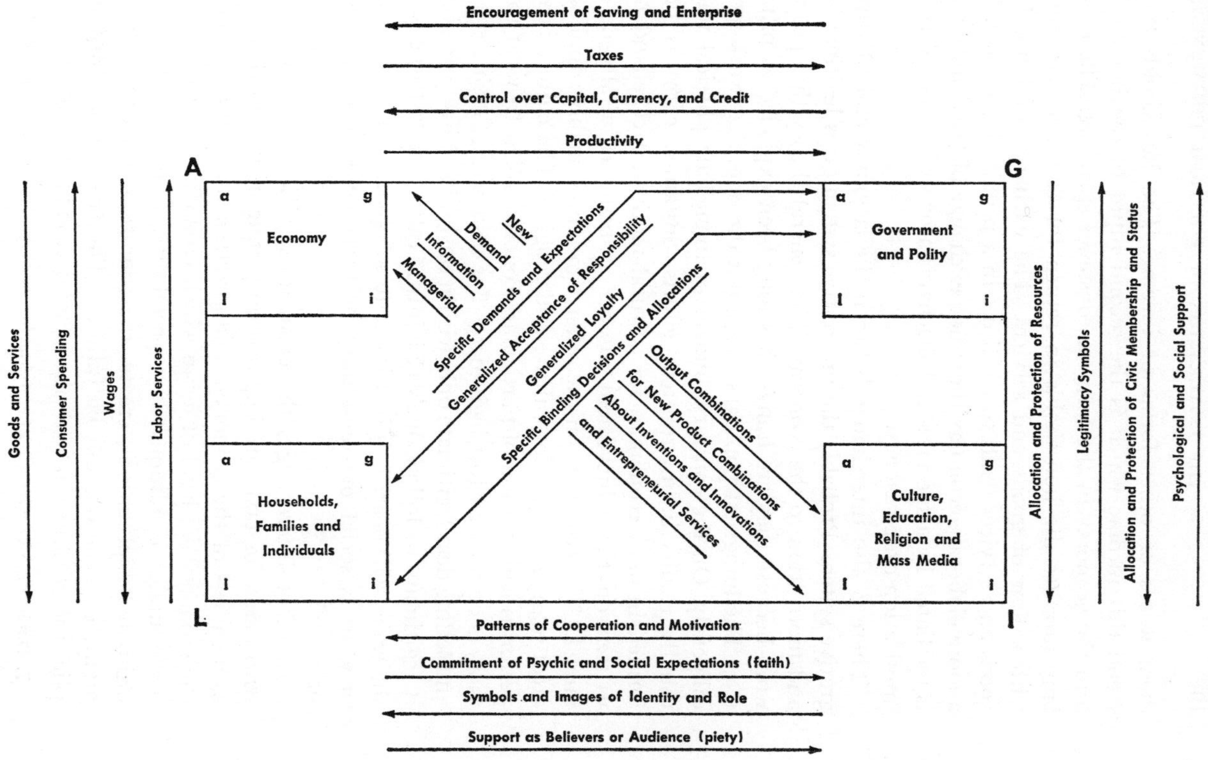

Encouragement of Saving and Enterprise

Taxes

Control over Capital, Currency, and Credit

Productivity

A

G

Economy

Government and Polity

New

Demand

Information

Managerial

Specific Demands and Expectations

Generalized Acceptance of Responsibility

Generalized Loyalty

Specific Binding Decisions and Allocations

Output Combinations

for New Product Combinations

About Inventions and Innovations

and Entrepreneurial Services

Households, Families and Individuals

Culture, Education, Religion and Mass Media

L

I

Goods and Services

Consumer Spending

Wages

Labor Services

Allocation and Protection of Resources

Legitimacy Symbols

Allocation and Protection of Civic Membership and Status

Psychological and Social Support

Patterns of Cooperation and Motivation

Commitment of Psychic and Social Expectations (faith)

Symbols and Images of Identity and Role

Support as Believers or Audience (piety)

them wages or other forms of income. The households then spend this income which is the second input of the household into the economy in the form of consumer spending. The economy supplies the households in return for consumer spending with a flow of goods and services. The exchange of labor for goods and services tends to be direct in a primitive economy. In a more elaborate economy the crude exchange of labor for goods is mediated by a special social mechanism or social code of communication called money.

There is also interchange between the economy and the integrative system. Probably the integrative system gives legitimation and motivation to the economy. The general theory that people work because they are hungry has long been exploded as primitive. The hungriest populations are not the ones that work most diligently. On the contrary, hunger or immediate physical want usually results in intermittent efforts. Sustained effort is performed in most economies for cultural motives. McClelland has written on the achievement motive as being culturally determined.[7] The economy, on the other hand, presumably supplies a great many resources for culture and religion. The culture again performs legitimation of particular economic roles. In what role, then, is economic effort legitimate? For instance, is buying cheap and selling dear legitimate only within the limits of just price, or is it legitimate to follow one's Calvinistic calling and charge what the traffic will bear? Is it legitimate to safeguard individual property, or is social or community property better than personal property?

In other interchanges the economy supplies the government with taxes, for taxes are imposed on people mainly in their role as members of the economy. The government, in turn, supplies the economy the legal order in which economic decisions can be made under conditions of expectability. Expectability, or coordinated expectations, creates the conditions under which economic expectations can be fulfilled. The economy in turn supplies the government with the general economic capabilities, the

7. David C. McClelland, *The Achieving Society* (New York: Norton, 1961).

productivity of a society. It is also the government which makes possible through its legal institutional systems the extension of credit and, therefore, the more complex channeling of investment. Credit and investment are not purely economic functions but assume certain political functions in the Parsonian scheme. They are political functions or aspects of the interchange between economy and polity. They partake as much of the political as the economic. Historically it was under King Henry II of England in the twelfth century that a statute was passed which allowed suits for recovery of debts in any court of the king, anywhere in the kingdom. From then on, demands from credit relationships were no longer collectible only at the place where the obligation had arisen but anywhere in the kingdom. This was a major political decision; but though it was a political decision, it created a nationwide possibility for credit. In a similar way, the full faith and credit clause of the American Articles of Confederation is highly relevant. It made claims from contracts and credit collectible anywhere in the Confederated States from 1783 to 1791. A clause of the federal Constitution added contracts to the direct jurisdiction of the federal government; later this was tested in the famous Dartmouth College Case by Justice Marshall. Credit could, of course, be used for maintaining patterns. For instance, a family incurring medical expenses on credit is actually borrowing money for pattern maintenance. Another case would be that of a society that requires 20 per cent of gross national product to be invested yearly for its sustenance as a larger economy.

This illustrates the difficulty in categorizing, even in a larger system. The attribution problem is a real one in the Parsonian scheme. Where do you put things? Ordinarily, the problem in abstract terms can be stated in advance by holding that all actual institutions in society can be divided completely into two classes: those which are predominantly attributable to any one of these functions and those which are not. As long as you accept the proposition that a very large part of social activities are more readily attributable to one rather than the other of those functions, the scheme has empirical possibilities. If it should turn out that the division of people into men and women is based on empirical fact and that hermaphrodites are extremely rare, then this division is meaningful. If 90 per cent of the electors were hermaphrodites and there were few men and women around, the scheme of dividing voters by sex for a Gallup poll would have very limited usefulness. The empirical fact that those who cannot be attributed to either sex are so few makes this particular division relevant. Similarly, you can divide the United States into regions—North, South, Midwest, Far West, Mountain States—because there are relatively few territories which could not plausibly be attributed to a section.

There is a second point. Suppose you had a few functions that could not be convincingly attributed into the Parsonian scheme. You could either distribute them evenly over the four, or you could experiment by attributing arbitrarily to see whether anything changes. If one were to place Oklahoma among the Western States or Mountain States or Southern States or Midwestern States, he could determine whether opinion poll data would be significantly thrown off balance by this change of distribution. So long as Ohio and Illinois are always in the Midwest, Georgia and Alabama in the South, and New Mexico and Arizona designated as Mountain States, the unstable attribution of Oklahoma might actually do much less damage than discarding the whole scheme. Perhaps the most important or interesting processes in society cannot be attributed, but one should never pretend that there is no attribution problem. We should bring the problem out and make it quite explicit for any particular piece of attempted research.

Interchange Between Government and Culture

What about the other interchanges and possible interchanges between government and the integrative, or cultural, system? It might be argued that the integrative system or the culture supplies the goal attainment system with a set of values, a generalized set of preferences in terms of which the different goals are integrated with each other. It might also be argued that the government supplies the members in the culture with a certain amount of leadership. Even in culture, the government can do much to set the style or tone of a culture. For example, the anthropologist, Douglas Haring, found an island off the coast of Japan which had never been incorporated into the Japanese police state. The Japanese on that particular island had a type of national character similar to the sixteenth century Japanese, and Haring thinks that one can show quite clearly to what extent the Japanese national character and culture were made more tense, more repressed, and more anxiety-laden by 300 years of police regime.[8] In a similar sense it could be argued that part of the highly authoritarian pattern of Europe was institutionalized by the absolute princes from the sixteenth to the eighteenth centuries which then gave rise to the German middle class autocrats of the breakfast table in the nineteenth century. A cultural pattern thus can be set off first by the government. Autocratic princes defeated non-autocratic princes in the sixteenth century. This in turn set reference group style models for the population at large until every German father was trying to be a little prince in his home. Government leadership in both general policies and style command acceptance, for the government gives individuals a sense of belonging. The sense of being a part of something or being involved in a great undertaking that serves the cultural religion of inclusiveness breeds a response by individuals in terms of identification. Then culture reinforces this by claiming that government is holy, sacred, and just and that it corresponds to the highest values of the culture. This can go all the way from laudable patriotism to all-out state idolatry.

Culture gives government legitimacy. A bishop annointing a king is a dramatic example of the integrated sub-system reaching out and symbolically conferring legitimacy symbols upon a

8. Douglas G. Haring, "Japanese National Character: Cultural Anthropology, Psychoanalysis and History," *Yale Review,* 42:3 (Spring 1953), pp. 375–392.

representative of a goal achieving system. When, on the eve of the First World War the clergy of all the belligerent states were ceremoniously brought to bless the draftees on the different sides before they were used against their foreign coreligionists, a performance of this function of legitimation could be observed.

To preserve its monopoly, a particular culture will often call on government to protect its institutions, not merely against material attack but against deviates. Most cultures have sexual and other taboos against which they invoke government obscenity laws. If a culture puts a high value on public health, it will call on the government to enforce vaccination laws. In Latin America and many other countries, a particular religion is a state religion. In this case the religious group calls upon the state to enforce its monopoly to make sure that no Protestants are tolerated.

Individual, Family, and the Cultural System: The Integrative Function

In the relationship of the individual to culture, individuals contribute to integration by internalizing and practicing, either directly or through the family, many of the values which are incorporated in the cultural system. For instance, Jewish homes may have some prayer scrolls, or there may be a Lenin corner in some Soviet homes. In addition to being generally pious, individuals and their households probably also supply the culture with contributions of creativity such as new cultural ideas, new symbols, new religious works of inspiration and insight, and so on. Thus the culture gets manpower and support from the individual.

Conversely, the cultural sub-system usually gives individuals reasons for legitimate self-respect as well as reasons for sticking to the family, thus contributing to their stability as integrated "sub-systems." For instance, in Latin America a person will be told to be faithful to his wife because it is God's law. In Russia, he will be told to be faithful to his wife because he would be a bad Communist and an unsatisfactory atheist if he were not faithful. So far as the pattern maintenance of the household is concerned, an atheist in Russia and the clergyman in Protestant Norway or Catholic Colombia give exactly the same advice—be faithful to your wife, stick to your family; parents, care for your children. If a culture should degenerate to the point where it would no longer supply legitimation or motivation for keeping families together, something very drastic would be likely to happen. There have been times when cultures have given far less support to families than at other times. Soviet Russia is a good example. Soviet Russian cultural ideology gave less support to the family thirty or forty years ago than it does now.

Thus, individual personalities and households get socially legitimate roles from the integrative sub-system. Whether a person should be proud or ashamed for having made money is clearly a matter of the culture. If two values are in conflict, such as the value of self-preservation and the value of military prowess, the question arises of whether a soldier in a difficult situation should retreat. The only way of answering or resolving the conflict between several values comes from the integrative system. If Spartan culture integrates by giving priority to warlike virtues, the American culture does so by telling soldiers in Bataan and elsewhere that, after having done their duty to the best of their ability, it is quite legitimate to surrender. The U.S. Army does not ordinarily fight to the death, but tells soldiers that after exhausting military usefulness for resistance, it is legitimate to be taken prisoner. The individual or family gets its self-respect precisely on the grounds of adherence to cultural norms. In an orthodox Jewish household, if a son joins a different religion, this is reason for utter disgrace. The same is true with all traditional religions. In American culture, on the other hand, the fact that a Presbyterian may switch to Episcopalianism may attract less attention. It is quite unlikely to be considered the reason for loss of self-respect. American culture asks: Is he still a good man?

All these are examples of interchange between systems. The interchange between the pattern maintenance system and the government might be visualized in the context of specific demands. Specific demands are made on the government such as a traffic light at the intersection, medical care for the aged, higher price supports for the farmer, law enforcement or protection against mugging on sidewalks, and so forth. The first service the government performs for individuals and families is to generalize specific demands into generalized assumptions of responsibility. That is, the government says: "I am in charge. Specific demands may indeed be legitimately directed to me." The assumption of the role of being in charge, of being somehow responsible for the attainment of goals of individuals, families, and others and therefore of being the proper place for demands to be addressed to is a function of government.

The government also, of course, eventually makes specific binding decisions in response to individual demands. When the decisions are acceptable to a certain number of individuals, general support for the government tends to increase. Making specific demands upon a government implies some offer of political support. If specific demands are met with reasonable frequency, given some threshold value, then generalized loyalty on the part of population results. The art of politics consists in finding enough groups for whom specific demands can be met sufficiently so as to generalize loyalty to government and support for it in its role of responsibility for goal attainment in society. Governmental systems, of course, have different sizes and levels, just as pattern maintenance is involved on the individual personality level or on the level of the family.

Some of these interchanges have been thoroughly explored and more thoroughly established than others. The labor, wages, consumer spending, goods, and service flow interchanges have been thoroughly explored and are well understood. The interchange between economy and government is less well understood, but, still, considerable work has been done on it and is reasonably clear. The interchanges from individuals in the population at large to politics, and from culture and ideology to politics are now under investigation, and probably a good deal will change and develop. Anthropologists are working mainly on the L-I interchange. Traditional political science used to explore most of the relationships of the A-G system, and, since Burke, Hamilton, and Marx, the interflow between economic interests and the government has also been studied. Modern political science very characteristically is trying to use the interchanges of the government sector with all three of the other functions. The political culture approach would be mainly concerned with the G-I, G-L, and I-L interchange, while the personality in politics approaches focus largely on the L-G interchange. Altogether they probably give a better picture of what is involved in politics and political systems.

The Governmental Function

There are questions of both historical and quantitative interpretations. For instance, historically the L-G interchange has undergone changes resulting in more and more specific demands addressed to government and in more and more spheres for which government accepts generalized responsibility. Historically, more and more individuals in each country have tended to turn to government for the attainment of more and more goals and for performance of other functions. The scope of government has been increasing throughout the twentieth century, which can be exemplified by the fact that the total governmental sector—federal, state, and local in the United States—was about 5 per cent in the 1890's and is about 32 per cent today. The figures are similar for Britain. There is a tremendous growth of this type in communist countries where the governmental sectors are much larger. Yet even in communist countries, there are certain spheres where the government explicitly denies any responsibility. If a young man finds that his girl does not like him, there is nothing he can do in appealing to the Communist Party or any other political agency in that country. This would be different where the government might accept responsibility for ordering genetically suited couples to marry for suitable offspring. But in most viable nations the government is not responsible for everything. The increase can be measured by discovering how much each society allocates to each of these four main sub-systems, how they differ from each other in this respect, and how their sub-systems differ. National governments presumably put more of their resources into goal attainment than into pattern maintenance, whereas municipal governments might be thought of more as instruments for pattern maintenance. This is Burke's point when he objects to Paine and others by saying that the state is not a partnership for a limited, transitory purpose such as the sale and purchase of pepper but is a partnership of the living and the dead and a partnership in all art, science, and religion. That is a plea for much greater attention to the integrative function of the state and, also, in Burke's case, one for sheer tradition.

Nevertheless, the notion that the integrative function is important is relevant. Even in traditional medieval political systems where military and power enforcement goal attainments were given to secular governments, most of the integrative functions were left to the Church. Even some of the economic functions were carried out directly by the monasteries. But in the Middle Ages, the integrative sub-system of the society had set itself up in business as an operating organization, which, at times, substantially overshadowed the secular government.

Thus, there are numerous ways in which the four functions can be performed. The amount of time, attention, and resources a particular society allocates to each of these four functions can be empirically established. Using empirical evidence it can be argued that modern Western industrial civilization is clearly oriented toward emphasis on the adaptive function. The adaptive function, in this sense, not only includes production of capital goods but also of invisible capital goods which we call skills and knowledge. The self-reinforcing, self-reproducing, and self-accelerating search for more and more knowledge, more and more productivity, and more and more power is characteristic of Western cultures. Yet there are exceptions in the West. Cultures such as southern Italy, characterized by tradition and family particularism, invest their meager resources in pattern maintenance

Lines of Empirical Inquiry

The Parsonian system, therefore, is quite adaptable to empirical investigations and lends itself to suggestive generalization. For instance, significant insights can be gained by discovering which functions tend to increase over time and at what time in what cultures. Second, inquiry can be directed toward the question of what specific functional balances have turned out to be more viable than others. The whole anticolonial revolt of today, as well as the communist revolutionary pattern, is based on the assumption of gaining control of the goal-attaining functions—the government. One set of anticolonial assumptions states that only by change in the governmental sector can there be further changes in the adaptive sectors. Marx, on the other hand, at times seemed to be of the opposite view. In traditional Marxist writings, the main autonomous changes are all initiated in the adaptive sector through economic development bringing on political changes and eventually the classless society.

A third line of investigation could focus on what goes on within the channels of a particular kind of interchange. When, for instance, in economic interchanges or societal changes, does labor become wage labor or the exchange of goods for services begin to go through monetary channels? Or, to what extent is the society run on credit rather than cash? Or to what extent does the government command generalized loyalty of people rather than merely the specific support of certain groups?

Pattern Variables

To answer the question of how societies do things we turn to the Parsonian concept of pattern variables. There are three pattern variables which are particularly interesting for the purposes of this discussion. One is the difference between *diffuseness* and *specificity*. A relationship is specific if it is limited to a sharply delimited class of situations or cases. For instance, one goes to a dentist for the specific purpose of looking after one's teeth. His advice on the stock market might not be trusted. Or, would you go to General Motors for an automobile? Yes. Would you go to General Motors for advice on the national welfare? Probably not, although Mr. Charles Wilson has been quoted as saying that what was good for General Motors was good for the country. Ordinarily we are inclined to go to specific agencies for specific advice. In traditional cultures, on the other hand, roles are usually diffused, that is, dealing with a broad class of situations and cases. The most diffuse role there is, is the role of a mother for her baby. From the position of a small baby, mother is everything: the source of life, warmth, protection, legitimacy, joy, fun, play, pleasure.

A *specific* relationship exists where there is a presumption that a personal agent competent in one case is not competent in another relationship. The burden of truth is on him who asserts competence or responsibility. A relationship is *diffuse* on the other hand, if the presumption of repsonsibility extends to general classes of events. This is, of course, an aspect of role specialization not only of individuals but of governments and other organizations. In a traditional culture, such as that described by Edward Banfield,[9] the extended family begins to assume diffused responsibility: it is the insurance company, health service, legal counseling service, and human relationship clinic.

However, the assumption of diffuse responsibility for many relations drains resources. Given a constant level of resources or

9. Edward Banfield, *The Moral Basis of a Backward Society* (Glencoe: The Free Press, 1958).

capabilities, an increase in diffuseness of responsibility must be paid for by reduction in the number of persons for whom the responsibility holds or a reduction in the range of situations, geographic or otherwise, for which this diffusion holds. In politics there is a choice, under limited resources, of either performing a few services for many people or a lot of services for a few people. Thus, given a limited amount of resources and capabilities that cannot be quickly expanded, an increasing diffuseness means increased particularity.

Particularism—the second variable—is related to diffuseness, particularly in poor societies. Particularism, the opposite of *universalism,* applies only to certain groups and areas. Freedom from want for every human being anywhere in the world is clearly a universalistic goal. Many religious imperatives are universalistic. Incidentally, the history of religions has shown that the particularistic religions were invariably replaced by the universalistic ones. Tribal gods usually gave way to Allah, to Buddha, to Jesus. Judaism is probably at the transition point. It is a universalist religion in intellectual content, but historically it has remained embedded in a particularistic situation.

The third pattern variable is the difference between *ascription and achievement.* Ascription assumes qualities based on previous patterns, traditions, heredity. In this sense, a young horse can be considered a crack racehorse and paid for accordingly before he has run his first race, if the studbook says he is a good racehorse. In human affairs, to consider somebody an aristocrat on the basis of pedigree is one thing, whereas Jefferson's concept of the natural aristocracy would in part become an achievement notion. However, in actual life we, of course, tend to ascribe a good deal; we see somebody with a commanding presence and we assume therefore he would be a good commander in a tight spot, but he might not be anything of the sort. A very inconspicuous fellow might actually be the man who would be more helpful if the going got rough. In society there is a good deal of ascription, both long range and short range. In achievement societies or cultures, one must prove over and over again that he mertis his status.

The three patterns can be combined. The society or culture that is diffuse, particularistic, and ascriptive is ordinarily a highly traditional culture, such as a small tribe or a feudalistic society. The lord has diffuse obligations of protection and jurisdiction in almost every aspect of the peasant's life. On the other hand, his jurisdiction only extends a short distance around his castle. The lord is supposed to be of noble blood because he is ascriptively of noble descent and, therefore, ascriptively the one with the virtues that go with nobility. This is not necessarily an authoritarian system of government. A closely knit tribe or family group might have diffuse responsibility with everyone in an egalitarian position. This society group could be particularistic and keep out outsiders and it could be ascriptive because it might consider itself the chosen people, chosen family or the chosen group regardless of what it actually does.

The sociologist, Ferdinand Toennies, called the closely knit, diffuse, particularistic, ascriptive community, the *Gemeinschaft* type of community. It was an idealized community, and it was described as being warm, emotional, limited to a few people, and secure. Once a person belonged, he always belonged, remaining part of the in-group by ascription. This community is rich in connotations but poor in combinations, because everything is already connected to everything else in some fixed fashion. Propensity to change is poor, and potential for adaptability is even poorer.

Toennies called the opposite type the *Gesellschaft,* one which is specific, universalist, and achievement-oriented. It is cool, rational, insecure, and directed toward goal achievement. The achievement society is potentially much more adaptable because it can easily give rise to universalistic ethics. It can carry particular purposes to much greater extremes than the warm, diffuse, somewhat immobile *Gemeinschaft* community. The *Gesellschaft* society exhibits an extreme commitment to one particular function, regardless of the connotations of other functions. The society is adaptable to fast changes and to wide varieties in conditions. It is poor in connotation but very rich in combinatorial possibilities.

From "Community" to "Society": The Social Effects of Industrialization

If the simplest English equivalent of a "community" would be a "brotherhood," the simplest equivalent for a "society" would be "task force." The community is forged from complementary, general communication habits so that people can talk to each other and communicate on a very wide variety of topics. Society, on the other hand, is based on much more limited special habits of working together for specific goals, including their rational willingness to collaborate for such goals. Parsons points out that historically, modern industrialization has meant a shift from community to society. This shift occurs as rationalization and bureaucratization develop. Societies are much more powerful than communities in some ways, but much less reassuring. They are, therefore, more likely to generate feelings of anxiety and alienation. If a house is thought of as a machine for living or a suburb as an engine for career advancement, then a highly societal, highly rational, highly specific universalistic and achievement-oriented attitude toward living results.

In the new suburbs there will be some secondary feedback of nostalgia in literature emphasizing the particular and close-knit combinatorial nature of the good old city square where everybody knew everybody else in a nice diffused way. The human richness of the old city block might become idealized in a nostalgic way. Numerous new books emphasize that the old neighborhood gave security and richness to individuals, and oddly enough this is probably in part true. The pursuit of specific goals in a suburb, such as a school guaranteed to get children into good colleges or a system making sure that one will ride on the train or drive or play bridge with nothing less than a junior vice-president from the same neighborhood, will have to be paid for by a loss of many other connotations and of much security. Suburban status is marked by constant achievement, whereas nobody much minded if old Mrs. Smith on the block in the old neighborhood had less money than she used to have. Her neighbors would still know her and like her.

The move from non-industry to industry increases achievement orientation, specificity, and universality; but it does not preclude traits of non-industrial society. Nevertheless, to say that increases in industrialization bring about increases in these pattern variables is an empirically verifiable statement.

One of the major, personal motives for people in achievement societies to become either socialist or communist in many cultures has been to protest against the insecurity, alienation, and specificity of relationships. The discovery which has been shattering to many who were sympathetic to communism, precisely on the grounds of this misunderstanding was that communist society requires the same type of achievement orientation as the capitalist society. There is a great deal of achievement orientation in economic production. Nothing is so deeply built into the needs of communist society as is its production plan; an annual 9 or 10 per cent gross rate of increase in the gross national product requires a lot of this.

In order to achieve its production goals, Soviet society has found that it must set up bureaucracies. It is inherent in bureaucracies that they devote much of their resources to pattern maintenance. These pattern maintenance objectives of a particular bureaucracy come into direct conflict with its productive functions in the larger system. The solution to this problem, which both the Soviet Politburo and the U.S. Congress have discovered, is to destroy many agencies every few years and start new agencies from scratch with very similar functions.

Building Large-Scale Communities: Functional Conditions

Given a vast increase in resources, can one build a community that is diffuse and yet particularistic with regard to much larger numbers of people? The modern nation-state assumes very diffuse responsibilities for the particularistic defined group of persons, but these groups are now numbered in the millions and in some cases by the hundreds of millions, rather than by the hundred as in kin group, or tribe. Instead of progressing from small particularistic groups to large, universalistic societies, one of the most interesting and most powerful combinations in politics are the large diffuse societies of the modern nation-states. They are diffuse, particularistic, and ascriptive. By ascription, Germans are supposed to be heroic, Americans practical, and Frenchmen brilliant. Particularistic and specific enclaves can be found in universalistic, achievement-oriented organizations, thus composing a particularistic sub-system. Alternative types of organization at different layers of the state can be found. The opposite is also found where specificity breeds diffusion. Diffuse responsibility may often be the result of success in specific achievement. For example, the school principal in Crestwood Heights, having achieved success in a specific, realistic context, then became the diffuse authority for the community.[10] Furthermore, starting from a specific base, governments have become the focus of a number of additional service demands by populations and have, in this way, a huge amount of diffused responsibility.

In the Common Market arrangement, however, what has succeeded in the last fifteen years and is likely to succeed for a number of years to come is the achievement of a type of universalistic organization which concentrates on very particular functions—coal and steel, communications, trade—and difficulties will occur precisely whenever the functions become more diffuse or when the spectrum of functions broadens. Only by consolidating success and achievement along very specific lines will it be likely that enough habits and expectations are built up by the population to then permit the establishment of a broad, diffuse government. In this sense, it is not accident but necessity that there was a union of courts between England and Scotland before there was an

10. Cf. John R. Seeley *et al.*, *Crestwood Heights: The Culture of Suburban Life* (New York: Basic Books, 1956).

Anglo-Scottish union; that there were Articles of Confederation before there was a federal union in the United States; that there was a German customs union before there was a unified German empire; and that there are now specific European agencies before there is a government of Europe.

If this is true, then it follows that early steps toward the extension of a metropolitan government could be taken most practically through the development of very specific agencies and through their consolidation in each case into a single specific agency with universal jurisdiction over its specific field of competence for the whole metropolitan region.

VIII

The Influence of Values in Political Integration

Apart from social and economic prerequisites, the integration of political communities requires conscious decisions by policy makers. In the following chapter, Philip E. Jacob examines the ACTS *of politically relevant persons who make "the political decisions which either trigger or jam integrative relationships." Investigating the value components of these acts which relate to the process of political integration, he first develops an original conception of values which can be employed operationally in empirical research on political behavior, places this concept in social science perspective, and then focuses on individual policy makers and the norms which weigh on their decisions to integrate or not to integrate. Examining the influences on the integrative process at both the policy level and the over-all community level, he is primarily concerned with the* DECISION PROCESS *involved in political integration, the* PEOPLE *who actually make the decisions, and the* VALUES *upon which these decisions are based.*

THERE ARE AT LEAST TWO RESPECTS IN WHICH THE ANALYSIS OF values is crucial in the study of political integration. First, the cohesion of a community seems to depend very fundamentally upon the compatibility of the values of its members. Indeed, one might almost say that it is a condition of community, that the human beings who compose it share values with each other more widely and more profoundly than they differ in their interests or struggle over competitive desires. Hence, for integration to occur among two or more previously existing communities requires that the values shared within each become shared with each other; or at least that the area of shared values between communities becomes sufficiently great so that the principal differences between them do not block common action on common concerns.

The second respect in which values bear significantly upon the problem of integration is in shaping public policies that are conducive to, or block, intercommunity cooperation. It is very important to understand what values are influential in the choices made by policy makers because integration, concretely, is a set of political decisions made by those who have the authority to commit their communities to collective behavior. If one could assume that the democratic theory of representation always operated—namely, that the public policy maker would dutifully carry out the public will and that his understanding of the public will would always correspond with the facts, then it would be unnecessary to explore the impact of values at the policy level. But it is apparent that far more enters into the decisions of many political leaders than their perception of the values of their constituencies. One must therefore examine independently of the community's values what it is that activates leaders and determine whether the values which motivate them are conducive to the process of integration or interfere with it.

The purpose of this inquiry is, first, to delineate a conception of value which may have relevance to empirical research on political behavior and to distinguish this conception from other uses of the value concept. This approach is developed more fully in a monograph, "Values and Their Function in Decision-Making."[1] The point of this attempt is to provide a definition

1. Philip E. Jacob, James J. Flink, and Hedvah L. Shuchman, "Values and Their Funtcion in Decision-Making," *The American Behavioral Scientist,* Vol. 5, No. 9, Supplement, May, 1962.

which identifies empirically discrete elements in the policy process and generally in the dynamics of human action—in other words, to describe values "operationally" so that one can analyze how they influence behavior.

A second purpose of this inquiry is to consider specifically how values so conceived bear on the process of political integration and to suggest a few lines of research which would help to clarify and measure the influence of values in inter-community relations.

The essential propositions are these:

1. Political action is basically a function of human decisions. Societal characteristics become politically meaningful only as they affect the choices of persons, whether at the policy level or in the community at large. Hence understanding the processes of human decision-making is necessary to explain the processes of political integration, as well as all other political phenomena.

2. Modern behavioral sciences have demonstrated the particular importance of three factors in shaping decisions: the individual's own personality structure as it emerges through his socialization, the specific expectations which people around him have of what he should do in the social roles he occupies, and the characteristic behavioral patterns of the culture of which he is a part.

3. One effect of these factors is to introduce into the process of human decision-making a "normative component"—that is an imperative to make choices, not only in terms of what a person may directly want, but in terms of standards of what he has come to regard as legitimate or proper. His decision is affected not only by what he desires but by yardsticks which define for him what is right or wrong, praiseworthy or blameworthy. These criteria by which the propriety of action is judged, we identify as "values"—or more precisely, "normative values."

4. Values impinge on the political process as a determinant in policy-making and as a strong influence upon the response given to policy by the community.

5. At the policy level, decisions often reflect an attempt to reconcile or integrate divergent values in a way that sustains the policy-maker in his position of community leadership and at the

same time contributes to the cohesion of the society. But sometimes bureaucratic norms clash sharply with the traditional values of the community, especially under conditions of radical social change. Then the immediate impact of policy-making may be strongly disintegrative, followed, perhaps, by the development of a new basis for integration in an emerging pattern of values.

6. Social norms, that is, values which permeate widely throughout the society, are the bedrock on which political integration is built *within* the community that holds them. But conversely, they stand as a major impediment to integration *among* communities. Values which deviate from the social norms, though a threat to the solidarity of the existing community, may be the most potent political force for broader integration, especially if these deviant values are shared by groups in other communities.

Human Decisions as the Basis of Political Behavior

This analysis rests upon the assumption that political behavior is fundamentally a process of decision. It is the resultant of a complex of human choices. Hence it must be understood in terms of, and traced back ultimately to, the determinants of the *personal* behavior of all those who in one way or another have a hand in "politics," that is, in the process of directing or controlling the collective actions of the society.

Much political research tends to approach political institutions and structures as established social artifacts rather than as the direct outcomes of human actions and reactions. But when one focuses on change and movement in political phenomena rather than on the static (or apparently static) features, the decisional nature of political systems and processes comes sharply to the fore. The point is made simply and directly by Robert Dahl: "Political action, like other human actions, consists in making decisions—in somehow choosing alternatives, and then trying to make one's choices effective."[2]

2. Robert A. Dahl, *Modern Political Analysis* (New York: Prentice-Hall 1963), p. 93.

This does not necessarily imply that a particular individual exercises a large amount of personal discretion in political decision-making. His choices are customarily constrained both by the social institutions within which he operates and by his own personality structure. He is surrounded and influenced, for instance, by "role-expectations," that is by what others to whom he feels accountable think a person in his position should do.[3] On the other hand, the decision-maker brings to bear on the problem of choice a particular mix of learned experiences, his own peculiar pattern of standards, perceptions, and habitual responses to given stimuli. The net effect, both of institutional and personality factors, is usually to limit the practicable alternatives among which the individual perceives that he has an option. He is by no means an independent operator, free to chart a novel course. He may even feel so hemmed in by precedent, by the expectations of his peers, by his own sense of limited capabilities, by his prejudgments and biases, and, perhaps above all, if he is in a position of political responsibility, by his view of what this responsibility demands of him, that he will insist to himself and to others, that "he has no alternative."

Nevertheless, the individual decision maker ultimately remains the filter through which all external factors have to pass before entering the policy process, at which point they begin to influence political events. And because individuals always have at least some latitude within which to react no matter how structured their institutional environment or how rigid their personality may have become, it is important to carry the analysis of political determinants back to the point where we can see how they function to motivate personal decisions. (Some latitude results from the fact that the institutional and personality determinants of action may not push in the same direction. If the individual faces a conflict of pressures, he must decide which takes precedence. He is literally forced to exercise decisional judgment.)

The implication of this approach to political dynamics for the

3. See discussion of the influence of role, *infra*, p. 218.

study of political integration is that one must relate the kinds of social and political phenomena considered in previous chapters to the genesis of the political decisions which either trigger or obstruct integrative relationships. Transactions, or societal attributes such as structure and system, are meaningful only as they are translated into the acts of politically relevant persons. Otherwise, we can easily fall into the trap of anticipating similar results to flow from similar objective conditions when, in fact, given persons or groups may be impelled to act in a fashion quite different from others, either because they perceive through different lenses the significance of this set of conditions, or evaluate them by standards which are not identical.

In the analysis that follows we are therefore deliberately turning the coin of political integration to the other side from that observed in the book up to this point: to the side of the *people* who decide to integrate or not to integrate, instead of the social characteristics that do or do not tend to accompany integration.

This decisional view of political behavior sometimes invites an exaggerated emphasis upon the influence of the few as against the many in shaping the course of political events. There need be, however, no presumption of elitism in this approach. To be sure, decision-making analysis is concerned with appraising the *weight* of the decisions of the various participants in the political process. This tends to center attention on the conduct of those who exercise a large and easily identified measure of political responsibility. But rarely are a few so omnipotent in the control and direction of their societies that one can disregard the behavior of the many. A full profile of participation in the political process, informal as well as formal, shows that in most contemporary societies, a very large number of people have some hand in propelling political action. Even if the amount of influence exerted by a particular person in the anonymous mass may be relatively small and not related directly to a specific policy decision, the sum total of individual decisions throughout the society becomes a potent political force, even in countries with authoritarian systems of government.

In considering the integration of communities and the process of community-building, it seems particularly important to pay close attention to decision formation at the base as well as at the top of the structure of political power and influence.

The Making of Decisions: Implications of Behavioral Theory

If human decisions are the roots of political behavior, the analysis of political action must square with sound anthropological, psychological, and sociological findings on human motivation. There are three developments in behavioral science whose implications are particularly important for an understanding of the process of decision-making: (1) the "phylogenetic" view of the nature of human evolution, (2) the "field" theory of the dynamics of individual and group action, and (3) the concepts of "role" and "reference group" as social imperatives.

Significantly, each of these offers strong empirical justification, from entirely different perspectives, for the vital influence in human behavior of a distinctive normative determinant, which we shall define as "values."

1. ***From the phylogenetic point of view,*** values in the normative sense, are peculiar to man. They involve different psychological processes from the goal-setting processes of other species, reflecting capacities for self-awareness and self-evaluation, the culmination in man of "ego" and "super-ego" processes. Values are learned through experiences of group living and social interaction which are distinctive of human societies. They can be transmitted across generational lines through the unique ability of man to manufacture symbolic systems of communication. Values are thus both an attribute and a product of "culture," man's particular mode of adaptation. Hallowell puts the case as follows:

> As a result of self-objectification human societies could function through the commonly shared value orientations of self-conscious individuals, in contrast with the societies of non-hominid and probable

early hominid primates, where ego-centered processes remained undeveloped and rudimentary. In fact, when viewed from the standpoint of this peculiarity of man, culture may be said to be an elaborated and socially transmitted system of meanings and values which in an animal capable of self-awareness, implements a type of adaptation which make the role of the human being intelligible to himself, both with reference to an articulated universe and to his fellow man.[4]

2. ***Field theory*** visualizes the individual at the center of the behavioral process—interacting with a variety of pressures and influences that act on him as he relates to the environment which surrounds him.[5] Some of these determinants of action—Lewin calls them "vectors" of influence—are associated with the biological drives and psychological forces that function within the person himself. Others stem from the physical and social conditions of his environment. These influences push and pull in different directions with varying amounts of force. In the end, a pattern of action emerges reflecting the net impact of these pressures, including both immediate stimuli, and those that have become incorporated over time as a more or less fixed part of the individual's personality structure. The individual, however, is the key to action. No matter how conditioned his behavior may be by past or present "determinants," the person himself is the final determinant. He is the catalytic agent who transforms a vast complex of elements into specific behavior.

Applying this concept to the political process, one can envisage the decision maker as continuously at the nub of at least three lines of influence. One represents the impact of his own personality structure; a second has its source in the demands made upon him by the position he occupies in the policy apparatus; the third arises from the cultural orientations of the

4. A. Irving Hallowell, "Self, Society and Culture in Phylogenetic Perspective," in Sol Tax (Ed.), *The Evolution of Man* (Chicago: University of Chicago Press, 1960), pp. 356–357, as quoted in Jacob, Flink, and Shuchman, *op. cit.* p. 15.

5. For a useful summary of field theory, see Morton Deutsch, "Field Theory in Social Psychology," in Gardner Lindzey, *The Handbook of Social Psychology,* Vol. 1 (Cambridge: Addison-Wesley, 1954), pp. 181–222. We have somewhat modified Lewinian terminology for the purposes of this chapter.

society in which he functions. Perhaps we should distinguish a fourth line, particularly when considering the conduct of international or inter-societal relations—namely, pressures originating *outside* the society to which the individual belongs. The intentions and activities of foreign governments, for instance, come prominently into play as a behavioral influence in foreign policy decision-making; the intentions and actions of a central government or of neighboring communities form part of the behavioral field of a local government official. In terms of field theory, political action should be viewed as the result of the convergence upon a particular person of all of these influences and his consequent response to them.

Field theory, however, does not stop with the individual actor. Probably its most significant contribution has been the exploration of the dynamics of interpersonal relationships in the behavior of small groups. Decisions emerging from a group process are found to be strongly affected by the nature of the personalities involved and the way in which the group is organized.

As political decisions are almost always reached by some form of group process, the bearing of field theory is obvious. It provides a model which enables one to examine systematically the interactions of members of a decision unit in terms of the two variables of personality and organizational structure. For instance, drawing on the observations of small group dynamics, sound policy analysis should take cognizance of the relative rigidity of personality of decision-makers, the patterns of leadership established (authoritarian as against permissive) and the techniques of group management employed (consensual as against more highly structured).

From the standpoint of the influence of values in the political process, the significance of field theory has been to demonstrate an extremely close correspondence between particular patterns of group conduct and the norms which come to be applied in the making of group decisions and also to establish an inter-relationship between the values held by individuals and their personality structure. As yet there seems to be no clear knowledge as to which may be cause and which effect, whether the values are shaped by personality and group process or vice versa. At least there is evidence of mutual reinforcement. Democratic values tend to sustain democratic procedures; authoritarian patterns of leadership grow on a base of "authoritarian personalities" and in turn breed authoritarian-oriented values.

3. ***Social role theory*** probably has the most immediate relevance to the analysis of political determination. It stresses the tremendous influence on a person's behavior of the expectations which he confronts all around him as a member of a variety of social groups. "Social role" refers to the ways in which a person is expected to act in carrying out a social function. "It is an understanding," states Cochran, "shared more or less by members of a group as to what a given position or status entails for any individuals who occupy it."[6] In its simplest and most direct application, it represents the expectations of only a small homogeneous group with definite attitudes regarding the performance in question and nothing important can be done by the individual without their knowledge. But in the analysis of political behavior it is more useful to think of larger and more general prescribing groups whose expectations determine what a decision maker may do; and actually a particular person may find himself simultaneously trying to fulfill several roles, responding to several different prescribing groups, each with somewhat different prescriptions of what it expects him to do. The complete description of a social role in most organizations and surely in the political process requires knowledge of the expectations of the several groups involved.

On the other hand, role theory recognizes that the actor at the same time that he is trying to live up to the expectations of the prescribing groups has inner aims of his own to which he is

6. Thomas C. Cochran, "The Challenge to the Historian of Social Role," New York, Social Science Research Council. We are indebted to Professor Cochran's lucid and penetrating article for the substance of the ensuing remarks. For a major exposition of role and reference group theory, see Robert K. Merton, *Social Theory and Social Structure,* rev. ed. (New York: The Free Press of Glencoe, 1957).

responsive. A psychoanalyst might call these, "imperatives of the super-ego"; the role theorist identifies them as the "reference group."

Both role expectations and the reference group constitute norms by which the person regulates his conduct. Both constitute "values" in the sense in which we use the term—to describe criteria in terms of which an individual judges the propriety of action. Both have a profound impact upon the determination of political behavior.

Values as the Normative Component of Human Decision: An Operational Definition

In observing how human decisions are formed one is struck by the characteristic of *evaluation,* which seems to enter in varying degrees, but quite universally, into the experience of choosing. That is, the individual examines the action he is considering not only in terms of whether it is likely to satisfy his wants but in terms of standards. These standards may sometimes be compatible with his personal cravings or desires; more likely they will be standards that are common in his society; or they may be fixed within the individual personality, emerging as the dictates of conscience. The standards by which a person judges or evaluates his actions and the actions of others are rarely mutually consistent; nor will the same standards be applied uniformly in the evaluation of all actions. But it seems distinctive of human beings that their behavior is conditioned in part by such normative considerations. It seems to be an essential ingredient of the human experience to go through a simple or sometimes extremely complex process of judging, justifying, and ultimately deciding action on the basis of standards which the individual himself regards as external to his own being. He must, as it were, validate his actions—square them, at least to his own satisfaction, with the "norms" he has come to accept as necessary rules to control human behavior.

It is to this component of human decision-making that the term "values" seems most appropriate to apply, especially for the purpose of a systematic analysis of the process by which human beings determine their actions. The definition of values as "the normative standards by which human beings are influenced in their choice among the alternative courses of action which they perceive"[7] opens the way to identifying with considerable precision one major distinguishable and vital element in the determination of human behavior. In this sense, the definition is "operational." We understand that this definition conforms closely to the view advanced by Clyde Kluckhohn, fitting within the general conceptual framework of the general theory of action developed by Parsons, Shils, *et al.*[8]

It should be stressed that values, conceived as the norms which influence human behavior, are only one of the determining sets of influences. For instance, we distinguish values from "beliefs," which are existential propositions, or perceptions, regarding the structure and operation of the universe and one's place in it. Obviously, beliefs exert great influence on behavior. In practice they are often intertwined with values: values are strongly affected by what people believe to be true, and, in turn, the norms which people hold can have a profound effect upon how they perceive themselves and the world in which they live. Nevertheless, we think that in the decision-making process the parts played by values and beliefs are distinguishable, and that the

7. See Jacob *et al., op. cit.* p. 10.

8. Talcott Parsons and Edward A. Shils (Eds.), *Toward A General Theory of Action* (Cambridge: Harvard University Press, 1951). This concept is also compatible with the findings of cross-cultural research on value-orientations conducted by Clyde and Florence Kluckhohn and their associates. See especially Florence Kluckhohn and Fred L. Strodtbeck, *Variations in Value Orientations* (Evanston, Ill.: Row, Peterson & Co., 1961). Other relevant research is reviewed in Jacob *et al., op. cit.,* pp. 13–16, and in Allen H. Barton, *Measuring the Values of Individuals,* New York, Columbia University Bureau of Applied Social Research, Reprint No. 354, 1962 (*Religious Education* supplement to the July–August issue). The latter provides the most systematic and perceptive critique of the definition of values to come to this author's attention.

normative and the cognitive are fundamentally different types of determinants.

We think it is also possible to distinguish from both values and beliefs a group of motivational forces which may be called "impulses." These forces, whether innate or learned, influence human action without regard to standards of propriety, beliefs or considerations of "reality." They operate almost compulsively, leaving the person virtually no opportunity to exercise judgment or opinion.

What we call "impulsive" determinants of behavior cover indiscriminately what have been identified as biologically dictated *drives,* psychologically compulsive *needs* or *need-dispositions,* and positive or negative *cathexes,* regardless of whether these are primary or secondary in origin.

From the standpoint of operational analysis, we consider that it is also appropriate to include here deeply entrenched *habitual* patterns of response, however they arose, because these tend to have the same kind of compulsive impact upon decision-making, as drives, needs and/or cathexes. Habits may indeed be rooted in biological necessity; but for the most part they represent the culmination of a complex process of social learning, with given responses prompted almost automatically by given cues.[9]

Alternative Definitions

One must admit that the approach to values here proposed and the corresponding lines of analysis of their place in political decision-making differ substantially from the positions taken by a number of distinguished social scientists, even among the group of "empirical theorists."

Political analysts following the lead of Harold Lasswell have identified values with goals, or "goal-events."[10] Some psychologists have taken a corresponding view, considering that values or

9. Jacob *et al., op. cit.,* p. 23.

10. See Harold D. Lasswell and Abraham Kaplan, *Power and Society* (New Haven: Yale University Press, 1950) for the major systematic exposition of this proposition.

"basic" values are equivalent to human "motives" or "needs."[11] Central to these conceptions is the idea that a value is an entity or state of affairs which a person wants or requires. It is some *thing* that is desired or, in psychological terms, is necessary to keep the organism functioning.

Related to a decision-making situation where one must choose among competing goals or wants, this definition has been modified to allow for the exercise of *preference.* A value is identified as a preferred goal or event. A person's pattern of values then would be considered an inventory of his preferences, rank-ordered in terms of those things which are most preferred as against those which are less.

These concepts virtually bypass the whole normative aspect of behavioral decisions.[12] They ignore the question of what operates in a person to govern his choice among wants, to determine the priority of goals and to establish the grounds on which a person comes to prefer one object rather than another. It is not enough to know the full catalogue of a man's wants or to have a good record of his preferences in order to probe the motivational dynamics of his decisions. Intensive observation of human behavior indicates that men do indeed have a mechanism which enables them to make decisions by choice rather than by a compulsion of largely automatic responses to given stimuli. What we really need to know are the factors which enable men to make choices when they realize that they cannot get all that they want. If values are merely goals or preferences, then there are some other phenomena of human action which need another name. These

11. See Ralph K. White, *Value Analysis* (Society for the Psychological Study of Social Issues, 1951).

12. White, however, explicitly differentiates *goals* and *standards of judgment.* He insists that the latter must be included as a distinguishable component within an adequate definition of values. *Ibid.,* p. 13. He concedes that this is an aspect of human motivation that has been relatively little explored by the "list-making psychologists." But, on the basis of extensive empirical content analysis of varied materials, including clinical data, personality inventories, public-opinion surveys and propaganda, White maintains that "standards of judgment are expressed by people in our culture as frequently as are goals" and are clearly distinguishable from them.

phenomena are the standards, yardsticks, or norms which form an integral part of the operational mechanism of human beings.

It was suggested in the University of Pennsylvania Seminar on Political Integration that what we have called "values"—that is, the norms to which people refer in the making of their decisions —correspond to what Lasswell calls "predispositions" including a considerable range of factors, such as "expectations," "identifications," and "demands" which form part of personality and incline an individual to perfer some events over others or to respond in one way or another to a situation where he has to make a choice of action. But this view also seems to confuse or ignore the normative element. What a person considers *legitimate* is something quite different from what he expects *may happen.* This is not in the least to deny that expectations—calculations of the probable—are very important in the shaping of decisions. But this is not the same as judging whether a given action is "right" or "wrong," whether it "ought" to be striven for or opposed, whether it is something of which one can feel proud or ashamed. The normative calculation represents an entirely different dimension of evaluation from estimating the chances that a given event will or will not occur. Decision results from a combination of processes which include both an estimate of the probable outcome of action and an estimate of its legitimacy. We would agree that the norms which have become incorporated as part of an individual's personality would "predispose" him toward preferring one goal over another. This *is* the normative component at work in the decisional process. It is necessary, however, to identify clearly and precisely this distinctive aspect of a person's predispositions—precisely because it is distinctive, yet is so often sloughed over in behavioral analysis. It is indeed, as has been suggested above, perhaps the most distinctive attribute of human beings.

Deutsch has suggested that what we have called "values" might be considered "second order preferences," that is, preferences among preferences. Such a distinction between two levels of preferences may be useful. The second order of preference represents that group of standards which guide and influence the person in making his choices among immediate goals or desires, in other words, in determining his first order preferences.

Allen Barton has presented perhaps a more clear-cut formulation. He distinguishes between "normative values" and "preference values," between values as obligation or as desires. Both are included within his working definition but are typologically distinguished.[13] Perhaps because of the wide currency of the usage of the term "value" as equivalent to preferences, it would be well to follow Barton's practice and make explicit whether one is using the term "value" to cover all kinds of preferences or limiting it to those that represent a normative influence. What we are discussing here is Barton's "normative values," or "feelings of obligation."

There is one other necessary semantic clarification. Practitioners of politics and students of political action alike repeatedly talk about "interests." Usually the context of discussions of "interests" indicate that what is meant is usually the same thing as goals, wants, or what is desired. However, there has been a growing tendency in some areas of political practice to differentiate among interests and to act in a way which indicates that some interests are "higher" than others. Action is justified or legitimized in terms of the higher definitions of interest, such as "the national interest" or "the public interest." The concept of interest may have, therefore, normative significance, in contrast to the idea which is usually associated with the term "special interest," that is, merely a statement of what a particular individual or group wants to grab for its own advantage. This is a very good illustration of the confusion that has arisen in political analysis because of a failure to isolate clearly the particular function in decision-making performed by normative values. The "interest" obviously has an entirely different impact upon politi-

13. Barton, *op. cit.* Barton's formulation is as follows: "Values will be defined here as general and stable dispositions of individuals, verbalized by them or inferred by the researcher, involving preference or a sense of obligation."

cal decision depending upon whether it exercises normative control in the making of choices or whether it simply defines a single goal for which an individual or group is striving. When interests become standards of choice, they would indeed be what we have been calling values. When they merely define goals without providing a yardstick to determine whether this goal or the realization of it is justifiable, then it does not have the properties of a value. Vernon Van Dyke has contributed a valuable clarification of this issue:

> In common usage the words *values* and *interests* have approximately the same meaning and each designates two sorts of thing, approximately the same two sorts. What are called interests divide into categories that can conveniently be labelled "independent" and "dependent." What are called values divide into categories that can conveniently be labelled "goal" and "instrumental." Independent interests are equivalent to goal values and dependent interests are approximately equivalent to instrumental values, the difference being that the term "dependent interest" is not so likely to connote the notion of intrinsic desirability, whereas the term "instrumental values" may do so.[14]

Identification of Values: The Test of Legitimacy

The normative element in human behavior usually emerges in statements that have a distinctive judgmental quality. Among these operational indices of values are: (1) simple declarations of approval or disapproval; (2) obligatory statements, that is, statements of what should or ought to be done; (3) expressions of shame, guilt, or demand for punishment, directed either at oneself or more customarily at other persons.[15]

Set in the context of a social or political situation, these expressions often take the form of claims of "legitimacy"—or of "illegitimacy." Individuals assert that such and such an action

14. Vernon Van Dyke, "Values and Interests," *The American Political Science Review*, Vol. 56, No. 3, September, 1962, p. 576.

15. See Barton, *op. cit.*, for a comprehensive and penetrating appraisal of indicators of values.

is "proper" while others are not. A policy is approved because it is in "the national interest" or "public interest"; another is condemned because it is held not to be. Implicit in such statements is the conviction that public action should be governed by concern for the welfare of the nation or the public, rather than by self-interest. On the other hand, someone else may vigorously defend self-interest as an entirely appropriate yardstick by which to judge the propriety of an action. Either way, the test of legitimacy is the political or social focus of the normative component of human decisions. When a person expresses a judgment as to the legitimacy or propriety of an action, he reveals that the normative process has been at work.

The question arises as to who sets the standard of legitimacy? Is this simply the same thing as the "social norm," the body of widely accepted criteria of conduct in the society of which the individual is a part?[16] From an operational point of view the answer seems to be that legitimacy is whatever a particular decision maker says is legitimate, rather than what may be the view of the rest of the society. The decision maker's view may coincide with what the bulk of his society considers a standard of legitimacy. But as we have noted before, it is quite possible for him to break with the social standard and feel that what is proper in a given case is different from, or perhaps outrightly opposed to, the prevailing code of "oughts."

How is it possible for a person to arrive at views of legitimacy that deviate from those of his society? If one assumes that norms, like beliefs or habits, are learned phenomena, then one must look to the particular experiences of the individual up to the point of his decision. Some of these may have led him to question severely the validity of the social code, especially where it ran against the values expressed by family, church, or other groups of persons he had come to respect or love. Perhaps the greatest incentive to the

16. Note the classic pioneer studies of the psychology of social conformity by Muzafer Sherif, in which the concept of social norm is developed as a basic analytical tool. See *inter alia* M. Sherif, *An Outline of Social Psychology* (New York: Harper, 1948).

development of a person's own particular pattern of values is the inescapable experience of conflict between his direct wants and the various sets of norms which he comes to observe around him and whose effect upon him is to deny, at least to oppose, the direct satisfaction of his ego desires. The individualization of norms is less the result of socialization—that is, the passive acceptance by the individual of what he finds others approving—than it is the result of witnessing a profound conflict among alternative values and being forced to make a choice among them.

Much of the process of learning values goes on without anyone's being very much aware of what is happening so that by the time individuals are politically relevant, their structure of values is well defined. The observer is inclined to take them for granted as a fixed part of the individual's personality. Using the indices mentioned above, one identifies the norms that are actually brought into play as decisions are made, compares these with the corresponding expressions of others in the society, and concludes whether and to what degree the individual and the social norms coincide.

Our point here, in brief, is that the test of legitimacy must not be confused with whether norms are socially prevalent. Legitimizing is a *personal* procedure; it is only when a person himself has come to accept what "society" prescribes as legitimate that the social norm becomes an active component of the individual's decision and hence meaningful from the standpoint of the analysis of action.

Because we know that individuals are prone to respond favorably to what is socially approved, we are justified, however, in paying a great deal of attention to ascertaining the modal distribution of values in the society. They represent one of the most important reservoirs on which individuals growing up and performing in the society will draw as they formulate their particular body of operational norms. At the same time we must constantly remember that, typically, societies are not monolithic and that there are tiers upon tiers of social groups within a political community whose norms with reference to certain areas of human action may differ substantially from what may be the dominant pattern in the society at large. It is essential, therefore, in political research to identify the groups to whom an individual decision maker feels most closely attached and then to identify the characteristic tests of legitimacy used by these groups. What we are suggesting, then, is that the normative component of decision, that is, "values" as we use the term, is broadly derived from three sources: the body of standards largely accepted in the culture or society of which the individual is a part, the standards held by the social groups within that society with which the individual is closely associated, and third, standards established as a result of life experiences peculiar to the individual himself. (See Table 14.) In

TABLE 14

THE BEHAVIORAL FIELD OF PUBLIC POLICY DECISION:

Determinants: Motivational Influences

Type of Policy Determinant (e.g., vector of influence relevant to the decision at hand)	Social Base of Policy Determinant		
	Individual Idiosyncrasies (of the policy-maker)	Role Attributes (attached to each policy relevant role in which the policy-maker functions)	Common Cultural Characteristics (of the society to which the policy-maker belongs and which are germane to the decision at hand)
1. Values			
2. Beliefs			
3. Impulses			

the end, each person's pattern of values will be a composite which is distinctive for him but which will overlap at a great many points with the pattern of others. As will be evident in the discussion that follows, it is largely out of the areas of overlap that politically significant values emerge.

Hence it is appropriate in political analysis to turn to data which will contain indices of values held in common by the makers of policy, their important reference groups, and the general political community. One important body of such data is the public rationalization or justification of a decision. To be sure, this may only represent what the person who has made the decision thinks *others* will accept as valid ground for making the decision. The values expressed in such a statement might then be intended to manipulate public acceptance of the decision, or of the decision maker, or both; rather than reflecting the genuine normative considerations which the decision maker himself used in reaching his decision. The externally expressed norm may not at all coincide with the internally operational norm. This would be particularly the case were the decision maker's norms to be severely at odds with those accepted by the society or by social groups whose approval he cherished.

Recognizing this problem, however, there is still considerable insight to be derived from an analysis of the value-laden content of rationalizations of decisions.[17] The very process of rationalization testifies to the importance of the normative component to the individual who is doing the rationalizing. It is *prima facie*

17. Barton, *op. cit.*, after appraising a wide range of empirical studies of values, concludes that in certain cases, at least, it has been successfully demonstrated that "the explicit, abstract standards which people verbalize are related to actual, important behavior."

Ralph K. White has done important pioneer work in identifying values through content analysis of verbal materials, *op. cit.* See also: Robert Angell's effective comparative study of elite values using content analysis of selected Soviet and American periodicals, *A Comparison of Soviet and American Values and Foreign Policies* (Ann Arbor: University of Michigan, mimeo); also, the massive application by Robert C. North and associates of content analysis to official documents, newspapers, periodicals and personal records in an exploration of the genesis of international conflicts: Stanford University Project on International Conflict and Integration.

evidence that he deliberately and consciously took into account the external norms which he is expressing in his statement. It is particularly important in the analysis of political decisions where the decision maker inescapably confronts the necessity of relating himself to others if his decision is to have any effect. The significance of values expressed in policy rationalizations, therefore, is at least twofold: (1) it indicates the estimate made by the policy-maker of what are socially potent norms in the society which have to be taken into account if decisions are to have a social impact; (2) it is a measure of the regard in which the decision maker holds the social norms and therefore a clue, though not a decisive one, to the part which the external social norms played in the original formulation of the decision.

The problem remains of how to probe to the norms other than those recognized in the public rationalization which had an effect on the individual's decision. To some extent these may be discovered through expressions and reflections made privately to "in-groups" or shared with an interviewer who establishes a relationship of confidence. Even here, however, the element of rationalization enters in, perhaps even unconsciously.

The question arises as to whether there are *actions* of the decision maker, in contrast to statements, which may provide indicators of the values he holds. Can one read back from a decision or action into the norms which influenced it? Our conclusion is that this procedure is highly susceptible to misinterpretation by observers. A given action may have been the result of a number of possible different influences, and how can the observer tell which of these was in fact effective? At most it would seem that performance or action might serve as a secondary check of the validity of the individual's expressed rationalization.

A better check, however, would seem to be a comparison of public with private statements and a comparison of public statements, made to different audiences. If these were largely consistent with one another, perhaps one could have reasonable confidence that the values expressed were those which in fact influenced the decision. Where statements were markedly inconsistent, one would suspect the presence of manipulated values alongside operational values.

Perhaps the most telling evidence is provided by the histories of particularly difficult or critical decisions. When the individual finds himself in a position where no available course of action seems to be able to satisfy all of the norms he has come to accept as basic, he is obliged to establish priorities and, in the process, to clarify and sharpen his awareness of the normative components of his personality or of his role. Or, in case the individual's decision runs head-on into conflict with the judgments made by others in a situation where a group has the responsibility for collective decision, he must try to convince others of his approach or find some means of accommodating his norms with theirs. Where material is available describing from the inception of the decisional crisis to its conclusion the conflicts of value which were involved, very real insight can be gained both as to the character of the values at work and changes occurring in the relative weight of the different values.

This brings us to the further question of how values can be measured, that is, in the sense of estimating the relative weight of different values in the influencing of decisions.

The Measurement of Values[18]

One of the major problems in estimating the relative weight which persons give competing values in making their decisions is to find measures that are actually used by the decision maker. There are really two problems of measurement. One is to establish the relative influence which a particular decision maker gives to different values, that is, to discover the priorities which he establishes among competing values. The second problem is

18. Allen H. Barton, *op. cit.*, provides a definitive methodological critique of the principal attempts to measure values empirically. See also his *Studying the Effects of College Education: A Methodological Examination of "Changing Values in College"* (New Haven: The Edward W. Hazen Foundation, 1959).

to compare the priorities set by one person with those that are established by others with whose decisions we are concerned. In each case it is necessary to find measures which are authentic, that is, which represent the individual decision maker's actual accounting system.

In comparing the value influences bearing upon two or more people, it is necessary, in addition, to make sure that the measuring stick is applicable to all who are involved in the analysis.

Much of the misunderstanding among those who have attempted to resolve these problems arises from the adoption of measures which *seemed* appropriate to the observer but may not in fact accurately reflect the "pricing mechanism" in use by the decision makers. For instance, in a wealth-oriented environment, which the United States seems currently to represent, it is tempting for the social scientist to think of values in terms of "utilities" and try to weigh values by the amounts of money or time which persons are willing to invest to achieve different wants. Not only does this approach confuse outcome of a decision with its normative motivation, but it presumes that each decision maker does in fact weigh his value by a materialistic utility standard. The unreality of this approach is like that of asking a person who has no interest in gold how he would rank his wants according to a gold standard.

Valid measurement of values probably requires a "self-anchoring" approach, to use the term with which Hadley Cantril describes his method of comparing human aspirations and fears across cultural lines.[19] From this standpoint one can approach the problem of measurement by discovering what in fact seems to decision makers to be the highest possible reward which they might obtain and, conversely, what they actually consider to be the worst possible punishments or deprivations that could be

19. F. P. Kilpatrick and Hadley Cantril, "Self-anchoring Scaling, a Measure of Individuals' Unique Reality Worlds," *Journal of Individual Psychology,* Vol. 16, No. 2, November, 1960. See also, Hadley Cantril and Lloyd A. Free, "Hopes and Fears for Self and Country: The Self-Anchoring Striving Scale in Cross-Cultural Research," *American Behavioral Scientist,* Vol. 6, No. 2 Supplement, October, 1962.

inflicted upon them. Having discovered this scale, one could then seek to measure values and the weight attached to each by a given decision maker, in terms of the amount of striving he was prepared to invest on behalf of a given norm—striving, that is, to obtain rewards or avoid punishments as he himself conceives of them. To compare the weight given a norm by two or more individuals, one would compare not the particular object of their striving but the *degree* of striving which each put forth or was ready to put forth in comparison with the maximum and minimum points on his personal scale of reward and punishment.

In a sense, this means that we use *sanctions* as the principal means of measuring the influence of values. But it should be stressed that these are the sanctions that are meaningful *to the decision maker,* not necessarily those which are practiced by his society and, most particularly, not necessarily those which the observer or analyst would feel controlling upon his own behavior. It may be that to many people the act of killing or being killed is just about the ultimate conceivable penalty. Readiness to sacrifice one's life, or, in turn, take another's, to such a decision maker would be the highest price that could be paid for implementing one of his norms. Probably the generally held view in the humanist-oriented and self-centered civilization of Western democratic countries would be to rank the sacrifice of one's own life higher than the taking of another's; and one would also draw a distinction between the nature of the person whose life one was prepared to take or had taken. Those considered closest to oneself, such as family, would be considered of higher worth than anonymous fellow nationals, and these in turn are of more worth than anonymous persons of another nationality. Where one would fit personal friends of another nationality in this order of worth would probably vary considerably from individual to individual and culture to culture. Also, the expression "women and children first," once accepted as the basis for survival in a sea disaster, suggests that the worth attributed to human life has age and sex variables. A rough attempt to develop a measuring scale along these lines was made in an analysis of atrocity propaganda during the Second World War, using as indices estimates of how the populations of belligerent and neutral countries ranked atrocities.[20]

Two major efforts to identify and measure variations in values among cultures have recently been completed. One is the anthropological study of value orientations in five cultures conducted by the Kluckhohns and their associates.[21] The other is David McClelland's psychological analysis of patterns of motivations as revealed through children's stories and other educational materials in forty countries.[22] Each of these brings out highly significant differences among the cultures and goes far toward developing "culture-anchored" scales, indicating the priorities among values prevalent in particular societies.

On the other hand, McClelland also points out some forms of sanctions that have almost universal impact and can therefore be used as common measures of value, crossing cultural lines. He says, for example, that the killing of women and children of one's own ethnic or cultural group is very widely accepted as an extreme form of sanction. Readiness to do this is in the implementation of some value or norm is, therefore, a measure of that norm's high priority to the executioners.

Returning to the fundamental point, it would seem that effective research on the measurement of values depends on the discovery of each person's own hierarchy or set of priorities rather than the attempt to draw up a uniform and universally applicable scale.

The approach suggested—that of measuring the significance of a person's values in terms of sanctions which are meaningful to the individual concerned—may be supplemented by a procedure in which the influence of each value is measured in terms

20. See Philip E. Jacob, "Atrocity Propaganda," in Harwood L. Childs and John B. Whitton (Eds.), *Propaganda by Short Wave* (Princeton: Princeton University Press, 1942).

21. F. Kluckhohn and F. Strodtbeck, *op. cit.*

22. David C. McClelland, *The Achieving Society* (Princeton: Van Nostrand, 1961).

of the readiness of the individual to sacrifice the implementation of other values which conflict with it. This is a truly operational approach because it tests the ordering of values by the extent to which they prevail over others in concrete situations. Where, for instance, the judgment of a policy maker is influenced simultaneously by concern for the well-being of the country as a whole and the friendship which he has established with a special interest group, which will take precedence in a situation in which the two clearly cannot be reconciled? One could, with a sufficient number of decisional histories, determine the number of times in which a particular norm took precedence as against those in which it yielded to others. The ratio would need to be modified by the number of incidents in which the decision maker evaded a choice, indicating his unwillingness to establish a clear priority (such incidents would include those in which the individual asserted to himself or others that there was indeed no conflict and convinced himself that he was subordinating none of the norms at issue).[23]

Values in the Political Process

Values affect the political process in at least two important ways. First, they are an effective component of, or influence upon, the decisions that are reached by policy makers. Second, the values prevailing in the community at large act as a limiting condition of action.

In the first instance, we view the political process from the level of policy decision, while in the second, we are considering the political process from the level of social response. In both instances the process involves decisions, but in the second, that

23. With regard to the measurement of conflicting values, see Samuel Stouffer, "Analysis of Conflicting Social Norms," *American Sociological Review,* December, 1949, and Samuel Stouffer and Jackson Toby, "Role Conflict and Personality," *American Journal of Sociology,* 56, March, 1951; and the re-analysis of the implications of the Stouffer data by Philip E. Jacob, *Changing Values in College* (New York: Harper, 1957) pp. 23–24.

is, in the case of the response of the society to the decisions reached by its leaders, the decisions do not appear so specific. The response of the mass of citizens is usually unstructured and widely diffused; but nevertheless it is deeply influential not only as it impinges on the policy makers themselves as a factor in the political landscape of which they must take account but also because the response of the society very largely determines how effectively the policies which have been decided on at the governmental level can be implemented.

Integration at the Policy Level

Considering first the relevance of values to decisions made by policy makers, one important point of inquiry is the source of the norms which carry particular weight in the making of choices. Typically, one may distinguish four groups of values which bear upon the policy maker and to which his decisions may be responsive in varying degrees: the *social norms,* that is, as we have defined them, the prevailing standards of legitimacy accepted in the community; the *role values,* that is, the norms that a person performing his function is expected to respect (by those to whom the policy maker feels that he owes respect); the *interests of special groups* which have established a claim on policy makers' loyalties; and, finally, the strictly *personal values* held by the policy maker himself. It is rare that all these will coincide, although it seems in the nature of the political role that policy makers will try to minimize the conflicts emerging among these differing value demands.

Deutsch has presented a significant explanation of how political decisions may arise as the policy maker seeks to fend off threats to his personality structure or to the cohesion of the community for which he feels responsible, cohesion which provides the very foundation of his political position.[24] He suggests that

24. Presented at the University of Pennsylvania Seminar on Political Integration, 1961.

to a policy maker (or, indeed, to any actor) an event or action is viewed as immoral or illegitimate if its effects are believed to endanger the integrity of his own personality structure or the cohesion of the community which made him relevant. In other words, the value judgments which ultimately carried weight with the decision maker would be those that were compatible, on the one hand, with the set of facts which were embodied in his personalty structure (with the "map of the world" as he saw it), and on the other, with the standards which formed the cement of the community. Deutsch conceives of a kind of homeostatic mechanism operating to produce decisions through which the individual on the one side and the community on the other protect and preserve themselves. In other words, he posits an intrinsic integrating force within the individual, an integrating force operating in three associated relationships: (1) to preserve the internal integrity and coherence of the personality; (2) to maintain a harmonious and mutually reinforcing relationship between the particular individual and the community of which he feels a part; and (3) to maintain the viability of the community itself as an integrated functioning human association among those whose personalities are sufficiently compatible to form it.

One of the most significant parts of his contribution is his suggestion that effective political decision-making is dependent upon a successful integration of the various norms which bear upon the policy maker. Thus, special group interests must somehow be reconciled with broad considerations of the public interest; role values must be reconciled with the personal values which have emerged as a vital part of the policy maker's personality, and so forth. Failure to integrate these competing values spells the political incapacity of the decision maker; he must retire from the scene or risk the breakup of his personality on the one hand or the undoing of his community on the other.

There is some evidence to suggest that what happens in highly structured societies with strong governmental bureaucracies is the submergence of the personal values of the policy maker to role values in which a concept of social responsibility is accepted as the dominant controlling norm for the policy maker's official life. In such a situation the social norms of the community and special interests likewise become subordinated in the hierarchy of politically relevant values. A bureaucratic norm is set, and its acceptance by the bureaucrat is the condition of his being accepted into the bureaucracy and allowed to make policy decisions. Satisfactory integration will occur if it is generally agreed in the community that it is indeed the bureaucrat's function to apply norms set in the bureaucracy to decisions affecting the entire community or a part of it.

This solution may be challenged, however, if either special interest groups or the large majority of the community should insist that it is the policy maker's job to implement *their* norms rather than the bureaucracy's. It seems to be at this point that much of the tension in modern democracies arises. Neither the public nor the conflicting interest groups that largely compose it seem willing to surrender their values, without vigorous protest, in favor of the values held by the bureaucracies. Though the policy maker may insist that he is making his decisions "in the public interest," many of those who have to live with his decisions will disagree. The disagreement is rarely expressed in terms of an outright rejection of the norm of public interest. It is usually asserted, rather, that the bureaucrat has failed to recognize what is *really* in the public interest. However, at root, the conflict is not between varying conceptions of the public interest but between the consensus of values accepted by the government group and the values which prevail outside, either among special groups or perhaps even in a very large portion of the community.

In rapidly changing or developing societies, the conflict between the social norms and the role values of the bureaucracies is even more apparent. Here, the bureaucracy is likely to be demanding a radical change in the traditional values of the society in order to accord with its own conception of what is legitimate and proper for the emerging society. The intensity of the struggle between new and old leadership, the conflict between the governmental center and the political base, and the many evidences of passive resistance and sometimes violent resistance to change throughout the society as a whole are all evidences of the unwillingness of political leadership in these societies to function integratively. They refuse to submerge their personal values to those of any competitors. They are willing to act directly and self-consciously to destroy the integration of the community whose leadership they have assumed. To be sure, they espouse a new integration in a different kind of community where cohesion is achieved on the basis of a new set of values. But they make no bones about their determination to have integration result from the acceptance of *their* values rather than from successful brokering of existing values in the society they govern.

Values and Planning

The attitudes of "planners" toward values require special consideration, because planning has become established as a central and discrete function of organizational decision-making in modern societies. It intrudes increasingly upon the formulation of public policy as governments extend their responsibilities more widely over the activities of people and confront rising demands to insure long-run security and welfare for communities they govern.

Within the decision-making processes of government, planners are pre-eminently the custodians of integration. They are expected on the one hand to pull together the disparate elements of social behavior within their community into rational, coordinated series of actions which will produce desired outcomes. They are supposed to know the relevant variables which affect individual and group conduct and to be able to prescribe patterns of cooperative effort, which, if put into effect by the ultimate political powers, will make their societies more viable and satisfying. On the other hand, broad-gauged planners, alert to factors which impinge on their communities from the outside as well as from within, should be unusually sensitive to the imperatives of interdependence which press for closer inter-community relationships. They are thus in a pivotal position to understand the processes both of intra- and inter-community integration.

One might think that the planning function, preoccupied as it is with the achievement of social goals, would engender a profound concern with standard setting, with the evaluation of the goals themselves. Curiously, as public planning has become professionalized, the planners have deliberately, almost fanatically, tried to divest themselves of any normative responsibility. Somebody else, they insist, must set the goals; their job is to devise means of getting there. To buttress this position they turn to the value-fact dichotomy propounded by logical positivism and claim in the name of scientific method that values, being "subjective," must be ruled outside the competence of the planner: His is "not to reason why" but "to do and die." *Facts* are his province, not values; means, not ends.

There are signs of reaction against this constricting position from within the ranks of the planning profession. Refutation is grounded or empirical re-examination of the philosophical distinction between fact and value along lines charted by Churchman.[25]

The essential thrust of the argument is that a statement of "fact" is itself a statement of judgment affected by the whole set of the mind and outlook of the person making the statement. Hence, to distinguish the "is" from the "ought" is both impossible and meaningless. To confine the decision maker to taking account only of so-called facts would not assure his objectivity or neutrality. Decisions will always be a function of value judgments; and the decision maker need not worry about being "unscientific" because he has been unable to limit himself strictly to assessing the import of facts or calculating the probable factual outcomes of his decisions. Davidoff and Reiner put the

25. See C. West Churchman, *Prediction and Optimal Decision* (Englewood Cliffs, N.J.: Prentice-Hall, 1961). The implications for the theory of planning are effectively developed by Paul Davidoff and Thomas Reiner, "A Choice Theory of Planning," *Journal of the American Institute of Planners,* Vol. 28, No. 2, May, 1962.

point trenchantly: "Planning is overloaded with value judgments masquerading as fact."

The planner's responsibility under these circumstances should certainly include the testing and verification of values. He should ascertain their consistency with other values and open up for choice by his clients the full range of possible goals. (This point of view still reserves to the "client" rather than the planner the responsibility for final decisions on transforming values into policy commitments.)

Deutsch takes a somewhat different position.[26] He proposes that one can properly reverse the Davidoff-Reiner argument and consider values as predictive statements of the "is." In other words, the values could themselves be subjected to empirical verification if they were viewed as estimates by the decision maker of the probability that a given state of affairs would result from a given set of actions. What *ought* to happen would be his estimate of what the chances were that it *would* happen, given a certain course of action.

Neither party, however, seems to have come to grips with the influence of values in the normative sense. Deutsch, in using the expression "ought"—as it may quite properly be used—refers to a high degree of certainty, or rather probability, that a sequence of events will occur, for instance such a statement as "the population of the United States *ought* to reach 180 million by the year 1975" on a given set of presumptions and projections of variables. From this standpoint one could effectively argue that decisions are the product of empirically verifiable judgments which could be substantially immunized against interference of subjective biases. On the other hand, Reiner and Davidoff are not troubled by the inclusion of normative value judgments in the decision-making process but rather by the problem of subjective perception in which the things that "are" are really only the things that people see them to be, thus bringing an element of uncertainty and illusion into presumably rigorous calculation of factors which are presumed to be absolutely and intrinsically real.

26. As presented at the Seminar on Political Integration, *supra*.

Deutsch's proposition may well open the way to controlling the play of the perception variable in policy-making. It does not obviate the necessity, however, of confronting directly the influence of normative values. These are "oughts" of a different species; they have little relation, if any, to what may or may not happen. To be sure, the values a person holds are influenced by things that in the past have happened to him or around him; they are indeed the product of his experiences. But in terms of their influence upon him in the actual reaching of decisions, they stand quite independently of the "facts" which he takes into account. Indeed, they form the basis of his judgment as to whether his actions should be directed toward maintaining the existing set of facts or attempting to alter them if they are judged unacceptable by the norms which he holds.

The value-fact distinction seems to be a useful one to keep for purposes of behavioral analysis, particularly if one uses "facts" as, in effect, statements by individuals of what they *believe* to be true and real within the skein of their accumulated experiences. What he knows or believes to be true obviously has a tremendous amount to do with how an individual will act. But parallel to his assessment of the factual goes the process of evaluating the means and the ends of his conduct in terms of the norms to which he has become attached and which, in turn, modify substantially the way in which he reacts to the facts as he sees them.

Social Values and Integration

We turn now briefly to a consideration of the relevance to the political process of social values, that is, of the values which operate in the community at large below the policy level.

Here we are concerned with at least two sets of values: first, the "social norms" which represent the widely held uniformities of standards, the great modal distributions of salient values; second, those values which deviate strongly from those held by the mass.

Social norms are relevant to the political process, as we have seen, in that they may significantly affect the decisions of those responsible for public policy. The policy maker has himself grown up in the society in which these social norms prevail and has not been immune to their influence upon his own personality structure. He may well have incorporated the social norms, or some of them—"internalized" them—so that they have become part of his battery of personal values. Furthermore, it is likely that the role values to which he responds are to some extent grounded in the social norms, because his function is of such wide import to the society that expectations of what he "ought to do" will be widely held outside the bureaucracy as well as within. The concept of the "legitimate" ruler, for instance, seems historically to be one of the most pervasive norms held in a political society. In general, the political function of social norms is to constrain the decision maker, setting the limits within which he may make his decisions.

From the standpoint of integration, one might say that the social norms represent, at the same time, the principal guarantor of the solidity and cohesiveness of the community in which they are held and the principal barrier to action intended to promote unity and cooperation across community lines. The more widely diffused and the more firmly implanted the social norms of a community, the more stable, predictable and cohesive it is likely to be; but, at the same time, the more resistant it will be to political and social change except on terms which will allow it to preserve and extend its particular mix of social norms. The community which is strongly committed to its social values will make a good aggressor or empire builder; but it will be a hard cooperator and a recalcitrant minority in a broader community where its values are not as fully influential. Monolithic societies will tend to be "loners;" pluralistic societies will find it possible to reach out their hands to others.

This means that in international relations, and perhaps also in metropolitan relations, we confront a paradox. The more viable the separate communities, in the sense that they are united on their goals and responsive to similar values, the more difficult it will be to find solutions which incorporate them or relate them effectively to their neighbors. At the same time that one is concerned with nation-building as a solution for some of the problems of transition from an imperial system—that is, forging a new basis for integration which establishes values along national rather than along intra-national lines—we are in danger of creating tight little islands which will try to seal themselves off from the outside world, or worse, try to impose their newly found values upon others.

There are two escape hatches. It is conceivable that the social values of the community may include elements that are conducive to harmonization with the rest of mankind. This is more likely to be true of mature or long-established communities which feel relatively secure, at least within themselves. An old and well consolidated nation may indeed develop a strong sense of responsibility for the well-being of other than its own members. One thinks of modern Britain in its relationship with the Commonwealth as a country whose political norms include such an outward-directed sense of responsibility.

The other escape hatch is found in the perception that people hold of the necessities for survival within the real world or at least the world the members of the community perceive as real. If people become convinced that they cannot square their social values with the physical and political demands and pressures of the "real" world, the stage is set for some give in the social values. They become more flexible to change. The community recognizes that it cannot have its cake and eat it too. If it wants to save its way of life and maintain at least a portion of its treasure chest of social values, it may have to prepare to give up some of them or at least alter them sufficiently so that people can live by letting live in the world that exists. "Facts," actually what people *believe* to be facts, are a catalytic agent which may dissolve one strongly entrenched pattern of social values and make possible a new integration through a broader, more inclusive sharing of values.

The Effects of Deviators

This brings us to the second set of values below the level of policy-making—deviant values—that is, norms shared by minorities which are at odds with the general pattern of social values. There are at least two effects of deviant values upon the process of integration. They represent, first, the potential for disintegration. They are the irritants which disturb and excite—the dissidents—within the community. On the other hand, one or more sets of deviant values may form the nucleus about which may grow the elements of a new integration if the conditions in the world make the maintenance of the more widely prevalent social norms unrealistic. A deviant set of values thus becomes the "emergent" system of values, in due course replacing the norms which have become anachronistic.

It is not at all certain that deviant values, as they threaten the disintegration of the old cohesive society, will become the pivot for integration of broader scope. It may quite as likely happen that the new integration will take place on a much more restricted basis, that the values will be shared by fewer rather than more people. Unfortunately there is nothing in the record of modern political history to sustain the illusion which was fostered by the American experience with federation that there is an "inevitable" progression from smaller to larger political communities. Fragmentation seems more the order of the day as deviant values succeed in bringing about the disintegration of the older traditional societies. In one sense, we should expect it to be this way. The very fact that the values *are* deviant means that they are held by a much smaller group than those who accept the "social norm."

On the other hand, it is possible that those who hold deviant values may succeed in becoming so politically effective that they make the values they hold prevail over the previous political community. If it should happen that the values that are deviant at one point within one political community are similar to or shared by those who become politically effective in other communities, then there is a possibility that integration of a broader scope may occur. Referring to an example previously cited by Karl Deutsch above, the integration of Germany can be explained as the result of the rise to political influence in various states of central Europe of persons whose political values diverged from the ones commonly accepted in their particular home states. Those who felt they were Germans first and Bavarians second, and those who felt they were Germans first and Prussians second—each at one point a small minority among their fellow citizens—became the effective political forces and joined hands. Something of the same order may be happening in Europe today as minorities within Germany, France, and other member states of Western Europe who have come to feel that they are Europeans first and Germans or Frenchmen second gain increasing political influence. Integration then comes about on a broad scale as a result of a kind of conspiracy of deviators within existing political communities. One might almost say that the integration of political communities—in the sense of extending the area of integration—requires first that there be "traitors" within each existing political community; second, that these traitors themselves be united by norms which they hold in common; and third, that they be more skillful in seizing the reins of power and keeping them than those who have chosen to be loyal defenders of the established norms of the society.

IX

The Learning of Integrative Habits

In the following chapter on psychological aspects of integration, Henry Teune points out that certain variables related to integrative behavior—such as identification with political units; inducements to cooperation; and similarities in experience, values and attitudes—are psychological in dimension. He attempts to explain how people acquire the dispositions which contribute to, or inhibit, political integration. Basic concepts and propositions of learning theory are applied in the examination of several social science theories and variables concerning political integration.

MUCH OF THE BEHAVIOR OF CITIES, COUNTIES, AND TOWNS RESEMbles that of nation-states. The ferocity of resistance to territorial changes between cities often matches that of nation-states in border disputes. Negotiations between mayors are not unlike those between prime ministers. A major query of Deutsch and others is whether explanations for present and future relationships between nation-states will have the same form and perhaps the same content as explanations for relationships between semi-sovereign local governments.[1]

If political integration refers to such things as merging political institutions, combining resources for common ventures, agreeing

1. See Deutsch, Chapter 2.

to share facilities, consulting on differences, and avoiding harmful confrontations, then it is a fact that these forms of political integration are present at the intra-national and international levels of government. A question, however, remains. Are the variables which are related to political integration both between nation-states and local governments similar? An affirmative answer to this question can be assumed. What is said, hopefully, will elevate this affirmation from the bottomless storehouse of social science assumptions.

Why do people identify with a nation-state, a region, a county, or a city? What are the conditions under which people give up or alter their political identifications? What are the inducements for inter-governmental cooperation? What are some of the characteristics of governments, of groups, or of individuals that correlate with integrative behavior? What similarities or dissimilarities in experiences, in values, and in attitudes are related to activities leading to political integration?

These questions are obviously important both at the international and local levels. They are questions directly related to explaining the phenomena of political integration. They call for psychological statements. They require psychological theory.

The major point of this presentation is that known facts about political integration can be explained by a psychological theory —learning theory. These psychological factors will be similar for political integration at any level. In short, they are highly generalized statements about human behavior of which political integration is one part.

Some aspects of learning theory will be used to prompt some insights into the process of political integration. Learning theory will also function to piece together some seemingly isolated bits of knowledge into a more general framework. Learning theory will be taken out of the laboratory, stripped of many theoretical refinements, and applied to some facts known to be relevant to political integration. Although learning theory will not be equally helpful in explaining all aspects of political integraton, it should, at the very least, produce insights into the processes of change leading to political integration or its opposite, political *dis*-integration.

The first part of the paper sets forth some groundwork for the subsequent analysis of some specific variables in political integration. Since the major effort is to restate one kind of knowledge in the language of another, a few statements justifying such an effort are first offered. Second, some of the concepts and propositions of learning psychology are presented in the context of social and political behavior. Third, some familiar variables or referents used in definitions of political integration are re-interpreted into psychological language. It must be admitted that no tight, unambiguous definition or statement of referents for the use of the term "political integration" is given.

The second part turns to some categories of variables or some propositions relating to political integration. These selected areas are: (1) the spill-over theory of political integration and cooperation; (2) the "rational" calculation of payoffs for political integration and cooperation; (3) shared values and expectations in political integration; (4) the political integration of elites; and (5) political identification and political integration.

The Functions of Restating Knowledge

Most social "theorizing" or speculation, reduced to its simplest component, is the result of combining two or more apparently different bodies of knowledge. It involves placing the structure and content of one kind of knowledge against another. Mechanical "models" are fitted to human behavior; biological functionalism is welded to social systems; engineering of communications is fixed on the interaction of people.[2] Using learning theory of the laboratory to explain social and political phenomena is, in a sense, transferring knowledge from one area of inquiry to that of another, but with an important qualification. Learning theory is a theory, not a model, of human behavior.

2. See Teune, Chapter 10.

Even if it is possible to restate most of what is known in the social sciences as some form of crude learning theory—a theory which would resemble that of modern experimental psychologists—the advantages of such a restatement are not clear. Restating one theory in the language of another does not automatically produce new knowledge. But such a restatement may prompt new insights. The theoretical importance of these insights may be difficult to determine immediately. In any event, restating knowledge is inexpensive. It costs little except the time of a few men.[3]

Cheaply acquired knowledge, however, can never be a substitute for observation. Transforming what is already known into different language can yield new insights but not confirmed or verified knowledge. The primary function or the result of restating knowledge is to contribute to scientific discovery.

It would be a mistake to confine all the results of reformulating knowledge to the context of discovery. Another result of reformulating what is known is to fit fragmented and seemingly isolated knowledge into generalizations of greater scope. Restating knowledge of a fragmented nature into categories of knowledge of greater scope can give some truth to more specific knowledge if that specific knowledge stands, even if roughly, in a deductive pattern with more general statements that are true. Thus what has been confirmed in one area can serve to throw light on less well confirmed or verified knowledge in another area, if the knowledge of both areas seems to be related to the same and more general propositions.

Still another purpose of restating knowledge into fewer and fewer categories is to organize knowledge for more efficient communication, and, if learning is a part of communication, for more efficient learning. Human minds are conditioned to use general facts to order specific facts for communication and recall.

Learning Theory and Social Behavior. The common sense core of behaviorism—a position in the debate about what man can

3. The attractiveness of cheap knowledge poses a danger for scientific inquiry. I define "cheap" as speculation about "what is the case," or about the world of fact.

know about man—is that what is known about individuals comes from observing behavior under certain circumstances.[4] By observing directly a person's past responses under specific conditions, it is possible to predict or explain a response if the specified conditions are present. How similar the circumstances must be to past circumstances depends again on the past experiences of the individual. Individuals learn to generalize or to discriminate, depending on the kinds of associations and rewards which were connected to the situation or stimuli.

Past experiences or learning are described in dispositional terms. Dispositional terms, such as attitudes, values, and opinions, refer to the fact that particular responses will occur when certain stimuli or situations are present. Descriptive statements, such as "John is a coward" and "John is brave," mean that under certain circumstances, such as a battle situation, cowardly or courageous behavior will be manifested. John is disposed to act bravely or cowardly under certain circumstances, and the only way to infer a disposition is to observe him under these circumstances. The test of whether or not salt is soluble, without knowledge of chemistry, is to place salt in water.

Dispositional characteristics of individuals are inferred from (a) certain objective criteria, such as occupational affiliation, socio-economic status, sex, or manner of clothing and (b) observations of behavior, including reports of past experience. Objective criteria, which indicate certain dispositions, are known to be related to certain experiences. The fact that an individual is a female indicates that she probably has had experiences characteristic of most females in a particular society. Knowing that an individual is an American, a Britisher may infer that he has had experiences which make him "outgoing," "friendly," "hard-working," and "practical." Confronting the American with a problem situation, the Britisher, knowing that the American probably has been rewarded by his fellow Americans for being "practical,"

4. See Gustav Bergmann, "Ideology," pp. 304 and 305, in Gustav Bergmann, *The Metaphysics of Logical Positivism* (New York: Longmans, Green & Co., 1954), pp. 300–325.

expects a practical solution or approach. Using one socio-economic characteristic to infer a complexity of dispositions is commonly called "stereotyping." Socio-economic characteristics, especially if used alone, are poor indicators of dispositions.

Dispositional concepts, such as attitudes, personality traits, opinions, values, and the like,[5] are in principle dispensable. There is no need in principle to use dispositional terms. It should be possible, in other words, to say almost everything about an individual in the language of a complex network of correlations of past stimuli and responses. The laboratory rat demonstrates this point. If all the experiences of the rat in the maze are recorded, it probably is not necessary to summarize his maze experiences. But if the rat is used for several experiments, he may be described with the dispositional term of being a "right-turning" rat. A mother usually does not ascribe learned dispositions to her young child. She may say that the child cries when left alone to eat because the child lost the bottle the last two or three nights. Dispositional concepts, nonetheless, function as efficient summarizing statements about past experiences of individuals.

Dispositional terms are also used at the group level.[6] A family is cohesive, an organization is aggressive, a nation is warlike. These dispositional terms refer to what collectivities of people will do under specified circumstances. Again group level dispositional terms are inferred from certain objective characteristics known to be related to certain collective experiences and from observations of group level behavior. Being warlike may be

5. For an extensive compilation of disposition terms in the behavioral sciences, see Donald T. Campbell, "Acquired Behavioral Disposition" in *Psychology: A Study of a Science,* Vol. VI, *Investigations of Man as Socius: Their Place in Psychology and the Social Sciences,* edited by Sigmund Koch (New York: McGraw-Hill, 1963), pp. 94–172.

6. What is said here may blur the distinction, insisted upon by some sociologists, between psychology and sociology. For a brief example of a statement of this distinction, see Albert K. Cohen, "The Study of Social Disorganization and Deviant Behavior," p. 462, in *Sociology Today,* edited by Robert K. Merton, Leonard Broom, and Leonard S. Cottrell, Jr. (New York: Basic Books, Inc., 1959), pp. 461–464.

ascribed to a nation with a large number of soldiers and a record of hostile engagements.

Various dispositional terms reflect permanence and generality. It is important to differentiate between temporary and relatively specific dispositions and those which are more permanent and general. For example, personality characteristics may refer to the most stable and most general dispositions, attitudes to less permanent and less general dispositions, and opinions to the least permanent and least general dispositions. Translating some of these individual level dispositional terms to some group level terms, culture may refer to the most permanent and general patterns or dispositions, national character to less general and less permanent dispositions, and public or national opinion to the least permanent and least general dispositions.

That dispositional characteristics influence behavior is a tautological issue. How dispositions are acquired and how they change is a question of theoretical importance. A fairly well defined and confirmed "theory" (or if a more rigorous definition of theory is held, a well-defined "conceptualization") which attempts to explain how dispositions are acquired and how they change is learning theory. Dispositions are acquired largely as a result of past experience or learning. The conditions necessary for dispositions to be acquired are contained in certain statements of stimulus-response (S-R) learning theory.

Several stimulus-response psychologists have systematically applied the S-R conceptualizations to social behavior. Perhaps the most well-known work in this area is John Dollard's and Neal E. Miller's *Social Learning and Imitation,* in which an account was given, consistent with S-R theory, of the process of socialization or learning from others. Earlier, Dollard used learning theory to explore some facets of Negro-White relationships in the South in his *Caste and Class in a Southern Town.* Then came the theoretical contribution of *Frustration and Aggression* by Dollard, Miller, Doob, Mowrer, and Sears. John M. W. Whiting and Irvin L. Child have attempted an S-R explanation of cross-cultural differences in their *Child Training and Personality.* B. F. Skinner took his theories out of the laboratory for an analysis of social behavior, in his *Science and Human Behavior*. David C. McClelland, although less concerned with an S-R explanation, has used the disposition—the need to achieve—to explain the phenomena of economic development. Donald T. Campbell has recently offered a statement of integration between the concepts of the S-R psychologists, the *Gestalt* psychologists, the social psychologists, and others who have used psychological notions in their work.[7] Other well-known social scientists have used some form of learning theory in their works.[8]

Most systematic attempts to utilize learning or other psychological theories to explain social phenomena or behavior have been by psychologists. Although the works of the above-mentioned psychologists are known to many social scientists, few social scientists have explicitly and systematically exploited these psychological concepts and propositions. Perhaps lack of psychology in social science is due to a bewildering array of different psychological conceptualizations. As it turns out, social scientists are generally the recipients of cognitive psychology, perhaps because cognitive language fits common forms of expression. Typically, interpretations of social survey data include references to "perceptions," "images," "frames of reference," "cognitive arrangements," and the like.

7. The full citations of these works are: Neal E. Miller and John Dollard, *Social Learning and Imitation* (New Haven: Yale University Press, 1941). John Dollard, *Caste and Class in a Southern Town* (Garden City, N.Y.: Doubleday, 1949). John Dollard, Neal E. Miller, Leonard W. Doob, O. H. Mowrer, and Robert R. Sears, *Frustration and Aggression* (New Haven: Yale University Press, 1939). John M. W. Whiting and Irvin L. Child, *Child Training and Personality* (New Haven: Yale University Press, 1953). B. F. Skinner, *Science and Human Behavior* (New York: The Macmillan Co., 1953). David C. McClelland, *The Achieving Society* (Princeton, N.J.: D. Van Nostrand Co., 1961). Campbell, *op. cit.*

8. Several years ago a prominent psychologist offered "learning theory" to political scientists at a time when the political science curriculum at one university was undergoing examination. See Charles E. Osgood, "Behavior Theory and the Social Sciences" in *Approaches to the Study of Politics*, edited by Roland Young (Evanston, Ill.: Northwestern University Press, 1958), pp. 217–244.

Even if a decision is made to use S-R psychology and not cognitive psychology for explanations of social behavior,[9] there is still a possible problem of deciding which modifications of the theory to use. Will it be the reinforcement theory of Clark L. Hull, the contiguity theory of E. R. Guthrie, or certain modifications of these theories proposed by O. H. Mowrer and others?[10] The crude facts of social science, especially facts involving behavior of governments, perhaps do not require sophisticated or refined theory. A crude or unrefined learning theory, not useful in the laboratory, may be of great utility in piecing together some scattered knowledge of social behavior, particularly when that behavior relates to nations, counties, or cities. A social scientist can be outfitted with a general theory of behavior if he takes some core elements of basic S-R theory and its amendments.

Some major, but here unrefined, propositions or principles of S-R learning theory which seem to have a good deal of relevance to social and political behavior are the following:[11]

Stimulus Strength. The more distinct or intense the stimuli, the more rapid the learning; that is, habit patterns will be estab-

9. The differences between stimulus-response psychology and cognitive or Gestalt psychology are avoided here. Two points of difference are: (1) cognitive psychologists tend to emphasize perceptive processes as intervening variables between the stimulus and response; whereas S-R psychologists tend to treat perception as a response; and (2) cognitive psychologists emphasize the *present* field or situation of the individual; whereas S-R psychologists tend to be more concerned with past experiences of the individual. Some would argue that it is impossible to make sense of human behavior without the notion of cognitive processes as intervening variables.

10. For a statement of the theoretical differences and refinements in S-R theory see William W. Lambert, "Stimulus-Response Contiguity and Reinforcement Theory in Social Psychology" in *Handbook of Social Psychology*, Vol. I, edited by Gardner Lindzey (Reading, Mass.: Addison-Wesley, 1954), pp. 57–90.

11. For introductory but thorough statements of learning theory see, R. Bugelski, *The Psychology of Learning* (New York: Henry Holt, 1956) and John Deese, *The Psychology of Learning* (New York: McGraw-Hill, 1952). There are numerous texts which present the propositions of learning theory. For a statement of learning theory for political scientists, see Osgood, *op. cit.* A thorough statement of all schools of learning is Ernest R. Hilgard, *Theories of Learning* (New York: Appleton-Century-Crofts, 1956).

lished with fewer associations of the stimulus with the response and with less intense rewards than would be necessary to establish a habit pattern if the stimuli were less distinct and intense.

Contiguity. The response must accompany or follow the stimulus in a relatively short period of time (and the reinforcer must follow the response in a relatively short period of time).

Reinforcement. Rewards, or a set of events associated with a particular response, tend to increase the likelihood of that response occurring again under similar circumstances. Punishment, or a set of events associated with a particular response, tend to decrease the likelihood of that response occurring again under similar circumstances.[12]

1. Learned Reinforcers or Secondary Reinforcers. Stimuli or events, when associated with other rewards, tend to become, in and of themselves, rewards or reinforcers. Most of what is rewarding in a social sense is learned (approval, achievement, saving, imitation of others).

2. Habit Strength. Learning or the strength of a habit is a function of the frequency, the contiguity, and the intensity of the reinforcers.

Generalization and Discrimination. Learned responses are generalized to similar stimuli if responses to similar, but not the same stimuli, are reinforced. Discrimination between relatively similar stimuli is learned if responses to similar but not the same stimuli are not reinforced.

1. In the first stages of learning the responses are general, or similar stimuli will elicit similar responses.

2. The learning gradient is steeper, or learning is more rapid, if the responses are punished rather than reinforced.

Extinction. Learned responses or habits which are either not

12. What is a reward and what is a punishment is a bit problematical. For a discussion of "primary and secondary" rewards and punishments, and for a statement on the problem of the circularity of the definitions of rewards and punishments, see Kenneth Spence, *Behavior Theory and Conditioning* (New Haven: Yale University Press, 1956).

reinforced or are followed by punishing events are extinguished.[13]

A Psychological Definition of Political Integration. Political integration is a group level dispositional term. The term seems to be applied to at least two general categories of behavior: (a) when certain stimuli are responded to in roughly the same way by a "significant" number (possibly a majority) of people and (b) when collectivities of people respond to each other as relevant stimuli. In addition to both learning to respond to the same stimuli in roughly the same way and learning to respond to others as relevant stimuli, there would also be the disposition or learned response among at least the adult segments of the population to teach these response patterns to their children, to reward other members of the collectivity for responding in the same way, and to punish deviations. For example, the stimuli of the American flag and the words "freedom," the Fourth of July, or the President of the United States, are responded to in relatively the same way by most people in the United States. These stimuli bring different responses in Canada, or the same set of responses occur in Canada to a different set of stimuli. If people living within the borders of the United States and Canada responded alike to the same stimuli, then these "nations" would, of course, be indistinguishable except on maps.[14] Responding to almost the same stimuli may occur in small states where differences in stimulus-response patterns occur only on a narrow range of matters. The stimulus strength of the surrounding country is too strong for independent or distinct political stimuli to endure.

Not all the people in a highly politically integrated nation-state would have to respond to the same stimuli in roughly the same way. There could be substantial differences. Only certain

13. Whether any learned stimulus-response pattern is extinguished or merely submerged into the unconscious is a question of interest. Whether the human being is a storehouse with or without leaks and exits, however, is not crucial problem. What is important to this discussion is that certain specific stimulus-response patterns are no longer observed.

14. This, of course, is oversimplified. It may, however, be enough to be different only on maps.

kinds of individuals would have to respond so that the group level characteristic of being a "nation" would not appear as something else. Only a minority of the people of India respond in the same way to the same political stimuli. But although India is not highly politically integrated, it is considered a state. It may have enough people responding to some shared stimuli so that at least as far as relations between nations are concerned, it responds as a "state."

The other major psychological criterion of political integration is that people respond to each other as relevant on at least a selected number of variables. On some stimuli most individuals in a political system do not discriminate, even if only with respect to considering all capable citizens as potential soldiers.

The Negro in America, in this sense, is politically integrated even if only partially so. The Negro is expected to enjoy the Fourth of July, to pay taxes, to serve in the Army, and to abide by a good many of the laws of the government. On other political stimuli, the Negro, however, is differentially integrated. He is unable to vote or voice certain political opinions in certain subsections of American society. But being responded to as relevant with respect to some political matters, the American Negro now has generalized his political experiences and expects to be responded to as relevant on all political stimuli. Being responded to as a relevant and undifferentiated political stimulus may generalize to economic and social forms of interaction. Because of this tendency to generalize experiences, it is difficult to maintain discriminatory practices. If a person is treated as a "citizen" with respect to taxes and military service, he probably will generalize being treated as a citizen to other areas of political importance. "No taxation without representation" is a manifestation of generalizing certain political experiences to other political matters.

An example of psychological factors in political integration is the definition given by Deutsch and others of a security community.[15] A security community in the above terms could mean that

15. Karl W. Deutsch *et al., Political Community and the North Atlantic Area* (Princeton: Princeton University Press, 1957), pp. 3–9.

the people, or leaders, respond to defense related stimuli in a mutually learned way and respond to each other as relevant stimuli. The stimuli of the security community may be explicitly defined in a treaty arrangement such as NATO, or may have evolved as a result of past experiences of responding in a mutual way, such as may be the case with the United States and Canada. Leaders in the various countries of a security community have learned to regard each other as relevant considerations on certain questions. American action against Cuba in 1963 was a source of frustration for the United States' allies who apparently thought that they should have been responded to as relevant stimuli when the question of Russian missiles became an American issue.

The Spill-Over Theory of Political Integration and Cooperation

Research was conducted to test the proposition of E. Haas[16] that treaties beget more treaties between nations. On the local level the spill-over theory of international relations would direct that the greater the number of inter-governmental agreements, the more likely further agreements between the governmental units would occur. Specifically, local governments with agreements on the mutual use of school facilities and libraries would be more likely to have agreements with respect to the mutual use of police facilities than would local governments who had only one agreement. To test this hypothesis, the total number of inter-governmental agreements in the Philadelphia metropolitan area were totaled and the relationship hypothesized that most of the agreements would be found among those governmental units, physically contiguous, with several agreements; and a large number of governmental units would have none or only one agreement.[17] Thus, an expected number of agreements was calculated, and data

16. Ernst Haas, *The Uniting of Europe* (Stanford: Stanford University Press, 1958).

17. For a report on this research, see, Toscano, Chapter 4 in this volume.

were examined to determine if there was a statistically significant aggregation of agreements among high agreeing governmental units.

The spill-over theory quite obviously involves some learning theory principles. One aspect of learning theory in the spill-over theory is that frequency of association or reinforcement leads to habit strength. A number of trials with intergovernmental agreements should contribute to a general pattern of making agreements. The other aspect of learning theory involved in the spill-over theory is the process of generalization. Thus, negotiating agreements for mutual use of fire protection facilities should generalize to similar stimuli, such as mutual use of police facilities, and then to less similar stimuli, such as library facilities. The greater the similarity in function, the greater should be the generalization or spill-over. The spill-over theory involves, then, two principles of learning theory, that of frequency of association and that of generalization of stimuli. The first principle was tested. The second, the generalization of stimuli (which would predict that agreements on more similar governmental functions, such as police and fire, would be more likely than agreements on less similar functions, such as police and schools) was not directly tested in the report mentioned above.

The spill-over theory has its common-sense counterpart in predictions that tariff agreements will establish a response pattern which will generalize to broader economic agreements and that economic agreements will further establish a response pattern which will generalize to political agreements. Small inter-governmental interactions would be followed by larger and broader ones. Agreeing to beat a mutual enemy should generalize to agreeing to mutual activities to keep the peace.

Data on intergovernmental agreements in the Philadelphia metropolitan area showed an indifference relationship for the spill-over theory in terms of number of agreements. Agreements were scattered and did not follow a pattern of being concentrated among governments with a large number of agreements.

Without important distinctions, social science theory retains the comfort of having a stock of plausible propositions for every situation, including negating ones. The plausible explanation that interaction leads to favorable attitudes is contradicted by the explanatory observation that familiarity breeds contempt. The distinction that was not used in the research on intergovernmental agreements in the Philadelphia metropolitan area was the important one of whether the agreements were rewarding, non-rewarding, or punishing. If these data had been included in the research (a simple questionnaire might have been sufficient), then perhaps the spill-over theory would have been confirmed. Of course, the capability for agreements, as limited by laws and by geography, has to be calculated into the research design.

The Rational Calculation of Payoffs for Political Cooperation. Discussions about "rationality" probably cause some uneasiness among social scientists. Nonetheless, developing "rationality schemes" to gain insights into human behavior has been found useful in providing some interesting hypotheses about political integration.[18]

Individual goals are not "rational," but techniques or means selected to obtain given goals can be evaluated as either inhibiting or facilitating achievement of goals. The idea that other goals are affected by selecting a course of action for a particular goal is summarized in the notion of "cost." Rationality, then, involves some statement about what means would maximize the chances of achieving a goal at a minimum "cost."

Calculating alternative costs of given courses of action in the context of certain stated goals is one thing. Projecting a system of costs and goals on a population and then using that system of costs and goals to explain and predict behavior is another. It is obvious that a system of rationally calculating costs and goals, when projected on a population, will enable explanations of behavior only in certain cases and only to a certain degree. Thus, the phenomenon of rationally calculating payoffs and costs from alternative courses of action must also be explained. Rational

18. See Deutsch, Chapter 6 in this volume.

behavior requires explanation. The facts that some people are "rational" and that, in a large population, all modes of behavior other than rational behavior may cancel each other out do not help to explain rational behavior.

It happens that behavior resulting from rationally calculating rewards fits, even though not tightly, with learning theory. The simple proposition underlying any system of rational calculation of payoffs is that changes in reward patterns will significantly alter human behavior—that habits can be changed or new habits will be sought if older habits are not rewarded or are punished. This is a directive from the reinforcement principle of stimulus-response learning theory. There is an important complication. Not only do people learn what is desirable, what is good, and what is rewarding, but they also learn specific habits on how to achieve what is desirable, how to do good, and how to get rewarded. Changing these habits could be an important factor in rationally calculated costs.

Cooperation, alliances, and mergers between political communities—instances of political integration—can be explained as the result of rational calculation of payoffs or rewards.[19] Integrating certain minority groups in a society could, for example, be accomplished by manipulating the reward structure. If the American Negro is given things which he has learned are rewarding, such as higher education, higher income, and higher social status, then habits of criminality will disappear; and he will behave in a middle class manner. If the anti-Negro white is confronted with business losses for continuing discriminatory practices, he may learn to change his habits and perhaps to advertise for Negro customers.

Of course, there will be wide individual differences in the impact changes in rewards can have on changes in beliefs and behavior. These differences depend on how strongly certain behavior patterns have been established as well as on how well a population has been conditioned to accept authority for beliefs,

19. *Ibid.*

to change belief patterns, or to be tenacious in holding to the content of beliefs. It may be that the White Citizens Council member would rather die than change his beliefs and habits with respect to Negroes. There may be other members of White Citizens Councils who will alter their behavior for a 2 per cent increase in profits.

There are some interesting avenues of speculation, fostered by an analysis of rational calculation of payoffs, with relevance to the general question of political integration. What do suburban leaders gain by keeping their political boundaries and institutions intact? What does the city resident gain by moving to the suburb? Moving to the suburb, for example, can be analyzed as a rather rational calculation on the part of middle class parents to provide a middle class education for their children. The costs of providing a private school equivalent of a public school suburban education could be used as a standard in calculating the gains of buying a house in the suburbs.

What are the benefits and costs of political separation? Leaders of suburban communities have a set of optional strategies to keep out "undesirable" elements. By excluding "undesirable" residents, certain suburban communities can operate with substantially lower welfare and police expenditures per capita than the central city. Keeping up the price of entrance to the suburb by manipulating real estate prices often means that the suburbs can devote most local revenue to the highly valued educational program.

What is the price any nation would have to receive in order to surrender some of its sovereignty? How much of an increase in trade, how large a rate of growth in the national product is worth the cost of casting decisions on tariff rates into the hands of a less predictable, and possibly unfriendly, international body?

These questions are one way of approaching the problem of political integration. This approach involves strength of habits and learned patterns of rewards. Rational calculation of rewards or payoffs, although not capable of giving data on who has learned what habits, is a means of analysis that is associated with some propositions of learning theory.

Shared Values and Expectations in Political Integration.[20] A persistent hypothesis concerning political integration is that shared or mutual values or value systems ease the way for greater political integration or cooperation. Contradicting this hypothesis is the adage that "politics make strange bedfellows." According to this hypothesis, viewed in the perspective of S-R learning theory, shared values reflect similarity in conditioning and similarity in conditioning facilitates a mutual transfer of stimuli or symbols. If all nations were paired on the basis of similarity in what is valued, then this hypothesis would predict that greater political integration in terms of tariff agreements, treaties, shared decision-making institutions, avoidance of war, and the like should obtain among the more similar nations. More specifically, in so far as socio-economic characteristics may indicate similarity in conditioning, nations with similar socio-economic status should also have a greater degree of political integration with each other in comparison to nations which are dissimilar in socio-economic characteristics.

Research in the Philadelphia metropolitan area was conducted to test the relationship between similarities-dissimilarities in socio-economic characteristics and voting patterns between communities and number and kind of intergovernmental agreements. Of the 380 physically contiguous community pairs, there were no significant differences in intergovernmental agreements between communities with more similar socio-economic status and more

20. The term "values" as used in this section differs from the operationally stated normative definition set forth by Philip E. Jacob in his chapter, "The Influence of Values in Political Integration." The reason for this divergence is that a learning theory interpretation of Jacob's definition, although in my opinion possible, would involve complexities I wish to avoid. My use of value is "what is desired." Learning theory should be capable of explaining the conditions in which people make normative statements, such as "This is right" and "It is our duty." Jacob's definition, for reasons not given here, is more in line with cognitive psychology. A definition of value as "What is desired" fits more comfortably with learning theory.

similar voting patterns.[21] The one relationship that did show up was that similarity in both socio-economic characteristics and political or voting patterns was significantly related to school agreements.

The data both on the intra-national and international governmental levels seems highly chaotic. Historically, Christian nation fought against Christian nation. Historically, relationships between the United States and Great Britain have been fraught with wars and antagonisms. The plausibility of the hypothesis that a greater similarity in values leads to political integration, involves the propositions that the greater the similarity in past conditioning, the greater the probability (a) that predictability of mutual behavior will be high (a factor which leads to trust), (b) that stimuli from individuals in one political grouping will be meaningful or understood by individuals in the other political grouping, and (c) that one nation will not do something that the other nation violently dislikes. These plausible propositions are at least not inconsistent with the propositions of learning theory. But the S-R theory of acquiring behavior dispositions also prompts some cautions.

First, the degree to which values and goals are shared does not

21. Miss Johanna Turich, a senior student of mine, examined the relationship between similarity in values, as reflected both in similarity in socio-economic status and in presidential voting, and political integration. All physically contiguous pairs of communities in Delaware, Bucks, and Montgomery counties in the Philadelphia area were ranked according to similarity in socio-economic status and in presidential voting, 1948–1960. The general hypothesis was that the greater the similarity in voting and socio-economic status, the greater the likelihood of intergovernmental agreements. A social rank scale, developed by the Fels Institute of State and Local Government, along the lines suggested in Eshref Shevky and Wendell Bell, *Social Area Analysis* (Stanford: Stanford University Press, 1955), was used to construct the socio-economic similarity-dissimilarity scale. She compiled her own data for the similarity-dissimilarity scale based on election returns for President. School agreements were found to be significantly related to both similarity in socio-economic status and voting (Chi square at significance level of .05). There were no other significant relationships between either the number or type (police, sewer, library) of intergovernmental agreements and similarity in socio-economic status and in voting. This senior thesis is on deposit at the Fels Institute of State and Local Government.

indicate the degree to which the habits or means are shared. Learning what is desirable[22] and how to achieve or acquire what is desirable should be distinguished. Men of good will, seeing that ends are shared, find it strange that differences do not dissolve. In certain contexts, this distinction between habit ends and habit means is quite obvious, as is the case of talking about "peace" with the communists. In other contexts, this distinction is slighted. The desirability of obtaining and having money, for example, is valued widely in the United States. This end generally cuts across social, ethnic, and occupational differences. But habits of acquiring money are obviously not shared. For some groups, outright robbery is both a well-known and legitimate means. For other groups, business enterprise is the preferred means. In the same sense, "economic independence," as accepted by the median German and the median Frenchman, may be highly similar. For the median German, obeying the law and working hard may be the way to acquire "economic independence." For the median Frenchman, the same end may be attained by not paying taxes and being as occupationally unencumbered as possible.

Second, shared values may be the result of different conditioning. This is the case with shared ends among different socioeconomic classes in America. Thus, learning to respect property of others may have been learned by Mr. A through a set of rather direct rewards. Mr. B, however, may have learned not to damage property because of a rather harsh set of punishments. Mr. C learned not to damage or take property of others because of the learned drive to please his mother and father. The same set of stimuli occurs, damage to property, and all three men will respond in the same way—showing respect for property. Do they

22. This is the notion of incentive motivation. In social psychological terms, it would be knowledge (used broadly) about the desirability of ends. See Ernest R. Hilgard, *op. cit.*, pp. 128–136, for a discussion of Clark L. Hull's notions and pp. 414–420 for some remarks on Kenneth Spence's ideas. For the relevance of this notion in the social sciences, see Campbell, *op. cit.* pp. 135–149.

share values? If only a snapshot is taken of that society, as in a national sample, it might be concluded that values are shared. But the socialization process of acquiring these values was quite different.

Behaving toward stimuli may indicate similarity in values. But each manifestation of behavior in the context of these values may have different implications for future responses, depending on the type of conditioning that established the response. Thus, Nation A may choose to reward another nation for instituting reforms Nation A wants. Nation B, wanting the same reforms as Nation A, may punish another nation for not making these reforms.

Learning theory may be able to refine our propositions concerning the importance of shared values in political integration. It points to the process by which these values are acquired and requires more than satisfaction with just noting that values are shared.

The Political Integration of Elites. Established patterns of social behavior reward people differently not only in quantity but also in kind. One set of individuals with relatively high stakes in an established pattern of social interaction is that of political, economic, and social leaders. Collectively, and roughly, this category of individuals will here be referred to as an elite. The notion of elite involves a persistent pattern of behavior, including that of recruitment, in which elite members in certain contexts are responded to *as if* such responses were rewarding. The business executive, often without regard to actual consequences, will be responded to on certain stimuli and by certain people as if such a response would be rewarding or as if not responding in a specific manner would be punishing. This is a simplified statement of the complex referrents of the concept of "elite." But this simplified notion of elite can be useful for an interpretation of some of the activities of the elite in political integration.

In addition to the learned reward acquired by non-elite individuals for responding to an elite stimulus, members of elites have also acquired a learned reward or drive to respond *as* an elite. Thus, being a politician and responding as one is in itself rewarding. Having politicians around is also rewarding. This learned drive or reward is similar to the concept of imitation.[23] As a child learns to imitate and the imitative behavior is reinforced, he generalizes the response of imitation to the point that imitation becomes a reward in and of itself, irrespective of the outcomes of the imitative response. In much the same manner, learning to respond to certain individuals as members of the elite—given a set of elite symbols or stimuli—is in and of itself rewarding to both elite members and some non-elite segments of the population. This fact may explain the sometimes "irrational" nature of the stake in the *status quo*. Being a member of the elite may actually deprive the person of other goals or may even lead to his destruction. But cases of maintaining older learned patterns of reward in the face of extinction are well known.

Deutsch and others have found that political integration seems to accompany a rapid change, a circulation, or a broadening of the elite in a society.[24] What probably happens in the case of a broadening of the elite is that the non-members of the elite begin to lose the learned drive to respond to a certain segment of the elite or to a particular elite stimulus. Hereditary symbols of the elite are effective as long as the population does not generalize exceptions to this rule. But once people learn that behaving as a member of the elite is largely a matter of acquiring certain symbols, then the relevance of the elite symbols is changed. The population may even be able to generalize their drive of responding to an elite or to authority across governmental lines.

If the population has generalized its elite response outside of a particular governmental boundary, it is obvious that the members of the local elite may, nonetheless, continue to respond as if they still were the most important elite stimuli. The local-cosmopolitan scales measure this generalization to broader cate-

23. Miller and Dollard, *op. cit.*
24. Deutsch *et al., op. cit.,* pp. 53–54 and pp. 148–149.

gories of the elite.[25] A person whose score places him at the cosmopolitan end of the scale would, among other things, have more interest in national than in local issues and follow national standards rather than local customs. When this generalization to national elites happens, many forms of local government may continue. Examples of this in local governments throughout the United States are plentiful. The form of making decisions on the part of local politicians remains the same even though no one attends meetings and there seems to be little interest in what is going on.

The broadening of the elite then may be the result of generalization of elite stimuli. It may also result from a lack of rewards for continuing to respond to the established elite. The first possibility should engender conditions for political integration at a different level. The second possibility should contribute to stopping or extinguishing responses to particular stimuli and may precipitate political disintegration. If generalization occurs, the former elite may be replaced by another elite. Anarchism would occur if the learned pattern or secondary reward of responding to any elite were extinguished, and there were no effective or rewarding elite stimuli.

Following some of the same directives of learning theory, there may be an increased orientation to local and visible elites if there has been a drastic change in the established national elites, whether through invasion, death, revolution, or peaceable but rapid withdrawal (colonial powers). The establishment of new elite stimuli would be facilitated by the personal presence of local leaders who would be the most salient stimuli. Further, one would predict that the symbols of the former elite would contribute to the legitimacy of the new elite.

Political Integration and Political Identification. An indicator of the degree of political integration is the proportion of people

25. See for example William M. Dobriner, "Local and Cosmopolitan as Contemporary Suburban Character Types," in *The Suburban Community* edited by William M. Dobriner (New York: G. P. Putnam's Sons, 1958), pp. 132–143.

verbally "identifying" with certain political symbols. "Identification" may be defined as a learned pattern to respond to one set of stimuli as the most relevant for a given range of activities and to ignore significant competing stimuli for that range of activities. A person "belongs" exclusively to one set of ethnic, religious, or national stimuli. Other competing stimuli will be considered of little importance. Expressions of intensity and permanency of political indentification could further indicate the degree of political integration. Whether or not some group of people has the characteristic of nationhood could then be determined by the number, the intensity, and the durability of individual statements of identifications of being German, French, or American. Political identifications, which endure serious deprivations may becloud the proposition that political integration is the result of shared mutual stimuli eliciting roughly similar responses.

This section will briefly present (1) a psychological interpretation of the phenomenon of political identification, (2) the relationships between political identifications and political stability, and (3) an analysis of the processes of establishing, strengthening, changing, and extinguishing political identifications.

The psychology of political identification. In the language of learning psychology, political identification is a learned drive. It is again similar to the description of "model" learning discussed by Miller and Dollard.[26] After the response of imitation is rewarded for a period of time, responding in an imitative way or responding to "models" becomes in itself a reward. Identification becomes a learned drive in much the same manner. But identifications are learned largely as a result of responding to models, or largely as a result of political socialization. The child is told that responding as an American is a desirable thing. He learns that "being an American" is in itself a reward. He must later find that the predictions of his instructors in social learning are true.

If a substantial portion of the population living within a po-

26. Miller and Dollard, *op. cit.*

litical boundary has learned that political identification is rewarding or has a learned pattern to be politically identified with a specific set of political stimuli, then this collectivity of people could be called a political community. Although learned drives may be generalized, such as the learned drive to imitate, political identifications are usually specific or discrete. It is not to governments in general that the learned reward of identification applies, but rather to some specific governments. It is permissible for an American to identify with his city, his state, his region; but generally it is not permissible for him to identify with more than one national government. There is no reason why any individual may not have multiple political identifications at the same level. This is apparent in cases of residents of several cities. There is an identification as a San Franciscan and as a New Yorker. It just happens that such multiple identifications at the national level are not rewarded and are likely to be punished by symbolic sanctions of disapproval. Certain multiple national identifications, although discouraged by law and perhaps slightly punished by disapproval, are tolerated in the United States such as Jews with Israel, Irish with Ireland, or Italians with Italy. For most Americans these are nonpunishing governmental stimuli. There is greater disapproval for identifying with other governmental stimuli which are punishing or threatening. Although it is tolerated that an American Norwegian can identify with Norway, an American Russian generally is not allowed the same degree of freedom in expressions of identification.

The response of political identification can be very restrictive, as is the case when the term "patriotism" is used, or relatively general, as when the term "internationalist" is used. In spite of the seeming strict demands for political identification to be restricted to one set of national stimuli, most countries realize that the drive to have a "nationality" is generalized enough so that the response of identifying can be transferred from one set of stimuli to another by a simple indication of the willingness to do so. Immigrants to the United States seemed to have had little difficulty in this conversion process. In particular, immigrants who never were substantially rewarded for their older and more specific identifications are usually eager to try a different set of stimuli. This perhaps is not the case with the immigrants who lost wealth and status after the upheavals of World War II. One group remembers starvation and uncertainty; the other remembers castles and parties. One group has substituted a less rewarding set of political stimuli for generally more rewarding stimuli. The other group may be more interested in restoring the older and more rewarding stimuli.

Political Identification and Political Stability. As loyalty to the family develops as a function of early, distinct, and rather intense rewards and results in an identification with the family intense enough to withstand some rather serious deprivations, so a newly formed nation must be able to provide sufficient and early rewards in order that it may also continue to have the loyalty of its citizens in times of crisis. When a nation or a new regime is first formed, the citizens will be attuned to the particular rewards and punishments emanating from association with the new government or state. If these rewards are not forthcoming, there may be revolutions, riots, and secessions. The newly formed American state lost its British sympathizers, resorted to force to put down the Whiskey Rebellion in 1794, experienced the embarrassment of the Aaron Burr episode, listened to the phrases of secession at the Hartford Conventions, and finally suffered *de facto* dissolution during the Civil War. Through the rewards of abundant land and resources, through a relatively dramatic but successful process of industrialization,[27] and through sporadic punishments of dissenters, the orientation or disposition to respond to direct, visible, and rather material rewards was gradually replaced by the disposition to respond to American governmental stimuli as if they were rewarding.

27. For a general discussion of the relationship of wealth to the American "character," see David M. Potter, *People of Plenty* (Chicago: University of Chicago Press, 1954).

A misleading assumption is that experiences of any past generation are also the experiences of all or any subsequent generations. If the experiences of past generations are to be taken as relevant to the behavior of any succeeding generation, proof of the impact of those experiences on behavior and crucially on behavior related to the socialization processes must be offered. Of prime importance is how people learn to change their socializing behavior and why they feel it is important to instruct others, particularly the young, that they should behave as if they had directly experienced certain events themselves. Past political events are taught to others. Past political events are stored in the physical environment, such as in books, records, buildings, movies, and the like. The preservation of past experiences in the physical environment may indicate that some people had a message to tell. These stored physical stimuli must be responded to in a certain way in order for the experience to be relevant to other generations. Oral instruction by elders or others in the schools, churches, and youth groups continually instruct new generations in the meaning of this physically stored heritage.

Learning to respond to governmental stimuli *as if* such a response would be rewarding or *not* to respond in a manner known to be inconsistent with certain governmental directives *as if* such a response would be punished is a psychological definition of political stability. S. M. Lipset's proposition that effective governments become legitimate governments is a more familiar formulation of the principle of reinforcement in political science.[28] A new government, state, or regime must, in order to endure, reward the population and such rewards must be general enough to preclude the development of large-scale dissident groups. It must, in short, produce the goods. It must have the will and the capabilities to avert or alleviate disasters, to be associated with improving material conditions, or to relieve the miseries of those who know they are deprived. After a period of "effectiveness,"

28. Seymour Martin Lipset, *Political Man* (Garden City, N.Y.: Doubleday, 1960), pp. 45–96.

the government will become legitimate. Legitimacy in learning theory language would be the widespread presence of a learned drive to respond to the government as if such a response were rewarding, irrespective of the rewards that the government is, in fact, able to produce. Legitimacy may also in part be the result of the population's avoiding certain forms of behavior as if that behavior would be punished, again irrespective of the punishments or deprivations that the government as a matter of fact is able to produce. The statement, "This is the law, and we must obey it whether we like it or not," is a manifestation of this learned disposition of political identification, political legitimacy, and thus political stability. A politically stable and politically legitimate government, then, will appear effective and will be responded to as if effective, despite deprivations and *de facto* political weakness.

Although a legitimate, and thus politically stable country, may be able to maintain a high level of political identification among its population in spite of consistent and rather severe deprivations, certain rewards must be forthcoming, even if such rewards are a product of accident. Whether the government has anything to do with the rewards may be irrelevant. It is probably enough that the government is associated with the rewards. An example of this is the impact of prosperity recession cycles, occurring outside of governmental control for most of American history, on the legitimacy of the party in power as indicated by election results. Since governmental stimuli are so pervasive, any general improvement may reinforce political identification at least with the most salient form or level of government. Nonetheless, certain political or governmental stimuli will have to be present before changes in political habits will occur. One condition necessary for governmental change is the presence of political or governmental stimuli in frustrating situations. This, for example, is not the case in our metropolitan areas. The motorist, frustrated by slow-moving traffic, is not presented with governmental stimuli that would connect the frustration with the problem of local governmental coordination. To him, it is largely an engineering problem, not a problem of governmental change.

The foregoing should not imply, however, that only rich countries can be politically integrated or stable. It happens that richer countries generally are more politically stable; and higher per capita income does, in fact, seem to relate to political integration and stability.[29] The use of threat stimuli will have an effect on the political integration of a nation. War may tend to solidify nations, or so some have believed. Loss of a great war may rock the foundations of stability. But just as promises need from time to time to be met, so threats need fulfillment. The greater the number of times a nation has undergone threat stimuli without the predicted results, the greater the intensity of threat stimuli which may be needed on subsequent occasions. Threat stimuli, in other words, begin to lose their credibility. Re-occurring crises should gradually elicit less anxiety.[30]

In addition to rewarding complying or identifying behavior, there is the option open to poorer countries of punishing non-integrative behavior. Learning to behave toward political stimuli as if such behavior will be rewarding may differ in many respects from learning to behave toward certain stimuli as if such behavior will be punishing. For one thing, the learning curve will be steeper. It will take fewer punishments to wipe out non-integrative behavior than it will take rewards to establish integrative behavior. Punishment can be a solution to imminent possibilities of national dissolution. For newly constituted governments, without minimum learned habits of integration and with limited economic capacity, punishments for independence movements probably will have to be relied on. It also seems easier to mobilize punishment forces, for the process of punishment appears to be a more readily available and generally understood device

29. Lipset, *Ibid.*

30. This could be checked by an analysis of anxiety content in newspaper editorials from the Korean War to the present. It could be hypothesized that at least newspaper men have learned to discriminate threat stimuli and have learned to control their fears. There should be a reduction in the proportion of anxiety content with each passing of a crisis. It might be possible to arrive at a learning curve of crisis stimuli.

than that of reward. For political leaders, punishment may produce immediate results, even if those results lead to more remote but more frightening consequences.

The problem of using punishments to establish new or alter old political identifying behavior is that the punisher is also the frustrator. And given the familiar frustration-aggression hypothesis, punishing governments will also be targets of hostility and direct attacks. The government may find that it has to rely on long-term commitments to punish while only a few appreciate the nobility of its motives. This situation, then, should engender for both parties—government and people—further frustrations and aggressions. But punishments may still lead to long-term political stability if the punishments are coupled with a propaganda campaign to keep the frustrating stimuli distinct from general governmental stimuli. If the party is the rewarding agency and the government or secret police the frustrating agency, then aggression should be directed toward the secret police or government and not the party. Indeed, from time to time, the party or those who wish to establish their legitimacy may even participate in attacks on these punishing agencies. Developing local scapegoats is a well-known characteristic of punishment-oriented governments. But often these will be tangible, local scapegoats. International scapegoats are often of temporary use in directing and focusing aggressions.

In addition to focusing all punishments on a distinct set of political stimuli and thus having aggressions directed toward one set of political symbols, there is the possibility of keeping the punishing stimuli so diffuse that the population remains confused about the source of its frustrations. In highly fragmented political systems, substantial punishments can be used without embarrassment of direct attack. The President can blame the Congress, and Congress can say that the Supreme Court has so ruled. Congress can make references to the states and to lack of leadership in the White House. The result may be that aggression is shared and is not directed toward a particular political institution, with the result that the probability of a change in any one political institution is reduced. This is one function served by keeping authority and responsibility neither clear nor commensurate.

Changes in Political Identifications. Changes in political identifications will follow shifts, severe or incremental, in the social reward pattern, or alterations in governmental stimuli. Of course, socialization processes may be vigorous enough so that unfulfilled promises of rewards or constant deprivations may have little noticeable impact on the strength of political loyalties. Deprivations may reinforce existing patterns of identification. Indeed one of the well-known insights into this process is the despot's use of fabricated outside threats to enhance his legitimacy, particularly as he fails to produce results or positive rewards at home.

There are, nonetheless, millions of people in the world today who have changed their political identifications one or more times, both with respect to particular nation-states as well as with respect to political identifications with types of government, political parties, or political ideologies. Severe deprivations or particularly large-scale displacements of older reward patterns are usually followed by shifts in political identifications. Crop failures, the collapse of governments after wars, and depressions have been followed by migrations out and attempts at revolutions from within. The degree of a country's political integration may be indicated by the number of applications for emigration, by applications for foreign employment, or by statements to the effect that personal satisfactions and hopes would be better served in another country. It is further significant that the two historical events which explain a major part of the voting patterns in the United States today were both highly depriving—or punishing—circumstances the Civil War and the Great Depression. And both these events seem to be more important in those areas which suffered the greater deprivation—the Southern states and urban areas. It is further significant that attempts at political integration on a large scale followed the devastations of the World Wars—the League of

Nations and the United Nations both having emerged after the wars.

Consistent, severe, and widespread deprivations, then, serve as important conditioners for changes in political identifications. This is a result perhaps of the fact that punishing or depriving stimuli tend to be more salient than rewarding stimuli. This saliency of punishing stimuli or situations may be a function of the fact that many people compete to be associated with improving conditions or rewarding situations and that, in times of failure, all the heads claiming credit disappear.[31]

The amount of change resulting from deprivations should be a function of (a) the severity of the punishment or deprivation, (b) the proportion of the population who are relatively more deprived, and (c) the ease with which the deprived groups can communicate and reward each other. The first point is somewhat obvious. It also involves how far people "fall," what they have learned to expect, and the degree to which the older political habits are ingrained. Thus during periods of economic crisis it should be expected that the very poor, such as peasants, will continue as before. It should be expected that segments of the population who have recently gained some status should be the least willing to change. Deutsch and others have noted that peasants tend to resist attempts at political integration.[32] Negro leaders are known for their resistance to attempts to change local governmental structure.

Learning theory also predicts that the relatively more deprived should be more willing to change their habits, for their older habits have not been reinforced. Lipset's analysis of the 1860 election returns shows that the vote for secession was greater in areas

31. This could be checked by an examination of the relative losses of the party in power at various levels of saliency in times of deprivations. Thus the gubernatorial incumbent's party should suffer the most in the gubernatorial contest and proportionately less at various local levels. It may also happen that the party holding the presidency should do worse in an election in times of deprivations than the party at local levels.

32. See Deutsch *et al., op. cit.,* pp. 105–110.

of relatively greater deprivation.[33] The vote in the 1860 presidential election shows a high proportion of electoral support for Breckenridge, the secessionist candidate, in counties containing relatively fewer slaves and stronger support for the traditional Democratic Party in counties having relatively greater numbers of slaves, presumably the richer counties. The more highly rewarded Southerners, even though perhaps more significantly threatened by the outcome of the election, were less willing to give up their older and more rewarding political habits.

The impact of deprivations depends on the degree of segregation among more highly deprived groups. Probably the most important form of segregation in changing political habits will be geographical. Geographical segregation provided excellent opportunities for exchange of political stimuli and face-to-face rewards for Southerners before the Civil War, for the farmers, who literally attacked authorities and took over local governments during the depression, for laborers in the cities, and for Negroes in residential ghettoes. To turn this statement about, the probability of political stability during periods of crisis will be related to how well mixed the deprived groups are both geographically and socially. Or still another way, political stability will be related to the difficulty the deprived lower classes, or poor, have in organizing. As is the case with most social science propositions, the opposite of this proposition has its degree of plausibility—the safety valve theory of federalism or governmental fragmentation. The safety valve notion states that if the dissatisfied, the disaffected, the disgruntled are confined to one or a few local governments, changes will be localized. Both competing propositions need to be more explicitly defined in order to determine amounts of change. Fragmented political systems fragment aggression, but they probably also facilitate the development of the aggression.

Although widespread deprivations have perhaps produced more dramatic examples of changes in political allegiances and although rewarding situations perhaps generally function to de-

33. Lipset, *op. cit.*, pp. 344–354.

velop embryonic or to reinforce older political identifications, knowledge of prospects to increase rewards may lead to changes in political identifications. In a certain sense, all changes in identifications result from some anticipation that other political stimuli may be rewarding. Possibilities of future rewards may, however, have little immediate impact on the strength of current political identifications. The probabilities of future rewards tend to add different stimuli to the pool of politically relevant stimuli. These different stimuli may in time result in different political identifications. The benefits of the Common Market, plus the possibilities of future economic gains, make the stimuli of Common Market institutions part of the political world of many Europeans. In time, this change in the world of political stimuli may lead to identifications with Europe.

Some conditions found by Deutsch and others to be important factors in political integration between nation-states include superior economic growth, at least in some countries, and expectations of joint economic rewards.[34] Diffused knowledge about the success of one country may prompt other countries to increased efforts to link their futures to countries of demonstrated success. Alliances, "cultural exchanges," participation in regularized consultation, and perhaps amalgamation of certain political institutions are examples of this behavior. This is the process of acquiring stimuli known to be rewarding to others. Incorporation of the stimuli of successful nations or peoples may be a way of obtaining these rewards. It also happens that the superior capabilities of one nation are the means of rewarding acts of friendship of other nations.

Outright imitation of a successful country or person is another result of the success of one nation or person. Changes in political behavior and political identification can be fostered by direct imitation. This obvious fact is reflected in statements of American political leaders to keep American economic growth high so that other nations will identify at least with the form of American political institutions.

34. Deutsch *et al.*, *op. cit.*, pp. 139–144.

It is possible that a lack of rewards or consistent punishments may completely extinguish the drive to identify politically. In most instances the drive is not extinguished, but the symbols or stimuli are changed. The learned drive to remain politically identified, once established, probably endures far beyond any identification with specific sets of identifying stimuli. It could be predicted, however, that punishments following a variety of different attempts to identify with specific sets of political stimuli would extinguish the learned reward or drive to identify with any political stimuli. This proposition may help explain the internationalist orientation of Jews, many of whom have been punished directly by a variety of governments and political systems or have been socially conditioned to fear political systems generally. Many groups that have either experienced punishments or have knowledge that others like them have been punished should develop internationalist orientations among at least some of the individual members of the group. Internationalism was the response of some Jews; attachment to a more secure set of political stimuli, a Jewish political state, was the response of others.

There are several other possible examples where learning theory could be applied to factors which are relevant to the processes of political integration. The propositions and concepts of learning theory contained in the spill-over theory, in the analysis of rational calculation of payoffs, in the concept of shared values, in the responses of political elites, and in the phenomenon of political identification were used to illustrate the central argument for the utility of learning theory in gleaning new insights into human behavior and in generalizing social science knowledge.

In speculative efforts, such as this, where the discipline of research is not operative, definitions are loose, and, consequently, most examples of data fit, but often fit unconvincingly. The examples presented were intended to illustrate some aspects of learning theory, however unrefined, underlying propositions about political integration. Using the propositions of one area of inquiry in a seemingly different area of inquiry demonstrates to some extent the similarities in concern, the transferability of language, and the interchangeability of research findings of all those concerned with behavior whether that of laboratory animals, of local governments, or of nations.

X

Models in the Study of Political Integration

Implicitly or explicitly, various models of the integrative process have been proposed in the analysis of this political phenomenon in this book and in other relevant literature in the social sciences. In Chapter 10, Henry Teune undertakes a systematic investigation of the uses and misuses of models employed in the study of political integration as well as in the social sciences generally. Firmly grounded in the philosophy of science literature, this chapter endeavors to clarify the various meanings of the term "model" as well as to provide the conceptual and methodological underpinnings for future studies of political integration employing models. Reviewing the various types of models and the functions served by models, his main contention is that while most models used in the social sciences are concepts, hypotheses, or generalizations they can, nevertheless, add to social science knowledge. This chapter, then, in the words of its author, "is an exercise in the clarification, or the explication, of a rather important methodological element in the study of political integration."

LITERATURE ON POLITICAL INTEGRATION RELIES HEAVILY ON "MODels." Various models suggested as applicable in discourses and research on political integration have included models of communications, models of rational strategies, models of decision-making, models to test distributions of intergovernmental agreements, models of biological functionalism, models of ideal political arrangements, and models for research.[1]

The complexity of the phenomenon of political integration, the difficulty of research, the long time spans of changes in integration have, among other things, contributed to a reliance on models for knowledge. It is not necessary to argue for the importance of understanding the processes of political integration to a generation of people who have experienced the horrors of disintegration—revolutions, governmental impotence, and the collapse of regimes. There is also little serious reservation about the significance of integrative behavior for empirical social or political theory. These felt needs for knowledge, in the face of practical difficulties of research, have promoted the use of models.

But are all of these models the same thing? Is there, in other words, a process common to all of the above-mentioned models? Even if the use of models entitles one to believe that their methodological import is unambiguous to most readers, what is the point in using models? What are the gains from using international relations as a model for explaining relations between local governments? Is the integration of ethnic groups just an analogy, not a model, for political integration of governments in a metropolitan area or for the formation of a united Europe?

This is an exercise in the clarification, or the explication, of a rather important methodological element in the study of political integration. What is said about models in the study of political integration applies to other areas of inquiry. Thus, models are discussed in a general context of social science inquiry.

It is the contention here that most models in social science are concepts (including statements of definition about what is "ideal"), hypotheses, or generalizations. There are two exceptions: (1) models of structural similarity between theories and (2) mathematical-logical models. These two types of models are discussed first. The first part of the chapter concludes with a pres-

1. These models, with the exception of a model of ideal political arrangements can be found in this volume.

entation of several models which could be simply described as concepts, hypotheses, or generalizations. The second part of the paper, "The Functions of Models," is an attempt to evaluate models as "more or less useful" in scientific discovery, in contributing to generalization, and in verification.

Nothing new will be said about the place of models in the structure of science. This contribution lies in the distinction between models as an aid to scientific discovery and models as part of scientific knowledge.[2]

Types of Models

The two meanings of "model" which are different from models as concepts, hypotheses, or scientific generalizations either refer to structural similarities between two or more theories or to structural similarities between an empirical theory and a mathematical or logical system.

Structural Similarity between Theories. Many theories share a similar form. When the structure or form of one theory is similar to the structure of another theory, the better known theory can be called a model for the less well-known theory. Apostel defines this: "Any subject using a system A that is neither directly nor indirectly interacting with a system B, to obtain information about the system B, is using A as a model for B."[3] The theory for the spread of diseases shares a similarity in structure with the theories concerning the spread of rumor. The structure of the laws concerning the passage of water through pipes tends to be isomorphic with the passage of electricity through wires. A hypothesis of economists is that the laws of population migration tend to be like the laws of gravitation. The storage capacity, combinatorial abilities, and communication facilities of computers

2. The distinctions used in this paper conform to Brodbeck's notions. May Brodbeck, "Models, Meaning, and Theories" in Llewellyn Gross (Ed.) *Symposium on Sociological Theory* (Evanston, Ill.: Row, Peterson, 1959), pp. 373–403. I thank Karl W. Deutsch of Yale University and Henry Wells of the University of Pennsylvania for their criticisms.

3. Leo Apostel, "Toward the Formal Study of Models in the Non-Formal Sciences," *Synthese*, 12 May 1960, 125–161. (Quotation is taken from p. 160.)

tend to be like those of the human mind (cybernetics). Noise blurs distinctions in sound in the same manner as social interaction distorts messages between people. Social distance may function to reduce interaction between people in much the same manner as geographical distance.

Formalization is the procedure for establishing the structural similarity between theories. Removing all empirical concepts in the theory and substituting "empty" marks, symbols without empirical referents, on a page will enable the researcher to determine whether the theories have a similar form. For example, if "when A increases, B/C increases," is like "when D increases, E/F increases," then these two propositions can be said to be structurally similar. The concepts from the first proposition can be substituted into the structure of the second, that is, the structure of relationships between the concepts of both propositions are similar. If new suggestions appear as a consequence of this substitution, then one proposition is a model for the other and the effort has been rewarding. Replacing the "empty" marks, the symbols devoid of empirical content, with empirical concepts is known as *interpretation.* If the concepts of two theories are interchangeable within the structure of either, then the two theories are structurally *isomorphic.*

One of the most practical uses of the structural isomorphism between two theories occurs when one theory is especially constructed to be isomorphic with another. Building physical models has enabled researchers to obtain rather inexpensive insights into projected plans. A simulated model of an airplane, traffic congestion, or battle situation, have prompted predictions about what would happen when the "real life" counterparts were substituted for the simulated ones.[4]

4. I include under physical models all electronic simulations of the empirical world. Simulated models are often difficult to distinguish from simple theory. A simulated model of the American voter, for example, usually includes most of those factors which are known to be theoretically relevant. Data about voters is then run in a computing machine with a model of the American voter. I would call this procedure the use of simple theory. But since the theory is often incomplete, it is called a model.

The process of uncovering the similarity between theories has the notion of the analogy or metaphor. Analogies have long been recognized as an aid for understanding the unfamiliar or the complex. Models in a sense are highly formalized analogies.[5] Both models and analogies have varying degrees of similarity with what they are models or analogies for. The extent to which theories are models or analogies for each other is a function of the similarity between the structure of the theories.

Establishing the structural similarity between two or more theories in the social sciences is, at least at present, a rather trivial goal. Often any one area is not any better known than another, and thus it is impossible to say which theory could serve as a model for the other theory. In order to use a model a certain amount of knowledge must exist about one area, and there must be knowledge about which area is better explained. But the more telling reason for the probable futility of determining structural similarities between theories of human behavior is the rather simple structure of the theories. Generalizations in the social sciences often stand alone. Most theories are collections of straightforward propositions, such as "If A, then B, under conditions $C_1 \ldots C_n$." That the proposition holds true only under certain conditions is sometimes expressed, "other things being equal." Since most of the generalizations of the social sciences are statements that two or more variables are related, most of the generalizations have the same structure.

Theories are sometimes thought of as similar if they employ the same concepts. Many of the concepts in international relations, for example, can be applied to local governments. Local governments compete for industry as do nation-states. Local governments in the United States have inter-governmental agreements; nation-states have treaties as well as inter-governmental agreements. But where the concepts are similar, the different areas to which the concepts are applicable may be an indication of the generality of the propositions, that is, the seemingly re-

5. Ernst Nagel, *The Structure of Science* (New York: Harcourt, Brace & World, 1961), pp. 107–117.

stricted concept or generalization may have greater scope. Similarities in levels of wealth may be related to interaction between local governmental units as well as to interaction between nation-states. The more general proposition in this example is that wealthy collectivities of people engage in more "outside" interaction.

It is often difficult, however, to determine whether "conflict" between nation-states refers to the same things as "conflict" between cities or between small and large municipalities. The problem of surmising whether concepts apply to a variety of areas is a result of unclear meanings of those concepts. It is perhaps more useful, more productive of scientific hypothesis, to think of similarities in the concepts of two or more theories as an indicator of the possible generality of the propositions within the theories, rather than to think of one theory as being a model for another.[6]

Mathematical-Logical Models. If the structure of a theory is isomorphic with some mathematical or logical system, then the mathematical-logical system is a model for the empirical theory.[7] This is what Brodbeck refers to as "arithmetic representation."[8]

6. See "Models as Contributing to Generalization," p. 301. Most of the propositions in the social sciences use group level concepts. Group level concepts refer to individuals, their characteristics, and the relations between them. Concepts referring to collectivities of people will always have individual referents. Thus, irrespective of the level of social organization which the group level concepts describe, they will always share the similarity of referring to individuals, characteristics of individuals, or relations between them. See May Brodbeck, "Methodological Individualisms: Definition and Reduction," *Philosophy of Science,* 25 January 1958, pp. 1–22.

7. Mary B. Hesse, "Models in Physics," *British Journal for the Philosophy of Science,* 4 November 1953, pp. 198–214. Hesse thinks that it is not necessary to distinguish between these kinds of models, as I have done. "However, the main justification for the use of the word 'model' in the wide sense is the fact, which we are attempting to establish here, that theories of a purely mathematical kind may function in essentially the same way as physically imaginable models, in being capable of suggesting further lines of development in the explanation of experimental facts," (p. 200). In the section on the functions of models (*supra.*) I blur the distinction between mathematical-logical models as the structural similarity between theories.

8. Brodbeck, "Models, Meaning, and Theories."

Euclidean geometry is an empirical theory. It is structurally similar to analytical geometry, that is, the mathematics of analytic geometry will produce the propositions of Euclidean geometry. $Y = ab + c$ is an algebraic formula of a Euclidean straight line. Heat, the rapidity of the movement of molecules, is measured by the thermometer, a scale which is isomorphic with arithmetic. The mathematical rules of probability are isomorphic with certain games of chance.

Any theory can be formalized by substituting "empty" marks for the empirical concepts. As a matter of fact, however, it may be extremely difficult to translate an empirical theory into a formalized structure. But, in principle, formalization is possible. An existing mathematical system can be given empirical content by exchanging the empty marks for empirical concepts, that is, by interpreting the mathematical-logical system. There are "rules of correspondence" to which the scientist must adhere so that the structure of the empirical theory is not violated when interpreted within a mathematical system.[9] The symbolic system then represents the form of the theory. The structure of the mathematical system is similar to the structure of the empirical theory.

The purpose of formalizing a theory is to enable the researcher to demonstrate or "see" the relationships between the propositions of the theory. If a theory is formalized, then the derivation of the theorems from the axioms is facilitated. Axioms thus are defined as the statements from which it is possible to derive or deduce the theorems. The truth or falsity of the theorems depends on the truth or falsity of the axioms. Once the axioms are interpreted, that is, given empirical content, they take on the character of being true or false in the same sense that the theorems are empirically true or false. Although true theorems can be derived from false axioms, theorems must be true only if the axioms are empirically true and the deductions are valid. The truth of the theorems, of course, is some evidence for the truth of the axioms.

9. Nagel, *op. cit.* Chapter 2.

Thus mathematical-logical models are a means of giving logical form to empirical theories in order to "see" the relationships between the axioms and theorems. Assigning a mathematical form to an empirical theory, or inventing a mathematical form for an empirical theory is in no way related to the truth of a theory. Provided that the statements of a theory make elementary grammatical sense, the truth of a theory is independent of its logical form. It is fortunate that the rules of logic and the functioning of the empirical world to some extent coincide. If they did not, mathematicians would be disengaged from the realm of science and relegated to the realm of philosophy. To put it differently, it is a happy circumstance which gives men the imaginative capabilities to discover logical forms for their observations.

Three of the more familiar types of mathematical-logical models in the social sciences are measurement, probability theory, and game theory. Each of these three types will be briefly examined in order to illustrate some types of "mathematical-logical models."

Measurement. Almost everyone is acquainted with the logical system of simple arithmetic. Simple arithmetic is the minimum form into which scientists would like to cast most of their concepts. What is meant by a "quantifiable" characteristic is that the characteristic is isomorphic with some rules of arithmetic (the interval scale) or all the rules of arithmetic (the ratio scale).[10] In the ordinal scale the quality of more or less is assigned arabic numbers. Thus, someone who is more favorable toward federal aid to education receives a score of "5"; someone who is less favorable receives a score of "1." If every discrete number corresponds to an equal quantity of more or less of some characteristic, an interval scale has been achieved. Then someone with a score of "5" has 4 more units of intensity than someone who scored "1." If it is possible that the intensity scale completely corresponds to the

10. S. S. Stevens, "Mathematics, Measurement, and Psychophysics," in S. S. Stevens (Ed.), *Handbook of Experimental Psychology* (New York: John Wiley, 1951), pp. 1–49.

rules of arithmetic so that a "zero" point is obtained, then all of the rules of arithmetic are operative on the scale. Then the person with a score of "5" would have 5 times the intensity of someone who scored "1."

1. Probability Theory. There is a system of logical relationships known as probability theory. The every-day world seems to correspond to these rules of chance. In the mathematics of probability if two events are dependent on one another, the probability of the combined event is the multiple of the independent probability of each event. The chance of "one" appearing on one die is $1/6$; the chance of two "ones" occurring together on two dice is p $1/6$ x p $1/6$ = $1/36$. It happens that actually throwing the dice will result in the probabilities figured by the mathematics of chance, provided that an adjustment is made for a sufficient number of "tries."

A probability model, or the probability of any event or set of events, is sometimes called a "null model."[11] If there are no other factors operative in the designated variables, what would be the probabilities of this distribution of events? If an observed distribution of events could occur by the rules of the mathematics of probability only five times out 100 samples, then the possibility that the observed events are a result of the laws of chance may be rejected.

It is apparent that the isomorphism between the mathematics of probability and the functioning of the empirical world is very important for testing hypotheses in the social sciences, where the empirical laws are so complex that the chances of a perfect or one-to-one relationship between variables of all samples are quite remote.

2. Game Theory. Game theory requires the mapping of a social situation in an isomorphic relationship with the rules of simple arithmetic and the mathematics of probability. The game is played in terms of a "set" of individual acts. If the music of Beethoven is four times as desirable as that of Bach and if the probabilities of securing Beethoven's music are twice those of secur-

11. For an example of a "null model," see Toscano, Chapter 4.

ing Bach's, then the actor, according to the rules of the game, will pick Beethoven over Bach. There are many variations to game theory. The problems of the mathematician in solving these games are tremendous, but they are probably not much greater than the present seemingly insurmountable difficulty of the social scientist in interpreting the symbols of game theory or mapping the laws of human behavior into the mathematics of a game in order to achieve an empirical theory.[12] Only when the laws of human behavior are mapped into the mathematics of the game will game theory be more than just a suggestive means of scientific discovery.

Other Uses of "Model" in the Social Sciences

All uses of the word "model" which do not involve an explicit, that is, a conscious effort to determine the structural similarity between two or more theories or between an empirical theory and a given mathematical-logical system, are either (a) some more or less confirmed, quantified or non-quantified propositions or (b) some form of quantified or non-quantified concepts. But what else could these models be, if they are in any way related to the empirical world? Scientific knowledge is knowledge about the empirical world, and this knowledge, to put it simply, is expressed in terms of verified or publicly verifiable statements about the relationships between things or characteristics of things, designated by some more or less explicit concepts.

Four categories of meaning which are sometimes implied by the word "model" are the following: (1) replica, (2) ideal, (3) ideal type, and (4) development of hypotheses.

Replica. One meaning of the word "model" is replica. A toy train is a miniature of a large one and thus a replica of it. Some characteristics of the replica are like, or isomorphic with, the real train; for example, the relation between wheel size and train

12. Discussion of rational calculations of payoffs pertains to this kind of model. See my "The Learning of Integrative Habits," Chapter 9.

size. There are "systematic" distortions in size. Some of the characteristics may be impossible to reproduce, such as the coal-fed steam engine. Making replicas of things involves objects, that is, one object stands for or represents another object.

Ideal. "Ideal" is a second meaning of the word "model." This meaning is reflected in the expression, "she is a model wife." The wife in this case exhibits certain characteristics to which approval or a normative value is attached. These characteristics are empirical characteristics, but the importance or value attached to these characteristics is non-empirical, or something different from empirical, even though expressions of the evaluations are empirical. Political scientists have developed many model states and discuss model governments, constitutions, societies, and the like. This kind of model building requires moral philosophizing about the empirical world.

Ideal Type. A concept which, for all practical purposes, has no empirical instances, is called an "ideal type" or archetype, a third meaning of the word "model."[13] When discussing concepts, one is often tempted to go into a discussion of the nature of concepts. We will avoid this rather repetitious task by asserting some fragments of what concepts involve without building the arguments for the assertions.[14]

One of the empirical principles which is rather commonly accepted now is that concepts must have empirical referents in order to have "meaning," that is, in order to know what is being talked about, the characteristics or objects to which the concepts refer must be stated. But what about "ideal types" which at first glance seem to have no "meaning?" An ideal type does have empirical referents, even though the objects or characteristics to

13. Max Black, "Models and Archetypes," in Charles E. Bow and Roy F. Nichols (Eds.), *Both Human and Humane* (Philadelphia: University of Pennsylvania Press, 1960), pp. 39–65.

14. See Carl G. Hempel, "Fundamentals of Concept Formation in Empirical Science," in *International Encyclopedia of Unified Sciences,* Vol. 2, No. 7 (Chicago: University of Chicago Press, 1953). Also see Gustav Bergmann, *The Philosophy of Science* (Madison: University of Wisconsin Press, 1957), pp. 48–67.

which the ideal type concept refers have never been observed. "Unicorn" is a concept with empirical referents, although almost certainly no unicorn has ever existed. The point is that a unicorn or a Weberian bureaucracy would be recognized if one occurred. Ideal types are usually combinations of empirical referents, which are rarely, if ever, observed combined (unicorn=horse and one horn). Absolute zero is another concept with an empirical referent derived from the isomorphism of the temperature scale with common arithmetic. Although no scientist has observed absolute zero, the scientist knows what he is looking for. Thus, if 32° is indicated in such a way on the scale, absolute zero would be indicated in "this" way, taking into account perceptual and measurement errors. *Ideal type concepts have in principle empirical referents, if not in fact empirical instances.*

It may be argued that "ideal type" concepts as used in the social sciences are more than just concepts. They also contain some at least implicit explanatory or predictive notions. This is probably true, for builders of concepts usually hope that their concepts will explain or suggest explanations. Implicit in the Weberian ideal type description of a bureaucracy, for example, is the suggestion that certain societies will have certain kinds of bureaucracies.

Developing Hypotheses

The previous three meanings of the word "model" primarily involve concepts. But models which have recently invaded the social sciences appear more complex and are often sources of confusion. Often familiar forms of model building involve systematic speculation to develop hypotheses or efforts to state more precisely what already is known in order to make hypotheses more amenable for testing. Three kinds of hypotheses—building models are discussed briefly: exclusion and inclusion of variables, mathematical or quantitative speculation, and implicit models.

Exclusion-Inclusion of Variables. Few theories account for all possible relevant variables. Whether any theory can account for all possible variables is an empirical question. Almost no theory states all the conditions under which it holds true. Holding that a theory must explain or account for everything or nothing is a familiar anti-scientific argument, which, if true, would deny the truth of almost every known theory. If a theory accounts for everything which could possibly make a difference, it would be called a closed theoretical system. Celestial mechanics, for example, is defined as a closed theoretical system.[15]

Because of the extreme difficulty in accounting for all possible variables, social scientists in particular have "systematically excluded" certain variables in their theoretical formulations. A listing of variables thought to be relevant to political integration involves this kind of model. Concepts, sometimes designated as models, such as exogenous-endogenous variables and stimulus-response factors, demonstrate a recognition of the incompleteness of the theoretical formulations and reflect an effort to distinguish between "systemic" variables, those for which the theory explicitly accounts, and "disturbance" variables, those for which the theory does not explicitly account. Although the scientist knows that other factors are relevant to his observations, he excludes them from his theory on the grounds that certain distinctions are an important practical step in acquiring fuller explanations. Explicit exclusions of variables does not make the theory false; it rather states more carefully the conditions under which the stated relationships will hold true.

The models of "economic man" or "administrative man" state that these characteristics of people, rational calculation or fortuitous improvisation, will make a difference in what human beings do. Exclusion of variables requires some knowledge, for to say that some variables are not as important as others is to either make a hypothesis or draw a conclusion about some phenomena.

Systematic speculation on evidence available to determine what variables will be relevant in explaining some phenomena can be called a model of relevant factors. When looking at an underdeveloped society, a writer may argue, these factors will be

15. Bergmann, *op. cit.*, pp. 84–91.

relevant and should be taken into account. Thus, there are models of primitive societies, models about behavior in large-scale organizations, models about conflict resolution in small groups, and models of political integration. This kind of speculation is often called a "conceptual scheme," although there are other meanings for "conceptual scheme."

Drawing a line between hypotheses building and theory is often difficult. Most of the theories in the social sciences contain propositions which are very tentative. Where evidence is particularly sparse, social scientists often use the word "model" for systematic speculation or for setting forth of hypotheses about things which are not well explained.

Mathematical-Quantitative Models. All theories are expressed in terms of a set of symbols. If the symbols stand in a certain logical relationship to one another, the theory is called a mathematical system. "Mathematical models," however, often refer to a set of hypotheses with quantified expression. The concepts in these models are thus at least partially isomorphic with simple arithmetic. But the quantified nature of the concepts is often posited rather than established by the techniques of scaling. "Organizational loyalty" and "intensity of commitment to organizational goals," for example, may be given hypothetical arithmetic weights. Then, organizational loyalty is hypothesized to be a linear function of intensity of commitment to organizational goals. Hypothesization with conjectured quantified variables is sometimes labeled a "mathematical model," such as assigning weights to factors contributing to political integration. Some of the propositions in these mathematical models may be quantified expressions; others may not be.

Implicit Models. Implicit models are more familiar as "hidden assumptions" or unstated propositions on which subsequent explicit statements depend. By and large, implicit models do not impose any great difficulty on the development of scientific knowledge. Once the implicit model or hidden assumptions are uncovered, they no longer have whatever undesirable consequences an implicit model is supposed to have. Further, the presence of an implicit model does not reduce the truth of the empirical findings. Although the scientific management school, as represented by Taylor and Gilbreth, used many unexamined assumptions concerning human motivation, there is no doubt that their research findings led to true statements about human productivity. The complaint against the scientific management school was that their assumptions about human nature did not allow room for the introduction of more relevant factors into their findings on productivity, and thus inhibited the growth of theories with greater explanatory power, theories which would predict and explain more, more accurately and more completely.

The Functions of Models

Several "functions" have been ascribed to models. Deutsch, for example, discusses several ends for which the model may be an aid: classificatory, heuristic, predictive, and mensurative.[16] Apostel presents nine functions of models, such as theory formation, simplification of complex formulations, extension of incomplete theories, and information classification.[17] Chapanis notes that models help in understanding complex systems, aid in learning complex skills, suggest new relationships, and help predict the impossibility of experiments.[18] The above authors caution against possible pitfalls in the use of models.

16. Karl W. Deutsch, "On Communication Models in the Social Sciences," *Public Opinion Quarterly*, Vol. 16 (Fall, 1952), pp. 356–380 (p. 360). Also see Deutsch, "Some Notes on Research on the Role of Models in the Natural and Social Sciences," *Synthese*, pp. 506–533.

17. Apostel, *op. cit.*, p. 127.

18. Alphonse Chapanis, "Men, Machines, and Models," *American Psychologist* (16, March, 1961), pp. 113–131. For other discussions of the role of "Models" in science, see E. H. Hutten, "The Role of Models in Physics," *British Journal for the Philosophy of Science* 4, (February, 1954 , pp. 284–301; Roy Lachman, "The Model in Theory Construction," *Psychological Review* 67 (March, 1960), pp. 113–129; and R. B. Braithwaite, "The Nature of Theoretical Concepts and the Role of Models in an Advanced Science," *Revue Internationale de Philosophie*, 67 (March, 1954), pp. 35–40.

Within the preceding discussion, what place do models have in the structure of science? Several steps in theory development will be the context in discussing the roles of models: scientific discovery, scientific generalization, and scientific verification.[19]

Scientific Discovery. The logic or description of scientific knowledge does not include the discovery of new knowledge. What is not known cannot be described. Scientific inquiry is a social process. The use of scientific knowledge, it is commonly agreed, is an important social question. Scientific knowledge does not necessarily involve the asking of social questions, either of the scientist or of the non-scientist. Cabinet making is a social process. The use of cabinets is a social process. Cabinets, as such, are not part of the social process. Cabinets are still "cabinets" long after their creators have died and "exist" independently of their accessibility to human use. Cabinets may inform researchers about the social processes, but cabinets could still "exist" if every form of life disappeared. This is a philosophical problem without relevance for the scientist. Even though Pluto was not discovered until quite late, no astronomer would argue that Pluto was not "there" because no one had known about it, nor would he argue that there were no stars before there was a man to see them.

Because some social scientists continually refuse to distinguish between the contexts of discovery and verification, how generalizations are established as true or false, confusion enters academic discussions. This confusion is manifest in talk about a scientist's values intruding into his selection of a research problem or his biases distorting the verification of his hypotheses. Scientific knowledge in the same sense can be described without knowledge of the scientist who discovered and verified the knowledge. It is a fact that scientists are influenced by the general state of knowledge available to them (intellectual history), by their socio-cultural values (sociology of knowledge), and by their prior experiences (psychology of thinking). Within the context

19. This is similar to Reichenbach's distinction between the "context of discovery and the context of justification." See Hans Reichenbach, *Experience and Prediction* (Chicago: University of Chicago Press, 1938).

of scientific knowledge, the fact that a person has been conditioned by the world does not mean that the world is what the person's conditioning directs. The context of discovery, in other words, has nothing to do with the process of verification.

To use another well-known example, Einstein was, as a matter of fact, motivated by a strong esthetic preference to demonstrate the unity of the universe; and if his speeches and writings are correct, this drive kept him enthusiastically pursuing physics. But this was the psychology of Einstein's thinking and did not bear on the empirical verification of his theories, which was accomplished by other scientists. C. W. Mills, however, provided an example of the confusion of the process of discovery and the process of verification. Mills, in his plea for more creative sociologists, de-emphasized the rather difficult and important problem of verifying sociological insights. He seemed to be unconcerned with the development of scientific knowledge, but instead advocated the solution of human problems with knowledge not discovered and not confirmed.[20]

The purpose of using one theory as a model for another, or in giving mathematical-logic form to a theory, falls within the context of discovery. When the propositions from one area of inquiry are known, they may be applied to a less well-illuminated or understood area to discover the laws which are operative but unknown. The structure of the theory of one area may serve as a guide to the laws which function in another area. But, as has been pointed out, to use models in this sense is to assume that the laws have some kind of structure other than the familiar common-sense form of "if water is heated, it will boil" and that there is enough knowledge to ascertain which of the areas of knowledge is better known. Although various theories in the social sciences may be structurally simple and equally unrefined, it is still an empirical question whether using models for suggestions is productive.

Models as aids for scientific discovery can be evaluated as more

20. C. Wright Mills, *Sociological Imagination* (New York: Oxford University Press, 1959).

or less "useful." Other functions of models seem similar to the familiar categories of theory or concept formation. Whether models are useful can be judged by two criteria: (a) whether an important proposition, in the sense of the role it plays in a generalization or hypotheses, would not have been discovered without model thinking, and (b) how many hypotheses have been discovered from the employment of models for workable research designs.

Thought processes are often so complex that it is extremely difficult to identify the key factor in the discovery of an important proposition. Perhaps the analogy or model is discovered after the hypothesis has been formulated or the evidence collected. Few people bother to explicate their creative thought patterns. Where there has been a step-by-step description of creative thought, it seems to come after the creative idea was confirmed; and it usually has the mystical, and hence unknowable, property of the Aha experiences. Creative insights imply that the individual credited with the discovery was indispensable in the process. Manuals for creative thinking will, perhaps, rarely emanate from creative people.

The processes of political integration provide an illustration of one area of inquiry's serving as a model for another. Relations between nation-states were used as a model for the study of relations between governmental units within nation-states and vice versa. Some hypotheses about metropolitan government which resulted directly from the international relations model may give some indication of the usefulness of the international model for the American pattern of governmental fragmentation.

1. Treaties between nation-states which are mutually rewarding may generalize to more treaties with the same party or more parties. Governmental units with inter-governmental agreements will be more likely to have more agreements with the same party and different parties.
2. The conditions of Articles of Confederation preceding the United States, a German Confederation before the birth of a German empire, a union of crowns before the Anglo-

Scottish consolidation, may imply the necessity for at least limited successes from governmental cooperation before any structural consolidation of a more extensive nature can occur.[21] Joint single functions between governmental units in a metropolitan area may contribute to the conditions necessary for future intergovernmental cooperation.

3. Nation-states may shed responsibilities on allies or on neighboring states, such as defense, construction of joint communication facilities, and food supply. Local governments can also shed responsibilities on other local governments, such as the suburbs restricting immigration of potential welfare cases, or on different levels of government.

These are a few of the suggestions which grew out of the "international relations model." Although there is no blanket evidence for the utility of this kind of model thinking, our impression is that the model acted as a springboard for several ideas and functioned to put the ideas into a more generalized statement.

Models as Contributing to Generalization. Generalization makes deduction possible. Deductive form is central to scientific explanation.[22] Generalizing from several observations is, in a sense, similar to the process of discovery. Generalizations arrived at by models or analogies must, of course, be empirically confirmed. If poor people in the United States and Britain vote for the Democratic and Labor parties, respectively, and the Democratic and Labor parties can be characterized as "parties of change," then perhaps the following generalization may be true: deprived people (poor people) will support (vote for) instrumentalities (parties) of change (alterations in the *status quo*). But since "deprived people" and "instrumentalities" refer to more things than "poor people" and "parties," the more general proposition must be subjected to verification.

21. See Karl W. Deutsch, *et al.*, *Political Community and the North Atlantic Area* (Princeton: Princeton University Press, 1957).

22. Carl G. Hempel and Paul Oppenheim, "The Logic of Explanation," in Herbert Feigl and May Brodbeck (Eds.), *Readings in the Philosophy of Science* (New York: Appleton-Century-Crofts, 1953), pp. 309–352.

By comparing two areas of inquiry, generalization may be fostered. A highly generalized statement (insecure governments will restrict the rights of citizens) explains more than less generalized statements (the United States passed the Alien and Sedition Acts because it was uncertain of the government's legitimacy). A generalized statement from one area may be extended into another with an appropriate growth in the inclusiveness of the concepts. This growth in the inclusiveness of the concepts, or what some call "building abstractions," however, does not excuse vagueness in concepts. Broadening the concepts increases the generality of the statements and points to new categories of evidence to be examined. The use of one theory as a model for another thus may suggest that the two theories are talking about the same thing and that one generalization will explain what formerly two or more generalizations explained.

Verification. If the propositions of one area are structurally similar to the laws in another area, does the structural similarity suggest that the propositions in the less known area are confirmed by the observed structural similarity in the better known area? The answer is obviously no. For, as has been pointed out previously, most of the crude generalizations in the social sciences have the same simple structure. The truth of a proposition or theory is dependent on the empirical world not on its similarity with other true theories or propositions.

If the use of one theory as a model for another theory points to the fact that the concepts in both areas refer to the same things, then the composited evidence from both areas is evidence for the veracity of the propositions. For example, the facts that rewarding interactions seem to contribute to favorable attitudes both among nation-states and among units of local government are evidences for the general proposition that rewarding interactions contribute to favorable attitudes. The use of models, then, can be said to have contributed to discovering instances of the general propositions which serve as evidence for the general proposition.

Our discussion of models left out two important issues and

one important example, which a more complete discussion of models could have included: can group level concepts be defined in terms of individual level concepts (methodological individualism) and, thus, does every theory in the social sciences share the same referent, the individual. Can one theory be explained in terms of another theory (cross-sectional laws and reduction). The example left out is the "model" of the atomic structure of matter. These are important issues, but it is not likely that they will throw much light on the central question that has been examined—the role of "models" in social science inquiry.

Index